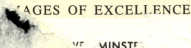
...AGES OF EXCELLENCE

...VE...MINSTE...

...uspension
...es.

IMAGES OF EXCELLENCE

Plato's Critique of the Arts

CHRISTOPHER JANAWAY

CLARENDON PRESS · OXFORD

Oxford University Press, Great Clarendon Street, Oxford OX2 6DP

Oxford New York
Athens Auckland Bangkok Bogota Bombay Buenos Aires
Calcutta Cape Town Dar es Salaam Delhi Florence Hong Kong Istanbul
Karachi Kuala Lumpur Madras Madrid Melbourne Mexico City
Nairobi Paris Singapore Taipei Tokyo Toronto Warsaw
and associated companies in
Berlin Ibadan

Oxford is a registered trade mark of Oxford University Press

Published in the United States
by Oxford University Press Inc., New York

© Christopher Janaway 1995

First published 1995
First issued as paperback 1998

British Library Cataloguing in Publication Data
Data available

Library of Congress Cataloging in Publication Data
Data available

ISBN 0–19–824007–4
ISBN 0–19–823792–8 (Pbk.)

Printed in Great Britain
on acid-free paper by
Bookcraft Ltd.,
Midsomer Norton, Somerset

Of all philosophers he is the most poetical. Yet if he will defile the fountain out of which his flowing streams have proceeded, let us boldly examine with what reasons he did it.

SIR PHILIP SIDNEY

ἄλογον γὰρ πρᾶγμα πῶς ἂν εἴη ἐπιστήμη;

How could a thing without a rational account
ever be knowledge?

PLATO

Preface

PLATO is the greatest writer ever to theorize about the arts, yet—to over-simplify again—everyone thinks he was wrong. My aim is to offer evidence pertinent to the first of these statements, and to argue that 'whether Plato was wrong' about the arts is a question as intricate and profound as any in philosophy.

More than ten years ago, as a newly appointed lecturer, I was simultaneously developing courses in Greek Philosophy and in Aesthetics. Encouraged by the example of my predecessor, Ruby Meager, I decided that Aesthetics need not begin with eighteenth-century authors, and tried to include Plato and Aristotle. I was struck by the power and lucidity of Plato's writings on poetry, inspiration, and artistic representation, and wished for a philosophically informed guide to them, something which I now hope to have written. I did not set out to write principally for specialist scholars of Greek philosophy, though the end-product has the ambition of interesting them as well. The more I have worked to clarify my own interpretation, the more I have been drawn into the vast field of scholarship on this topic. References in the footnotes give the reader the opportunity to retrace some of my paths, but I do not claim to offer anything like a comprehensive survey of the field. My governing aim remains to make clear Plato's philosophical position and what is interesting or important about it.

People occasionally describe aesthetics as the 'cinderella' of philosophy, perhaps feeling that it doesn't make it to the ball with its sister-subjects such as logic or ethics, or even that it ought not to (in a whisper: it's not much of a subject). It is a shame if people think that. Art, greatly more pervasive in history than science (for example), is one of the most characteristic things human beings do. Fine forms and sounds, depictions, and invented stories occupy most of us to some extent, and for some lives they provide the very backbone. But how important are they really? Aesthetics is not much of a subject if it takes for granted that we all know that the arts are valuable, and why. But if we assume that neither point is obvious, addressing these questions becomes a philosophical challenge of the deepest complexity and the widest import.

It is surprising that Plato should be able to teach us how central the philosophy of art is. For he stubbornly refuses to set the arts apart as having a value of their own, and always asks how they help us to be better people, what elements in our psychological make-up they engage and promote, how they make a community better to live in, or how they contribute to the search for truth; and he bids us wrench ourselves away from art which we love, if it fails to satisfy these stringent tests. But it is precisely this refusal to privilege or bracket off the arts which challenges us to say what importance they have. For Plato, the enquiry into the nature and value of the arts is simply philosophy, and in this I think he was right.

Parts of Chapters 1, 2, and 6 have appeared in earlier versions in the following places:

'Plato's Analogy between Painter and Poet', *British Journal of Aesthetics*, 31 (1991), 1–12.

'Arts and Crafts in Plato and Collingwood', *Journal of Aesthetics and Art Criticism*, 50 (1992), 45–54.

'Craft and Fineness in Plato's *Ion*', *Oxford Studies in Ancient Philosophy*, 10 (1992), 1–23.

I am grateful to audiences in Sydney, Melbourne, and Canberra, where some early material towards Chapters 5 and 6 was presented. Let me finally thank all those who have shown their interest by listening, reading, and offering support, and especially the following for giving me their views on later versions: Anthony Price, Stephen Halliwell, Roger Scruton, Adam Mills, Malcolm Budd, and Sebastian Gardner.

C. J.

London
September 1994

Contents

Abbreviations and Translations

References to Plato's works use the standard marginal page, section, and line numbers of Burnet's Oxford Classical Text. Names of the dialogues are abbreviated, where necessary, in the following way:

Apol.	*Apology*	*Phdo.*	*Phaedo*
Char.	*Charmides*	*Phdr.*	*Phaedrus*
Crat.	*Cratylus*	*Phil.*	*Philebus*
Euth.	*Euthyphro*	*Pol.*	*Politicus*
Gorg.	*Gorgias*	*Prot.*	*Protagoras*
HiMa.	*Hippias Major*	*Rep.*	*Republic*
Ion	*Ion*	*Soph.*	*Sophist*
Laws	*Laws*	*Symp.*	*Symposium*
Meno	*Meno*	*Tht.*	*Theaetetus*
Parm.	*Parmenides*	*Tim.*	*Timaeus*

Unless otherwise stated, quotations from Plato are either in my own translation, or (more frequently) from the following translators:

Apology, H. Tredennick; *Gorgias*, T. Irwin; *Hippias Major*, P. Woodruff; *Ion,* T. J. Saunders; *Laws,* T. J. Saunders; *Phaedrus*, C. J. Rowe; *Philebus*, J. C. B. Gosling; *Protagoras and Meno*, W. K. C. Guthrie; *Republic*, G. M. A. Grube; *Sophist*, F. M. Cornford; *Symposium*, W. Hamilton; *Theaetetus*, M. J. Levett, revised M. Burnyeat; *Timaeus*, H. D. P. Lee.

For publication details see under translators' names in the *Bibliography* (items marked *). Sometimes I have adapted these translations in minor ways without comment. Any important changes are signalled in the Notes.

Introduction

THE arts are seen to play a positive role in the lives of many people. Across cultures, times, places, and class-divisions, people sing, dance, decorate, enact, represent, narrate, and express, in conventionalized ways, to audiences who enjoy and participate in these activities, and often care about them deeply. It seems natural, if not highly informative, to call such practices 'artistic'. Many of them may also be religious, commercial, therapeutic, political, or educational in their motivation—but there is usually a fairly clear distinction between pursuing such ends artistically, and doing so in other ways. We tend to assume that the arts, however in the end they may be defined, are in general a good thing. Some artistic productions are better than others, some are good for one reason, others for another—but artistic productions as a whole are something it is better to have than not to have. More inflatedly, we think that the ability to engage in them is valuable because it is deeply entrenched in, or essential to, our being human. Such thoughts are often extremely vague. So what can philosophy do? Socrates tells us that 'the unexamined life is not worth living for a human being' (*Apol.* 38a5–6). Many of us live with the arts with few qualms—philosophy tempts us to step back out of that security and ask what account can be given, in a general way, of the nature and value of the arts.

The first attempt at such an examination in western philosophy is that of its great ancestral figure, Plato. Although Plato's thinking about the arts of his culture cannot really be described as a systematic theory, he has consistent preoccupations from his earliest to his latest writings, which reach a peak in the best-known work of his middle period, the *Republic*. We find a body of arguments addressing central questions about the arts, and engaging with themes that are centrally Platonic. If Plato initiates western philosophy's ethics and theory of knowledge, then—as part of the same project—he initiates its examination of the arts in an equally powerful way. Following Socrates' example, he asks naïve questions: Is poetry good for us? Why do we enjoy tragedies? What does Homer really know about, and what does he teach us about? The combination of his blunt, unflattering answers and the brilliance of the literary medium in which he conveys them gives Plato's critique of the arts its unique flavour.

Today's writers on the philosophy of art often discuss Plato's views, or allude to them while in pursuit of their own ends. Such mentions are not always unfavourable or dismissive;[1] nevertheless, Plato has been dubbed a philistine, his arguments have been pronounced bad, his critical attitude to art one-sided and prejudiced. I believe that this is too harsh a picture. Plato's arguments are by no means flawless, but they are not stupid. The claim of philosophy's pre-eminence over the arts, though perhaps too rigid, is there for good reasons. Most of all, as I hope to show, Plato was far from being a philistine—he did not lack appreciation of the arts, nor of their claims to importance. In his most extreme moment he wished to eliminate the chief forms of poetry from the city-state and from the republic of the soul, but not for philistine reasons; rather because, as his examination convinced him, they were incompatible with a life devoted to truth and the good, and hence, in his view, incompatible with what it was to be a human being in the noblest and healthiest of ways. This was an argued position whose premisses were central to his whole philosophy. If we consider that philosophy worth studying and think it worthwhile to have a view about the value of poetry, music, and the like, we cannot lightly bypass Plato's critique of the arts.

Arthur Danto has recently suggested that Plato set the agenda for the whole history of that philosophical subject which was to become known as 'aesthetics'. That Plato openly devalued art in comparison with its rival, philosophy, Danto believes is to his credit. At least the nature of the enterprise is honestly acknowledged, whereas Plato's successors have played the same game in more underhand fashion: Danto discerns a 'somewhat shabby history of the philosophy of art as a massive political effort either to emasculate or to supersede art', and thinks that 'from the perspective of art aesthetics is a danger, since from the perspective of philosophy *art* is a danger and aesthetics the agency for dealing with it'.[2] In that case, the philosophy of art has always been 'footnotes to Plato'. An equally broad-brush picture—perhaps equally plausible—might show us a long line of thinkers sensitive to the position

---

[1] In recent philosophical aesthetics Plato is taken seriously and maintains a substantial presence in e.g. Mothersill, and Danto (1981) and (1986). Schaper, and Halliwell (1991) argue clearly for his importance to contemporary aesthetics.

[2] Danto (1986), 16, 13. This piece has influenced me more than I suspected it would when I first tried to sum it up (Janaway (1989), 198).

the arts hold in our lives, and developing glowing philosophical accounts in order to atone for the blasphemy of their ancestor. (Perhaps both pictures are compatible. It is after all Hegel's philosophical elevation of art which, for Danto, serves as a way of neutralizing it as an independent force, by presenting it as a kind of philosophy in imperfect form.)

If the first western philosophy of the arts turns out to have this kind of enduring foundational role, then an elucidation of its arguments will have even greater import. The prime task, however, is to understand Plato's thought and the extent to which it holds credence. I shall seek to show how Plato's account of the nature, production, and experience of the arts (as distinct from the question of value) is often on the right lines: sometimes it is true, or the beginnings of something true. At other times it is probably false, but the beginnings of something arguable or worth entertaining. Either way, Plato provokes us into a more thorough re-examination (such as he himself envisaged[3]) of the questions we need to consider about the nature of the arts, if we are to assign them a positive value. To find that he occupies such a position in the dialectic of the philosophy of art will be good enough vindication of Plato against his less favourable critics, and against those who ignore him.

If this book regards the value of the arts, and especially poetry and drama, as open to question, it is because prior to an engagement with Plato we cannot afford to assume that we know what that value is, or, therefore, that they do have a value. Is art *per se*, and without extensive regulation, compatible with a rational and ethical life? We hope so. Was Plato then wrong about the nature of the arts, or only about the best way to live? Or was he wrong about both? Does art convey truth and enable knowledge? Does it harmonize essentially with the rationally chosen good? Or can it be guaranteed to do neither? Are these perhaps the wrong questions to ask about it? Should we be looking to a unique kind of pleasure with its own value, and leave truth and morality aside until that is accounted for? Can 'truth' and 'morality' even be ranked as some kind of construct on a par with what artists produce? These are the questions I shall regard as open at the start.

---

[3] *Rep.* 607c4–e1: 'If poetic *mimēsis* designed for pleasure has any argument to bring forward to prove that it must have a place in a well-governed city, [we] should be glad to welcome it . . . We should also give its champions who are not poets the opportunity to speak on its behalf in prose to the effect that it not only gives pleasure but is useful to cities and to human life. We shall listen to them in a friendly spirit' (slightly adapted from Grube's translation with help from Halliwell's). This is neither a philistine nor a totalitarian voice.

In any philosophical examination of the arts we must ask sooner or later how poetry, drama, or representational painting achieve what they do. Is some special understanding or other state of mind required for the production of these things? And what kind of entity does an artist really produce—something in the same class as a carpenter's table, or (as many have thought) something quite different? How is it that drama or painting acquires a content, presents an appearance that we recognize as something from the real world? How do these arts engage our minds—thoughts, emotions, appetites—as we take them in? Which parts of the psyche do they appeal to, and nourish? Plato initiates all these debates, which are still with us, unresolved in one degree or another. Not until we establish one or two answers here will we be able to explain art's relation to the world of real things or to the human mind, and not until these relations are understood will we have the basis for a proper answer to the question of value raised above.

When it comes to art and the community Plato's stance is notoriously uncompromising. He wants political control over the arts, from nursery tales onwards. He advocates explicit censorship and, for the most distinguished and impressive poetry, prohibition and deportation. All such measures are to be undertaken for the general good of the state—but so, we should remember, is every measure envisaged in the ideal *polis* Plato constructs. With this end in view, he advocates, for example, that deformed newborns should be abandoned to die because they will be of no use, and that the state should control human reproduction to ensure the breeding of the right kind of 'stock' (or 'herd'). In this context, anyone who is particularly enraged by Plato's willingness to censor Homer selectively for use in schools, or even by his ban on performances of tragedy, may have things a little out of proportion. It is not, at any rate, some peculiar blind spot about the arts that prompts Plato's harshness. So it is a worthwhile exercise, not to deny or to excuse the abhorrent political measures, but to push them a little into the background, to see whether there is any sense in what Plato says about the nature of the arts as such.

Plato insists on raising questions about the educational, political, and moral value of art, and about what outside itself it enables us to know or to do better. Such questioning can seem misguided if one is prone to a blanket-response of 'art for art's sake'. Plato prompts us to recognize an often disguised prejudice which bestows on the arts a self-contained, self-guaranteeing status. He reveals in us an adherence to aestheticism, the view that some form of pure pleasure or beauty which can be isolated from other states and values is the dominant or sole scale of evaluation for the arts. Aestheticism and 'art for art's sake' form an easy way of thinking which partly explains the lack of attention paid to Plato's views. We are the inheritors of a rather vague orthodoxy, built to an extent on diverse materials laid down in the eighteenth and nineteenth centuries, much questioned more recently, which nevertheless persists in people's minds and practices. What we may find it hard to forgive in Plato is the apparent arrogance with which he ignores our orthodoxy. However, if we avoid such an anachronistic attitude and suspend our prejudices, we can allow Plato's case to be heard. Art may have a self-contained value, but we should not get away with this as a lazy, unargued, or even unstated assumption.

A point of terminology: is it 'art' we are talking about, or 'the arts'? Plato discusses poetry (his main interest), drama, story-telling, dance, painting, and music on various instruments and in various contexts. In other words, he discusses the arts, or some of what we call the arts today, and it is these discussions that define my topic. We should hesitate a moment before placing any of Plato's writings in the modern genre 'philosophy of art'.[4] He certainly has no single word that translates as 'art'. But on the other hand, he makes explicit links between poetry and painting, especially when elucidating the notion of *mimēsis*, the making of appearances or representations. Further, he brackets music and poetry together under the wider Greek conception of *mousikē*. Of great importance too is the fact that poetry for Plato is usually publicly performed and, as tragedy and comedy, includes dramatic characterization and the music and dance of the chorus. We should remind ourselves that near to our time the model for the *Gesamtkunstwerk*, the total or complete work of art, has been found in Greek drama. Such works were fiction (or something close to it), they employed representation both of character and of scene, they used music, human movement, lyric poetry, and dialogue, and spoke directly to a whole community, moving them to intense emotion, and, they supposed, informing them about themselves, their common past, and their destinies. This was art, if anything was, whatever Plato and his contemporaries called it. The same can be said of the *Iliad* and the *Odyssey*, which were also publicly performed in Plato's day and revered for their fineness as poetry.

---

[4] Halliwell (1991) suggests that we should not hesitate too much: 'The often repeated claim that the Greeks had no conception of art "in our sense" is unjustifiably drastic, not least because of the thinness of the modern concept of "fine art(s)" itself' (325 n. 8).

Plato's continuing relevance to the philosophy of art lies here. What he lacks is, as it were, the concept of art with a capital 'A', the concept which prejudges questions of the value of artistic activities. Lacking this attitude to the arts, he raises the question of value with a vigour that proves hard for many modern readers to stand. Faced directly with what for us remain paradigmatic works of art, comprehending them, and indeed admiring them in some ways, he was prepared to reject them. It is because the rejection strikes deep at what we cherish that we are so uneasy with Plato, but that is precisely why he is important. If his case were to hold in the face of Homer and the great tragedians, there is nothing else we could show Plato—bringing him forward in time, educating him in the history of all the arts put together—that would weigh one iota.

Is there any single point to poetry, fiction, and drama which is also the point of music, painting, and dance? Should we pin our hopes on Art with a capital 'A'? Some may think the common factor in all these activities is 'aesthetic value': perhaps if we could explain what that means, we would have our 'answer to Plato'. Aesthetic value is usually conceived as a value which may obtain independently of all other values. Take a poem which we regard as a *good* poem. While it is legitimate to ask whether the poem is cognitively accurate, ethically commendable, or useful towards some external end, to ask only these questions is to miss the further, independent possibility of its being a good poem in an aesthetic way. And a particular poem might easily be a good moral judgement, a good description of a state of affairs, and a good means of inculcating attitudes in the young, without being a good poem in this further way which we incline to think is in some way privileged. The inclination is to say that to be good *as a poem* it must (whatever else is the case) be good *aesthetically*.

The second basic feature of aesthetic value is its relation to certain ways of experiencing things. A poem or building will not be said to have positive aesthetic value unless it has a propensity to bring about some kind of feeling in those who encounter it. This feeling, which aesthetic theory has found especially elusive, may be pleasure, satisfaction, elevation, or devotion, but is at any rate a feeling which is itself of positive value to the subject. We respond positively to things that have aesthetic value, and our doing so is intimately connected with experiential encounter. Aesthetic value is discerned by looking, listening, or reading, and opening ourselves to feelings about the objects of our own experience. This sketchiest of outlines is already enough to confront Plato with. For he seems to find no place for aesthetic value even thus outlined—is that not his chief weakness?

It is true that anyone expecting a *theory* of aesthetic value or aesthetic experience must look to more recent thinkers, for Plato has none to give. And perhaps one reason for this is that he does not regard aesthetic value as sufficient to justify the arts or our involvement with them. However, there are two different views which this summary statement might embody. One is the view of the crude, destructive Plato whose over-insistence in pressing questions of function and morality and truth blinds him to the whole glorious realm of the aesthetic. The more sophisticated Plato, however, is the one who has inhabited this realm, knows how sweet, wondrous, and divine the arts can be, knows the argument that pleasure should be the criterion of value, and knows that the human psyche will always be drawn to fine words, sounds, and pictures. This second picture is the right one. Only once we acknowledge the aesthetically sensitive side of Plato, the poet, speechmaker, and musician in him, can we understand the voice he adopts to resist the aesthetic spell. His resistance is to a part of himself, as he makes clear in the *Republic* when he declares his arguments a 'charm' to ward off the fine works of poetry which his education has taught him to approach as one approaches a loved one.

Why did Plato need such a defensive spell? In the Platonic dialogues we meet Socrates, who despite variations in style, mood, and apparent doctrine, is the steady paradigm of philosophy in its search for truth and the good. But let us consider who else we encounter. There is the reciter and poetry-critic, Ion, who claims that Homer is omniscient and that his submersion in the great poet's works makes him an expert on every subject. There is the teacher of rhetoric Gorgias, who cannot untangle fine talk from genuine expertise and insight, the sophist Protagoras, who extols the traditional method of educating the young by setting the works of the poets before them, and his proud and learned colleague Hippias, who cannot understand the distinction between beauty and this or that beautiful thing. There are Agathon and Aristophanes, fine poets in tragic and comic vein, who delight their audiences but may not speak the truth and cannot follow Socrates' arguments very well. Then Phaedrus, whose life is given up to the love of beautiful speeches, even if they are designed to praise people who cynically manipulate their sexual partners. We hear too of virtuoso musicians whose only expertise is in breath-taking displays which gratify all and sundry, lovers of sights and sounds who never miss any production staged at the festivals, devotees of Homer who argue that he must know everything to be able to write so finely, and clever, versatile people whose life is governed by the pleasures of dramatic artifice and empathizing with the violent emotions of fictional characters.

Again and again Plato confronts his dogged philosopher with the cultured class of his day. The philosopher overcomes them in argument, but they remain largely unruffled. Plato is showing us that unless we hold the arts off at some distance, we become disabled—powerless to distinguish the pleasing from the good, plausibility from truth, or cleverness from genuine expertise and wisdom. Unless we question the poetic, rhetorical, pleasure-loving culture in radical terms, it remains impervious to the very conceptual distinctions it needs in order to raise questions of value about itself. Unless philosophy is founded as a mode of enquiry that resists the arts, they will engulf everything. So I shall argue that Plato understands the basic premisses of one kind of 'aesthetic' defence of the arts. He is aware that some people assign the arts autonomous value on the basis of the pleasure they provide to those who experience them, and that some who attribute great moral and educational significance to the arts have not properly disentangled such achievements from that of giving pleasure. Plato's counter-campaign is not gratuitous, but is intimately linked with his concern to establish philosophy as an independent method of enquiry.[5]

My interpretation of Plato differs from a number of others. There are those who have argued that really, deep down, Plato is not opposed to the arts—he is opposed to pseudo-art, to misuse of art, to bad art, to bad as opposed to good *mimēsis*, or whatever, but really means us to see that art could (at least) be a good thing. I think that this way of interpreting Plato, sometimes born of wishful thinking and anachronism, is largely wrong. Plato is sensitive to the arts, and often respectful towards them; he is willing to grant some art-forms instrumental value in society, and to regard harmony, form, and proportion as profoundly educative of the human psyche. But there is no Platonic theory which proclaims 'good art' *per se*, as the modern world thinks of it, to be intrinsically important and good. Another camp consists of those who have thought Plato's views so absurd, or just so badly argued, that they do not even constitute a case against the arts that is worthy of the name. I offer to displace this view by presenting a set of tolerable philosophical arguments that serves at least as an initial case.

---

[5] Cf. Halliwell (1991) again: 'If . . . Plato lacked anything narrowly (or currently) describable as an aesthetic theory, this was not because he failed to see the need for one, but because he held reasons for actually *denying* such a need' (328).

Plato's fullest and most damning discussion of the arts comes in the *Republic*, to which Chapters 4–6 of this study are devoted. But there is some business to attend to before we reach the *Republic*. First (Chapter 1) an examination of the witty and puzzling early dialogue, *Ion*, which asks how poetry relates to knowledge. Poets themselves are praised—perhaps with irony—as 'divinely inspired', but in the same breath Plato makes a negative claim which he never relinquishes. It is that fine poetry requires neither poet, nor performer, nor audience, to possess or acquire any knowledge. Plato's greatest ridicule is directed at people who make extravagant claims to knowledge because they do not realize that this is true.

It is of course unclear what kind of knowledge we are looking for. What kind of knowledge might we want to attribute to a poet or a performing artist? To answer this we must confront the ubiquitous concept of *technē*—craft, expertise, expert knowledge, or, in a misleading sense, art. We can still speak of the politician's art, or the wrestler's or the carpenter's art. But clearly we do not mean thereby to embrace these activities among 'the arts', which, I take it, include music, literature, drama, painting, sculpture, dance . . . (The tinge of vagueness is harmless: when we turn to the 'arts page' of a newspaper, or discuss the funding of the arts, we are sure enough what we are talking about.) In speaking of the art of the politician, wrestler, or carpenter, we mine a more archaic layer of meaning, more closely akin to the *technē* of Plato's Greek. In the *Ion*, Plato makes the point that poetry does not succeed by the same kind of rational processes as these ordinary 'arts' or 'crafts'; nor does familiarity with poetry teach us any genuine expertise. It is in this sense that it neither proceeds from nor engenders knowledge.

In Chapter 2, looking especially at the *Gorgias* (a dialogue usually placed at the end of Plato's early period and regarded as transitional to the period of the *Republic*), I examine Plato's charge that arts such as music and drama aim solely at producing pleasure or gratification, and (because there are no generalizable principles of pleasure) can give no rational account of their mode of success. Once again the concept of *technē* is used, this time as the ideal of a rational understanding controlled by knowledge of the good. In Plato's early ethical thinking activities which do not measure up to the ideal of *technē* cannot be a route to knowledge of good and evil. How could a thing without a rational account ever be knowledge?

We are bound to wonder whether beauty is a relevant issue. Is not beauty what the arts primarily, and distinctively, have to offer? In

Chapter 3 I consider Plato's view of beauty. In his *Hippias Major*, for instance, some of the examples of beautiful things are works of art, but many are not. The Greek word *kalos* which we translate as 'beautiful' often means something which is fine or admirable, and is much wider in its connotations than our 'beautiful' tends to be. People, actions, political constitutions, and humble artefacts such as a soup-ladle, can without any strain be described, and thereby praised, as *kalos*. If we think that works of art are pre-eminent in possessing an aesthetic property we call 'beauty', *kalos* is the wrong word for this—and again Plato has no ready alternative. He sometimes calls poetry *hēdus*—sweet, pleasant, or pleasure-giving—but that could apply just as well to a wine or a summer breeze, and so gives no aid to the arts in their search for a value of their own.

And yet, although Plato has no word for 'aesthetic', he recognizes that there is aesthetic fineness or beauty. As he puts it, some things are fine because, through our sight and hearing, they give us a pleasure without any particular benefit. He acknowledges that people place value on the arts because they are fine things in which we take great pleasure. But he is not swayed by this. Even with an explicit concept of the aesthetic it would not be easy to convince Plato that the arts must have anything particularly valuable about them. Not all aesthetic things are art-products; and besides, the analysis of the aesthetic may not reveal it to have any peculiar value that overrides Plato's other concerns. He is alive to the charms of beauty, but will not rate them highly compared with the values of discovering truth and being an excellent human being. Furthermore, in his 'middle period' philosophy Plato has an account of beauty which reduces any mere beautiful *thing* to only secondary importance. 'Beauty itself', a beauty absolute, undimmed, and unchanging, becomes for him the ultimate value and the ultimate object of love, as we see in the famous speech of Socrates in the *Symposium*, with which I conclude my Chapter 3. Here we confront the theory of Forms. This absolute Beauty is a Form, shared in imperfectly by many perceptible things, but itself imperceptible and accessible only to pure thought. It is for Plato a supreme object of knowledge and a standard of all genuine value, akin to the Form of the Good which is the philosopher's highest goal in the *Republic*. Yet there is little reason to think this 'beauty itself' has much to do with the arts as such.

In Books 2 and 3 of the *Republic* Plato discusses the role of poetry and music in the education of the young citizens of his ideal city-state. All aspects of content and form, he argues, should be rigorously censored to control their effects on the characters of the young during their formation. As I hope to show in Chapter 4, Plato has interesting arguments for his view, and starts from premises that are sensitive to the importance of the arts. An example is the discussion of the nature and effects of dramatic characterization (*mimēsis*) on its participants: *mimēsis* alters people's characters because they tend to become assimilated to what they habitually enact. Pursuit of dramatic enactment as an end in itself distorts the personality, making a person 'double' or 'multiple'. Plato insists throughout that the arts be subservient to moral aims. It is not immediately obvious whether he is wrong to do this. We should not be blinded by the levels of political control which he thinks legitimate in furtherance of his aims. Looking more carefully, we find that the arts are accorded a strong positive role in early education, that of moulding the human soul, making it well-proportioned and harmonious, and hence receptive to right ways of thinking and acting later on.

Chapter 5 is devoted to an analysis of the concept of *mimēsis*, which emerges in *Republic* Book 10 as a wider conception of the way the arts present an appearance of reality. I shall argue that here *mimēsis* is best understood as what we today call 'representation', and that Plato has, in outline, a unitary account of how representation is achieved in the visual arts and in dramatic and epic poetry. Mimetic artists make no real thing, only an appearance of a thing of some kind. There is no need to believe that Plato limits the arts to a crude or mechanical copying or to the making of literal illusions. He has much subtler concerns, still linked closely with his discussions of ethics and knowledge. This is revealed in Chapter 6, where I consider the arguments Plato presents in Book 10 against mimetic poetry. He is highly critical of poetry and drama, on the grounds that they engage an unstable emotional part of us and subvert reason, while yet seeming to proceed from, and to transmit, knowledge. He is especially concerned that poets are regarded as possessing and conveying knowledge in the ethical sphere, when in fact they have only an ability to produce pleasurable and convincing 'images of excellence'. These arguments, both epistemological and psychological, form Plato's strongest critique of the arts. They are the arguments which must act as the charm to ward off mimetic poetry, whose banishment from Socrates' model city founded in words symbolizes its exclusion from the individual psyche.

Plato's thought about the arts and related matters did not cease with the end of the *Republic*. In later works he developed his thinking on inspiration and madness, pleasure, image-making, *technē*, and the place of the arts in the social order. In Chapter 7 I look at passages which may seem to evidence a change in Plato's outlook, chief among them the passages on poetic inspiration in the *Phaedrus*. But although we sometimes find Plato less vehemently antagonistic to the arts than he was in the *Republic*, there is no reason—or so I shall argue—to attribute to him any fundamental reversal of his position. The continuity of the later with the earlier Plato is shown in the discussions of *technē* and *mimēsis* in the *Sophist*, *Statesman*, and *Philebus*, and the well-considered view of the role of the arts which he constructs in the long late dialogue, the *Laws*. Many themes recur from the *Republic*, but in the *Laws* Plato no longer yearns for an ideal community. In the real world the arts will always be there, and Plato tells us in detail how they should be organized to contribute to a well-ordered and moral life. Arguing that pleasure should not be the criterion of evaluation in the arts, he nevertheless organizes the life of his citizens so that they will learn through play—music, dance, and poetry—how to feel pleasures correctly. He keeps the arts under strict regulation lest the horrors of experimentation break out, and he still will not tolerate tragic drama.

Allowing that Plato has made a case, what is its place within the philosophy of art? In the final chapter, I consider the challenge of providing a 'defence of art'. Is it possible, by stating what we know about the arts in the late twentieth century, to lay the Platonic critique to rest? Though the issue is vast, I consider a number of approaches. One line of thinking says that a proper account of aesthetic judgement will give us a defence of the arts. Another holds that the mimetic arts in particular have a direct input into our learning to be better human beings. Plato need not be left with the last word—yet our thoughts are liable to be more confused here than Plato's. It is not clear whether the concepts of art and the aesthetic can be relied upon to answer Plato's more radical questions. Is art a serious endeavour? Is its value aesthetic value? How does aesthetic value relate to other values? Do we not, on the one hand, sometimes expect to enjoy artworks 'for their own sake', locating them in an area where questions about ethical value and literal truth may be allowed to go fuzzy—or rather, where we may choose either to invoke such considerations or to ignore them? For Plato that is no truly serious endeavour: if truth and goodness matter, they matter absolutely, and if they do not matter absolutely in the arts, then the arts reduce to harmless play or amusement. On the other hand, do we not also find ourselves taking art with enormous seriousness as if it embraced every conceivable value and improved us in every way Plato could demand? One part of the problem is that modern views of art are so diverse: Plato poses his questions with a greater single-mindedness than we can muster in response. One part of the answer—perhaps the least tolerable part to Plato—is that art's values are in principle plural and elusive, and even to be cherished because they are so.

1

Rhapsody

IN many of Plato's early works Socrates is pitted against characters who claim some kind of knowledge which Socrates doubts they have. Ion, the poetry enthusiast who gives his name to the shortest of these elegant dramas, is not a demanding opponent. The dialogue is led from the front by Socrates, who inflicts a playful humiliation on Ion without his even noticing. Yet this brief piece is a good initial approach to the problems that concern Plato and will concern us.

Shelley translated the *Ion*,[1] and in his own writings he echoes the positive account of poetry which it appears to present:

A man cannot say 'I will compose poetry'. The greatest poet even cannot say it: for the mind in creation is as a fading coal, which some invisible influence, like an inconstant wind, awakens to transitory brightness: this power arises from within, like the colour of a flower which fades and changes as it is developed, and the conscious portions of our natures are unprophetic either of its approach or its departure.[2]

Socrates tells Ion that fine poetry and the poetry-critic's impressive discourse stem from a kind of possession or inspiration not within the mind's conscious control. Yet there is a puzzle for the modern reader: this apparently familiar Romantic[3] idea is not used to portray poetry as a thing of high value. Instead it purports to explain why poetry and discourse about poetry are less valuable than they are claimed to be, because lacking the all-important status of knowledge.

Ion is undoubtedly a master of the rhapsode's art. From the dialogue itself we learn that a rhapsode was a professional reciter of poetry to a public audience and could claim to be an expert interpreter—both performer and critic—of the works he knew. Ion is an expert interpreter of Homer, and Socrates at first expresses envy of his ability:

---

[1] See Shelley, 233–48.   [2] Ibid. 135.
[3] See Schaper, 35–8, 120–34, for a wider discussion of Romanticism in relation to this aspect of Plato.

Your art [*technē*[4]] makes it right and proper for you to dress up and look as grand as you can. And how enviable also to have to immerse yourself in a great many good poets, especially Homer, the best and most inspired of them, and to have to learn his thought thoroughly and not just his lines! For if one didn't understand what the poet says, one would never become a good rhapsode, because a rhapsode has to be an interpreter of the poet's thought to the audience, and that's impossible to do properly if one does not understand what he is saying. (*Ion* 530b6–c5.)

Ion laps this up: agreeing that he is to be envied, he adds that he is simply the best interpreter of Homer around. Later we hear that 'everyone agrees' on this point (533c6–7). What is it that Ion is able to do? Apart from performing scenes from Homer, which is discussed later, he can 'speak well (or finely) *about* Homer'. He knows his material so well from having perfected his performances that he can hold forth in a lecture or display,[5] bringing out convincingly Homer's qualities as a poet. This role is referred to as that of critic or judge (*kritēs*), but also that of eulogist (*epainetēs*) of Homer. Ion can judge how finely the poet speaks about what he portrays, and can himself speak finely in praise of the poet.

Ion's comic display of arrogance about his own talents does not go unpunished. Socrates trounces him in argument, showing (ostensibly, at any rate) that his success does not really stem from a *technē*: he does not, like a doctor or fisherman, have an expertise which counts as the systematic, transmissible knowledge of a definite subject-matter. Although Plato's use of the concept *technē* can be a fairly complex matter,[6] a basic point to grasp straight away is that a *technē* is a branch of knowledge. (The phrase '*technē* and knowledge [*epistēmē*]' makes no real contrast between the two terms.[7]) A *technē* is a branch of knowledge which guides some human activity to a successful outcome.[8]

---

[4] No single word in English captures the sense of *technē*. 'Craft' and 'expertise' are the least misleading translations, 'art' the most misleading.

[5] *Epideixis*. A good example of the practice is Protagoras' long speech about the origins of virtue at *Prot.* 320c ff. *Epideixis* was a method used by the Sophists, who also claimed to interpret poetry and 'considered themselves to be in the tradition of the poets and rhapsodes'—see Guthrie (1971), 41–4.

[6] See below, Ch. 2. The present chapter deals with the Plato's use of the concept in the *Ion* specifically.

[7] *Technē* is often synonymous with *epistēmē*, though the latter has a wider range of application. Exhaustive treatment of these and related terms is given in Lyons. See also Nussbaum (1986), 443–4 n. 10.

[8] 'An organized body of knowledge of the ways to achieve a certain end' (Annas (1981), 25); 'the systematic application of intelligence to any field of human activity' (Dodds (1973), 11). For more refined discussion see Woodruff (1990); Roochnik; Nussbaum (1986), 94–9 and 443–6; and below, Ch. 2.

Some have taken it that the aim of the *Ion* is to deny the existence of any rhapsodic *technē*.[9] Certainly Socrates repeats throughout that rhapsode and poet succeed in their activities not 'by *technē* and knowledge' but rather through an inspiration which comes from outside themselves. And yet, as we shall see, in the course of the work Socrates apparently assumes that there is both a rhapsodic and a poetic *technē*. One interpretation[10] reconciles these points by saying that Socrates assumes the craft-like nature of the rhapsode's activity only to refute it, that he traps Ion into an unsustainable claim to expert knowledge which will lead to absurdity. Part of the demonstration of that absurdity is the demonstration that not even poets, on whom rhapsodes depend for their supposed knowledge, have any genuine *technē* at all.

I shall offer an alternative interpretation. The dialogue is designed primarily to refute Ion's claims to knowledge in his *discourse about Homer*—i.e. in his role as critic or eulogist of Homer. His critical abilities are not an exercise of *technē* because they do not proceed on generalizable principles, and his intimacy with Homer's poetry bestows no knowledge of any of Homer's subject-matter. As regards poetic composition and performance, it is specifically their fineness or beauty that cannot be explained by way of *technē*. Poets and performers who delight us do not really know how they do it—they cannot explain their successes in terms of rational procedures they have followed. But, for all this, Plato assumes the existence of poetic and rhapsodic *technai*. He does not deny the common-sense view that being a poet or rhapsode is a form of craft or expertise. It is merely that whatever teachable, learnable expertise a poet or rhapsode may command is not the true source of the beauty of good poetry or good rhapsody, not the basis of artistic success (as we would call it). Seen in this way, the *Ion* becomes a less puzzling work. In the denial that *technē* is responsible for fine poetry we may see the beginnings of a separating out of the 'artistic' from knowledge-based activities such as medicine or building. That explains why modern readers find a positive evaluation of poetry here. The trouble is that Plato, while conscious of the wondrous power of the 'artistic', is highly suspicious of it.

The dialogue divides naturally into three sections. The first and third

---

[9] This is what Sprague means in saying 'the rhapsode is no expert and the rhapsode's art no art' (1976, 2). Flashar (37) holds that the concept of a rhapsodic *technē* is contradictory. Woodruff claims, with the *Ion* as witness, that Plato 'will not allow the poets a *technē*, even of pure style' (1982b, 145).

[10] Put forward by Flashar in his very detailed study.

(530a1–533c8 and 536d4–542b4) claim that Ion, in his capacity as eulogist of Homer, is not exercising a *technē*: his ability to discourse about Homer is not a case of expert knowledge. While Ion's claim to succeed as eulogist by *technē* is thus in the foreground, Plato allows Socrates the more or less common-sense assumptions that to be a poet or a performing rhapsode is to exercise a *technē*. Then, in order to give a positive account of Ion's success as a eulogist, the middle section (533c9–536d3) offers to explain the nature of fine poetry itself, using the Shelley-like notion of inspiration. Recognizing that a rhapsode 'speaks finely' about Homer, Plato is drawn to account for this by characterizing the fineness in poetry itself, which he holds to bypass *technē* altogether.

Socrates first pursues the seemingly trivial puzzle that this expert interpreter is an expert only on Homer: as Ion says himself, when anyone discusses any other poet, 'I pay no attention, and can offer no remark of any value. I frankly doze' (532b9–c2). But, in asking why this is so, Socrates introduces the principle that knowledge of a *technē* must be generalizable across all its possible subject-matter. Ion claims to make comparative judgements. Though Homer and Hesiod (or some other poet) may share subject-matter, such as warfare and the multifarious relationships of humans and gods (531c4–d1), still Homer does better as a poet—or so Ion judges. But if Homer and Hesiod write about the same things, then he should be able to interpret both equally.[11] And the point applies in particular to comparative judgements: to judge that *A* does better and *B* worse at the same activity requires only a single judging skill. Parallel examples are the *technē* of arithmetic applied to correct and incorrect calculation, and that of the doctor applied to good and bad diet. So, if Ion is exercising a *technē* in judging Homer, he is exercising the same *technē* in judging any other poet. Why then is he sure he has nothing authoritative to offer on any poet but Homer?

This is the explanation Socrates presses on him: 'it is obvious to everyone that you are unable to speak about Homer from *technē* and knowledge—because if you *were* about to do it by virtue of a *technē*, you would be able to speak about all the other poets too' (532c5–8). To possess a *technē* one must be able to apply some general principles to an appropriately wide range of objects—one does not have an

---

[11] *Ion* 531a8–b1. Plato confuses matters by talking about poets who do not 'say the same'. Does this mean poets who share subject-matter, but say different things about it, or poets who have different subject-matter? It is hard to see how the argument covers the latter case. See Sprague (1976), 2–4.

arithmetician's knowledge if one can apply the principle of subtraction only to the numbers 2 and 3, nor a doctor's knowledge if one can recognize and treat tonsillitis only in one or two patients. However, it is not clear how much weight this point will bear. Ion might have said that interpreting poetry in the role of critic *is* a *technē*, but that the range of poetry of which one must be knowledgeable in order to exercise it is in principle vague. Or he might have claimed that interpreting epic poetry, interpreting tragic poetry, interpreting lyric poetry, and so on, are separable *technai*; and if that is plausible, why can there not be a further separable *technē* of interpreting Homer? After all, this will be generalizable to cover not just a few lines or scenes, but everything that the *Iliad* and the *Odyssey* have to offer. ('That strikes me as enough', says Ion (531a3–4); and we might sympathize.)

But Plato does not allow Ion this reply. He has Socrates press home his point by stating that every *technē*, and the poetic *technē* in particular, exists 'as a whole' (532c8–d3). Parallel cases are painting ('Have you yet seen anyone who is an expert at demonstrating which paintings of Polygnotus . . . are good and which bad, but can't do the same for the other painters?' (532e7–533a1)), then sculpture, flute-playing, lyre-playing, singing to the accompaniment of the lyre, and rhapsody itself.[12] Rhapsody is assumed to be a *technē* along with the others, with the same point: if one can judge one rhapsode to be a success or failure in his endeavours, one must possess a general ability to recognize good and bad rhapsody among all-comers.

To see how the argument here works, we may distinguish between critical *technē* (that exercised by the sculpture-critic, music-critic, and so on), and object-*technē* (the *technē* judged—sculpture, music, and so on). The argument then goes as follows:[13]

1. If the exercising of an object-*technē* is to be judged by a critical *technē*, then the critical *technē* has principles generalizable across all instances of the object-*technē*.
2. Examples of object-*technē* which bear this out are sculpture, flute-

---

[12] Plato's examples of *technē* here are drawn from what we would call 'the arts'. But he provides no 'theory' of the arts in general—certainly none of 'Art'.

[13] For Flashar, poetic *technē* and rhapsodic *technē* are ironically assumed to exist in the *Ion*, only to have their existence refuted by the argument as it progresses (see 27–8, 59). But, while the present argument gives reasons why Ion as eulogist or critic is not exercising a *technē*, it relies on the assumptions that rhapsody (step 2) and poetry (step 3) are exercises of *technē* ripe for systematic judgement. If Socrates denies the existence of *technai* of poetry and rhapsody, he robs himself of this argument. (See Ferrari (1989), 95, for a similar view.)

playing, lyre-playing, singing to the accompaniment of the lyre, and rhapsody.

3. Poetry is a parallel example of an object-*technē*.
4. If judgements of poetry are made according to a critical *technē*, then they are made on the basis of principles generalizable across all instances of poetry.
5. Ion's judgements of Homer are not made on the basis of generalizable principles.
6. Therefore, Ion's judgements of Homer are not the exercise of a critical *technē*.

It is as if Plato were saying 'Critics of various arts are able to make judgements about these arts as a whole. They clearly use *technē*. But in the case of poetry, the ability to make judgements about it can bypass *technē* altogether.'

Faced with this thought, Plato has Socrates expound an alternative explanation of the rhapsode's critical abilities. The striking passage that follows is vital in explaining not only these abilities, but the rhapsode's ability as a public performer, the nature of the audience's response to his performance, and the nature of the good poet. The account has great economy, tracing all of these to a single source: an attraction by an exterior force one is unable to control, explain, or resist. The image Plato chooses to capture his point is that of a magnetic stone with the power to attract a metal ring and pass on the power of attraction to the ring itself so that it may attract others in a chain. The analogous description of poets is worth quoting at length:

Similarly, the Muse herself makes some men inspired, from whom a chain of other men is strung out who catch their own inspiration from theirs. For all good epic poets recite all that splendid poetry not by virtue of a *technē*, but in a state of inspiration and possession. The same is true of good lyric poets as well: just as Corybantic worshippers[14] dance without being in control of their senses, so too it's when they are not in control of *their* senses that the lyric poets compose those fine lyric poems. But once launched into their rhythm and musical mode, they catch a Bacchic frenzy:[15] just like Bacchic women, who when possessed and out of their senses draw forth milk and honey from

---

[14] A succinct gloss is provided by Saunders (1987), 55 n.: 'Corybants were mythical quasi-divine attendants on Cybele, a Phrygian goddess of nature and fertility; like them, her human worshippers engaged in frenzied dancing.'

[15] Saunders again (ibid.): 'Plato treats the ecstasy and dancing of Corybantic and Bacchic ritual as essentially similar. Bacchus (Dionysus) was the god of raw natural vitality.'

rivers—exactly what the souls of the lyric poets do, as they say themselves. You see, I understand the poets inform us that they bring their lyric poetry to us from certain gardens and glades of the Muses, by gathering it from honey-springs, like bees, and flying through the air like they do. And they are right. A poet, you see, is a light thing, and winged and holy, and cannot compose before he gets inspiration and loses control of his senses and his reason has deserted him. No man, so long as he keeps that, can prophesy or compose. (533e3–534b7.)

There are, Socrates says, distinct external sources of inspiration to which poets may succumb, inspiring them to excel at a different genre of composition, and, as he baldly puts it, 'each of them is hopeless at anything else' (534c4–5), an alleged fact[16] to be explained by the theory that it is 'not by virtue of a *technē*, but by a divine power' that they have their abilities. Further evidence for the same view is the phenomenon of a mediocre poet producing an isolated masterpiece. (Plato's example is one Tynnichus.) The best description of this, we are told, is that a god has spoken through the poet, using him as an instrument or mouthpiece.

The images in the quoted passage on poets are perhaps good examples of what Kant would call an 'aesthetic idea', or 'that representation of the imagination which induces much thought, yet without the possibility of any definite thought whatever, i.e. *concept*, being adequate to it'.[17] Plato uses 'literary' means to 'induce much thought' here. Abandoning the clipped dialogue style, he emulates the flow of poetry's language and its profusion of images, but always on the border of cliché and with a hovering sense of irony and ambiguity. Some have suggested that Plato's own literary sensitivities must detract from, or at least colour, his later attack on poetry. (According to Shelley, 'Plato was essentially a poet—the truth and splendour of his imagery, and the melody of his language, is the most intense that it is possible to conceive.'[18] He adopts the image of magnetism in his own *Defence of Poetry*.[19]) This issue needs careful handling, but Plato's literariness

---

[16] Apparently not a genuine fact, though. Tigerstedt (1969, 28) gives a salutary reminder: 'Everybody knew, for instance, that Pindar had composed both dithyrambs, encomia and dance-songs. Yet, it suited Plato to disregard this.'

[17] Kant, §49, 175–6. The central thought that crystallizes in this *Ion* passage is, incidentally, one Kant agrees with: 'No *Homer* or *Wieland* can show how his ideas, so rich at once in fancy and in thought, enter and assemble themselves in his brain, for the good reason that he does not himself know, and so cannot teach others' (ibid. §47, 170: almost an allusion to the *Ion*?).

[18] Shelley, 114.   [19] Ibid. 124.

(and not just in flights such as that quoted) is something we must acknowledge straight away.

Let us return to the argument. If this account of inspiration should prove to have some element of truth in it, how does it relate to what has gone before? How is Ion's ability to judge Homer without exercising a craft explained by Homer's composing his splendid poetry in a state of irrational possession? The answer is provided by spelling out the image of magnetic attraction with which Socrates' long speech begins. As the poet is an interpreter of the divine message, so the performer is in turn an interpreter of the poet for the audience (cf. 535a4–7). The performer's relation to the poet is the same as the poet's to his divine source. There is a single origin of magnetic power external to all the metal rings in the chain, which causes each to attract the next. And, just so, the single divine source of inspiration attracts the performer and the audience in turn to the poet's work. Because the poet is inspired, his work inspires its performer, and the performer's work inspires us.

It must then be shown that performer and audience are similarly affected by their attraction to the Muse through the poet. We switch attention from Ion's ability to discourse about his favourite poet, to his activities as a public performer. While performing one of the famous Homeric scenes involving Achilles and Hector, or Odysseus confronting the suitors, what is his state of mind? 'When you give a good performance of epic and stun your audience . . . are you, at that moment, in control of your senses? Or are you taken out of yourself, and does your soul, inspired as it is, imagine itself present at the events you describe?'[20] Socrates' question suggests a state in which the performer is 'out of his senses' or 'out of himself', being so wrapped up in the fictional course of events, and imagining them so vividly, that he no longer thinks of his actual situation as a person on a stage performing a fictional narrative, and so on. Ion picks up a related feature of this state: 'When I say something piteous, my eyes fill with tears. When it's something frightening or terrible, my hair stands on end with fear, and my heart thumps' (535c5–8). He experiences something like genuine emotions, with appropriate bodily manifestations, but directed towards events within the fictional scene. Plato senses that there is something odd about this, and the present passage is perhaps the very first in

---

[20] *Ion* 535b2–c2. Saunders has 'when you give a performance of epic', but the Greek is *hotan eu eipēis epē*, so I have amended to '. . . a *good* performance . . .' which reflects '*eu*'.

which the problem of 'fearing fictions' gets an airing, at least *en
passant*.[21] If these emotions are anything like genuine, then must not
the person who feels them be in a particular sort of cognitive state
directed towards the fictional events—perhaps something approaching
but falling short of a belief which is literally true? Conversely, if there
is nothing approaching belief here, then how can there can be genuine
emotion? Plato highlights two peculiarities of Ion's state of mind in
performance which contribute to the puzzlement:

SOCRATES. Well then, Ion, take a man dressed up at a feast or festival in
    elaborate clothing and golden crowns. If he has lost none of these things, but
    nevertheless breaks out in tears, or if he gets into a panic in spite of standing
    among more than twenty thousand friends, when no one is denuding him or
    doing him any harm, are we to say he's in his senses at that moment?
ION. No, by Zeus, not at all, Socrates, if the truth be told.
SOCRATES. And do you realize that you people have exactly these effects on
    most of your spectators?
ION. Yes, I'm very well aware of it. At each performance, I look down on them
    from up there on the platform as they weep and look at me with dire emotion
    in their eyes, in amazement at my story. You see, I have to pay a lot of
    attention to them—since if I make them cry I shall laugh all the way to the
    bank, whereas if I provoke their laughter, it's I who'll do the crying, for loss
    of my money. (535d1–e6.)

The dramatic performer must be disjointed from his ordinary beliefs
if he is to react with such emotional intensity to the unreal action he
relates—he must be at least to this extent 'out of his mind'. Yet at the
same time he must observe the audience and monitor their reaction.
The joke at the end has its serious point. Only if his performance is a
good one will he be paid: he needs to be cool-headed enough to know
that his performance is a good one. (The curious split in the performer's
state of mind is reflected in some remarks by a present-day actor, who
writes that 'unless it's your own lust, longing, or craving, the audience
will only be intellectually aroused: the thing will have been referred to,

---

[21] Gorgias had already noted fear and pity as characteristic effects of tragedy (*Encomium of Helen*, §9, in Sprague (ed.), 52—and see the discussion of Gorgias in Ch. 2
below). Aristotle remarks that in a tragedy 'the plot ought to be so constructed that,
even without the aid of the eye, someone hearing the story told will shudder with fear and feel
pity at the events in it' (*Poetics* 1453b3–6). But is genuine emotion here compatible with
understanding the context as fictional? Plato comes closer than Gorgias or Aristotle to
regarding this as a problem. A well-known recent discussion of the issue (to which I
allude) is by Walton. For a comparison of passages on pity and fear in Plato and Gorgias,
see Flashar, 68–72.

but not experienced', and yet at the same time: 'No matter how intense or painful the emotions of a part, the more you enter into them in a good performance, the less you are affected by them. . . . The emotion passes through you.'[22]) It has been suggested that Ion's conscious attention to the public's reaction is incompatible with 'a real state of possession'.[23] He cannot be literally in a trance-like Bacchic transport, and his implicit willingness to accept that he is is ironic. But his not being fully in rational control of what he is doing in performance, and his being genuinely moved to emotions disjointed from the reality he believes to obtain, need not conflict with his calculating attitude towards the audience. Plato merely grazes the surface of these problems, and his view concerning the mental state of the audience is even less developed. They simply 'weep' and have 'dire emotion in their eyes'—no hint of the special problem of emotional distancing that attends dramatic representation. Still, it is probably part of the truth that the performer and audience may be 'out of their senses' in being forgetful of their real-life situation and feeling temporary emotions out of tune with it.

So in the central section of the *Ion* Plato offers a single explanation for the ability of poets to write good poetry, of performers to perform it well, and of an audience to receive it in a way that they value. A good performance is one in which an audience becomes emotionally engaged, to the exclusion of their more self-possessed ordinary beliefs. The ability to produce a good performance requires the ability to become emotionally involved in the act of presenting the scene, so as to bring about the audience's emotional response, and again to the exclusion of some of one's more self-possessed beliefs. The basis of a good performance is a good poem to interpret, one that attracts the performer into the right emotional involvement. And a good poem is one written by someone possessed from outside by a force which they cannot understand, but which enables them to animate the emotions of performer and audience alike.

If this is how things stand, we can expect poets themselves to run into problems when posed certain kinds of question—something

---

[22] Callow, 167, 200. An anecdote reveals how actors learn to observe their own genuinely emotional behaviour in a detached way. The actor Micheál MacLiammóir heard, in real life, that a friend was dead: 'He burst into tears and ran downstairs to the reception desk. On the way down, he passed a mirror and caught sight of himself in it. "Oh," he thought to himself, "*that's* what one looks like when the dearest person to one in the whole world has just died"' (ibid. 174).

[23] Tigerstedt (1969), 21.

confirmed elsewhere by Plato. In the *Apology of Socrates* poets are among those Socrates says he has examined by cross-questioning and found to claim knowledge which they do not have. 'I decided', Socrates says, 'that it was not wisdom that enabled them to write their poetry, but a kind of instinct or inspiration, such as you find in seers and prophets who deliver all their many fine messages without knowing anything of what they say'.[24] A further remark intimates why this discovery should be so important: 'I also observed that the very fact that they were poets made them think that they had a perfect understanding of all other subjects, of which they were totally ignorant' (*Apol.* 22c4–6). While Ion's extravagant professions to knowledge are—as we shall see—ridiculous, Plato is also concerned that poets themselves claim wide-ranging knowledge which they do not have. But why do they have *no* knowledge?

> I turned to the poets, dramatic, lyric,[25] and all the rest . . . I used to pick up what I thought were some of their most perfect works and *ask them closely what they were saying* . . . It is hardly an exaggeration to say that any of the bystanders could have *spoken better about the poetry they had made*.[26]

Poets show themselves ignorant in interpreting their own 'meaning'. And in the *Protagoras* Plato thinks that nobody else can really do much better: 'most often when [poets] are introduced into the discussion some say the poet's meaning [what the poet means or thinks, *noein*] is one thing and some another, for the topic is one on which nobody can produce a conclusive argument' (*Prot.* 347e4–7). Poetry appears to express thoughts, but neither their utterer nor anyone else can give an authoritative account of what those thoughts are. This acts as further evidence for the view that poets lack full rational understanding or control of the making of poetry. If you cannot say what you mean, how can your fine words have sprung from the application of your intelligence? Paul Woodruff attributes to Plato the view that poetry, while it may express thoughts, even truths, is 'insulated from the belief structure of its author'.[27] If this is right, there is literally nothing that the poet

---

[24] *Apol.* 22b8–c3. The word rendered 'instinct' is *phusis*, 'nature'—compare the idea of a 'natural gift'.

[25] Literally, 'the poets [makers] of tragedies, of dithyrambs, and the rest'. Dithyrambs are discussed briefly in Ch. 2 below.

[26] *Apol.* 22a8–b8. Emphases mine, marking divergences from Tredennick's less literal translation.

[27] Woodruff (1982*b*), 144. Cf. Ferrari's view: 'a poem is not meant to be a set of opinions . . .; it is meant for performance' (1989, 103).

means or thinks, which would neatly explain the phenomena Plato remarks upon.

Here we may recall Socrates' opening remarks: the rhapsode must interpret not only the poet's words, but his thought (*dianoia*); one cannot be a rhapsode properly if one does not understand what the poet is saying. Ion presumably expounds Homer's pronouncements on many topics in a highly convincing manner, not just repeating the verse, but offering helpful elucidations. However, what worries Plato is that while poetry's words convey thoughts, the process by which these thoughts come to lodge in the mind of the audience is suspect. Homer, to start with, was far from being an authority on the truth of the thoughts in his poetry. He did not arrive at his words by rational means, and is no infallible authority even on which thoughts they convey. Then the inspired expositor sets to work, and may discern a great many thoughts conveyed by the poem, but another enthusiast may disagree—no one has over-riding authority or responsibility for truth anywhere in the chain. It can happen that a thought is picked up which announces something true and important, as Plato says elsewhere.[28] But this is only 'hitting on' the truth by an unreliable method, and is not sufficient for anyone to claim knowledge.

The chief negative point of the *Ion* is that Ion's ability to speak finely about Homer arises 'not from *technē* or knowledge'. Instead it is 'by divine dispensation (*theia moira*)' that our rhapsode is enabled to speak so finely of Homer. That he discerns value in Homer and has the ability to convey his *aperçus* to others stems from his being caught up, as a performer, in the power of a chain of inspiration. One argument was given earlier for the dialogue's negative claim; following the glimpse of Ion as performer of Homer, we revert (536d4) to considering him as the critic or 'eulogist' of Homer, and after one final reinforcing argument, Socrates offers Ion the choice of being considered the possessor of a genuine *technē*—but 'unfair' for not revealing it under questioning—or 'divine' because his ability stems from a state of possession. 'It's a much finer thing to be thought divine', says Ion (542b1–2), though in accepting ignorance and lack of a *technē* along with 'divine' status, he receives at best a double-edged compliment. It is in this final

---

[28] Cf. in the late dialogue *Laws*: Homer wrote some marvellous lines about the founding of Troy 'under some sort of inspiration from God . . . And how true to life they are! This is because poets as a class are divinely gifted and are inspired when they sing so that with the help of Graces and Muses they frequently hit on how things really happen' (*Laws* 682a2–5).

section that it is hardest to sympathize with Plato's direction of proceedings: Socrates appears to ask grossly irrelevant questions, to which Ion responds with sheer stupidity. I shall suggest that the argument nevertheless establishes something which is true, even if its point is obscure until more philosophical work is done.

Socrates has 'spoken well' of the divine power that produces good poetry and rhapsodic performance, but Ion is still sure that he is not 'out of his senses' when he eloquently praises Homer. To convince him, Socrates fastens attention on the question of subject-matter. Ion's subject-matter is what Homer says about various things. But which subject-matter in Homer is it that gives Ion the opportunity to 'speak well'? 'Every single one of them', is his claim—there is nothing in what Homer covers that Ion 'does not know about' (536e1–7). What are we to make of this? In a sense the claim is harmless. As a frequent reciter of extracts from the poems, Ion is familiar with the entire Homeric corpus and well aware of its dramatic successes, whatever is taking place within the narrative. Accordingly, we find that when Socrates mentions a random topic, chariot-racing, Ion replies with Nestor's speech before the chariot-race in *Iliad* Book 23. Whatever Homer speaks about, Ion could find a passage and discourse eloquently on it.

Socrates is concerned with Homer's portrayal of chariot-racing, medicine, fishing, prophecy, generalship—i.e. the exercise of some *technē* by a fictional character, whom the poet either describes as exercising expertise, or makes speak in a manner betokening it. But his key question is this: Does speaking well about a poet's depiction of a character with some *technē* require possession of that *technē* by the speaker? The question is ambiguous. Ion 'speaks well' in the sense that he is eloquent and convincing in his praise of Homer as a poet. Socrates, on the other hand, allows 'speaking well' to encompass only saying whether a craft is depicted correctly or not (e.g. 'Are we to assert that it is more the business of a fisherman's *technē*, or that of a rhapsode, to assess what [Homer] says [about fishing], and whether he says it well or not?' (538d4–5)). Obviously one does this best if one possesses the craft oneself. Once things are set up this way, each real-life exponent of a craft has certain portions of Homer's work on which they are especially competent to pronounce, and so it makes sense for Socrates to demand: 'Pick out for me the sort of thing which concerns the rhapsode and the rhapsode's *technē*, and which the rhapsode properly examines and judges better than the rest of us.' Ion dare not say 'Nothing'. But on the reasonable assumption that each craft must have its own circumscribed subject-matter, he cannot claim to know everything in Homer.

He must make a positive, but limited claim to knowledge; and his next suggestion is by no means foolish. A rhapsode in particular would know:

What may suitably be said by a man . . . and the sort of thing suitably said by a woman; the sort suitable for a slave to say, and the sort suitable for a freeman; and the sort of thing suitable in the mouth of a ruler, and the sort suitable in that of a subject. (540b3–5.)

Socrates insists, however, that it is only when such persons are exercising a specialized role that the question of what is appropriate for them to say arises (when a slave is a cowherd, a woman a wool-spinner, and so on). At this, Ion's last refuge is to select some specific craft depicted by Homer, and claim that it is in this sphere that he is knowledgeable. There is a great deal of generalship in the *Iliad*—so a rhapsode would certainly know 'what is appropriate in the mouth of someone who's a general, when he is exhorting his troops'. But to make Ion sustain this line, Plato reduces him to the ridiculous expedient of claiming to see 'no difference' between the craft of generalship and that which makes him a good rhapsode, and even to be himself the best general among the Greeks. (Iris Murdoch finds 'unspeakable charm' here,[29] but is the irony overdone when Ion adds, 'that too I learnt from the works of Homer'?) It is easy to show that the crafts of general and rhapsode are distinct, and to point out that Ion's life has shown no evidence of generalship. He is being 'unfair' if he has genuine military '*technē* and knowledge', and has carefully concealed it (541e1–3). Otherwise he must lack such knowledge; and, if he lacks it, the only explanation is that his ability to speak about Homer stems from the inspiration discussed earlier. He acquiesces in the final statement that, as eulogist of Homer, he should be accorded the status of being 'divine' rather than skilled (*technikos*).

The truth which this final passage establishes is that to speak well, in the sense that Ion can lay claim to, about Homer's depiction of any *technē*, does not require possession of that *technē* oneself. Plato does not make the false claim that a successful eulogist of Homer cannot have the knowledge of a general or a charioteer. Rather, he makes the point that such knowledge is not necessary, and would therefore be incidental to one's success in the role of eulogist. In the *Republic* he makes the same point concerning the poets,[30] and there is clearly a

---

[29] Murdoch, 8.
[30] *Rep*. 598b–601b. See the discussion in Ch. 6 below, and also Janaway (1991). Urmson (1982, 129–35) expounds the point and related issues with vigour.

connection between the two cases. How could Ion, whose ability is the derivative one of discoursing about Homer's writing, be required to have knowledge of generalship, when Homer himself can lack such knowledge and still write good poetry about its exercise?

A useful picture is that of different levels of *technē*.[31] A general or a charioteer has a *technē* which is basic, in that its subject-matter is simply directing men in warfare or driving a chariot. By contrast, the *technē* of the poet is at second level: its subject-matter includes the basic *technai*, along with their subject-matter. The rhapsode's critical or eulogistic art is at a third level: when he 'speaks well' of Homer, his subject-matter is the poetic *technē*. Now note two important points. In one sense, there is a transparency between these levels: in discoursing on Homer's exercise of the art of poetry, one obtains generalship and charioteering as part of one's subject-matter. But knowledge of the basic subject-matter is not transmitted up the hierarchy of levels. Already at the poet's level, including a *technē* in one's subject-matter, and having the ability to make fine poetry about it, does not require that one have knowledge of its subject-matter. How much less then, on the strength of his abilities, should a mere eulogist of poetry claim knowledge of any basic *technē*. As we shall see, these two theses, the transparency of poetry's subject-matter, and its non-transmission of knowledge, remain fundamental to Plato's thinking about the arts: the discussion of *mimēsis* in *Republic* Book 10 has equivalents of the same theses at its core.

Earlier we raised the question whether there are rhapsodic and poetic crafts at all for Plato. The rather rambling final argument tells us nothing more about whether there is a poetic *technē*. But it makes eight mentions of 'the rhapsodic *technē*', all put into the mouth of Socrates,[32] as if he affirms its existence. Of course, on one view[33] this should again be read as a temporary assumption of precisely what is to be refuted. But if we look carefully at the argument's conclusion, we do not find any statement that there exists no rhapsodic *technē*. The conclusion is

---

[31] Here I am indebted to Sprague (1976), 6–7.

[32] 538b4, c5, d5, 539e3, 540a2, a5, d4, 541a1–2. Three of these use the expression *hē rhapsōidikē*, omitting the word *technē*. In these passages Ion admits that the rhapsodic *technē* is distinct from those of the charioteer, doctor, and fisherman, is asked whether he sticks by his doomed claim that the rhapsodic *technē* is identical with that of the general, asked what the special subject-matter of the rhapsodic *technē* is, and forced to conclude that the rhapsodic *technē* does not know everything.

[33] That of Flashar.

that *as a eulogist of Homer* Ion is not master of any *technē*.[34] Moreover, the dialectical context requires only that Ion's own professions of knowledge are refuted, and what is contested is not his claim to be an expert rhapsode, or his claim that there is such a thing as expertise in rhapsody. The dubious assertions he has made are that he is an expert on everything that Homer writes about, and that he is an expert in the *technē* of generalship. The argument refutes these claims easily, using as premisses the general proposition:

If *technai* T_1 and T_2 are distinct, then the practitioner of T_1 does not as such have the knowledge enjoyed by the practitioner of T_2.[35]

and the specific assumption about the rhapsodic *technē*:

The rhapsodic *technē* is distinct from those of charioteering, medicine, generalship . . . (all the *technai* Homer portrays).[36]

Thus if the rhapsode's *technē* is distinct from any one of the *technai* Homer depicts, the rhapsode will not have knowledge of all such forms of expertise, as Ion initially claims. If it is distinct from every one of them, then the rhapsodic expert can claim knowledge of none of the *technai* portrayed in the Homeric poems. Conclusion: no *technē* explains the success of the rhapsode when he acts as judge or eulogist of his poet's handling of particular subject-matters. But this is not to say 'there is no rhapsodic *technē*'. It is compatible with the dialogue's ending that there should be a rhapsodic craft. The point is that, if there is such a craft, its practitioner speaks *finely* rather than *knowledgeably* when discoursing on his favourite poet, and that such fine speaking is precisely what cannot be explained by mastery of a *technē*.

This is all well and good, but we may feel that important issues have been evaded. As Iris Murdoch puts it: 'Ion, looking for something to be expert on, might more fruitfully have answered: a general knowledge of human life, together of course with a technical knowledge of poetry.

[34] In the final sentence he is said to be *mē technikon peri Homērou epainetēn*: not a eulogist about Homer by *technē* (542b3–4). The conditional choice offered him preparatory to this conclusion is in precisely the same terms: either he is able to eulogize Homer by *technē* and *epistēmē* (541e1–2), or he is not *technikos*, but speaks many fine things about the poet through being possessed by divine power and knowing nothing (542a2–5). Cf. 532c6–7, 536d2–3, 536c1–2.

[35] Cf. *kata pasōn tōn technōn, ha tēi heterai technēi gignōskomen, ou gnōsometha tēi heterai*, 537d1–2.

[36] 538b4–5 states this step explicitly for charioteering. The ensuing argument brings in parallel *technai* without stating this step again for each—a tactical suppression which enables the final skirmish in which Ion denies the distinction between rhapsody and generalship.

. . . The humane judgement of the experienced literary man is excluded from consideration by Socrates' sharp distinction between technical knowledge and "divine intuition".[37] There are two points here: firstly, if we are talking about technical knowledge at all, then it is false that poet and critic lack it, since they have specialized technical knowledge concerning poetry itself. Secondly, the discussion should not be restricted to technical knowledge, since there is also a 'general knowledge of human life'—dare we say 'wisdom'?—that informs the best poetry, and gives authority to criticism. Let us take the two points separately.

First consider 'general knowledge of human life'. Ion comes closest to this when he talks of 'what may suitably be said by a man . . . and the sort of thing suitably said by a woman; the sort suitable for a slave to say', and so on. It has been suggested that 'with this objection Plato shows that he is aware of the narrowness of his own handling of the problem'.[38] However, the issues become anything but clear once this is mooted. Are we considering the 'general knowledge of human life' which any ordinary person above a certain age would have acquired? If so, we still lack any specialist knowledge for the rhapsodic critic *per se*. Are we looking for an uncommon range of experience and depth of insight into human life? If so, why should that be the prerogative of the poetry critic? Why, indeed, should such wisdom be his at all? Ion manages to be a great eulogist of Homer without showing exceptional wisdom. The only 'knowledge of what is suitable for people to say' that is a plausible candidate as the rhapsodic critic's specialism is knowledge of what it is suitable for people to say in an epic poem—in other words, how characters are appropriately represented by a poet such as Homer. And why should that require any more than an ordinary knowledge of life itself? Julius Moravcsik suggests that 'poets and their appreciators' are likely to have more sensitivity than the average person to 'the cruelty and senselessness of war', for example; this is something which Homer 'knew as much about, if not more, than any general'.[39] But again would our best description be that Homer had a special sensitivity to the cruelty of war, or that he had the sensitivity to imagine and represent it? If the latter, we are in the province not of knowing about war, but of the ability to compose fine poetry, which Plato has already dealt with in this dialogue: it comes not from knowledge, but from inspiration.

---

[37] Murdoch, 9.   [38] Schaper, 33.   [39] Moravcsik (1982), 36.

Murdoch's other point is that Plato ignores the importance of that technical knowledge of poetry which Ion may have. I take it we mean such things as rules for writing or reciting in a set metre, what marks the difference in the epic genre between narration and a speech in character, perhaps even which modes of diction (vocabulary, syntax) are appropriate for poetry as opposed to prose. All of this can be learned, and is appropriately called the craft of poetry. The rhapsode's expertise in performance may be fed by such knowledge, and may in addition have rules of its own that can be learned. If Ion has such technical knowledge, it is strange that we hear nothing of its informing his discourse on Homer's good qualities, especially since the possibility was canvassed earlier of judging poetry by a genuine form of expertise. That possibility has receded by the end.[40] But in the final argument Plato shows not that Ion lacks any technical knowledge—only that the critic need possess none of the crafts portrayed in the poetry he judges. He neither affirms nor closes off the possibility of a proper craft of poetry-criticism. Thus on my reading Plato need not be denying specialist expertise to the poet and rhapsode. Their having it will not be very important, though: knowing in detail how to construct and enunciate hexameters is not evidence of knowing anything else.

So a poet's ability to compose fine poetry does not stem from '*technē* and knowledge'—while yet Plato appears to assume that there is a *poiētikē technē*. But this position is intelligible. What is at stake is the *fineness* of poetry and performance—and this may not stem from the correct exercise of the crafts of poetry and rhapsody, even if they exist. Plato makes clear in the middle section of the *Ion* that he is concerned to account for the fineness or beauty of what good poets say:

All good epic poets recite all that splendid [*kala*] poetry not by virtue of a *technē*, but in a state of inspiration and possession. The same is true of good lyric poets as well: . . . it's when they are not in control of *their* senses that the lyric poets compose those fine [*kala*] lyric poems.[41]

'These fine [*kala*] poems are not on the human level nor the work of humankind, but divine, and the work of gods', says Socrates at the

---

[40] LaDrière (31) suggests this is because the latter part of the dialogue is 'devoted to establishing that no such criticism can be found, or is in the nature of things possible'.

[41] *Ion* 533e5–534a2. *kalos* and cognate terms occur a further six times in Socrates' long speech up to 535a2. (This is well brought out by Dorter, 75.) Plato's phrasing emphasizes that it is *good* poets he is talking about: *hoi tōn epōn poiētai hoi agathoi . . . kai hoi melopoioi hoi agathoi* might be translated 'the epic poets — the good ones . . . and the makers of lyrics — the good ones'.

culmination of his long speech. There are bad poets, of whom Tynnichus is said to be one, but the gods proved themselves the true origin of fine poetry, when Tynnichus of all people produced the finest [*kalliston*] lyric (534e2–535a1). The rest of Tynnichus' output demands no explanation in terms of divine inspiration. It is the fineness or beauty of poetry that is inexplicable even to the poet and requires the theory that he is a mouthpiece for an external agency. Bad or indifferent poets, who may yet be *bona fide* poets composing according to the poetic *technē*, are bad or indifferent because they are not visited by the right divine power. This appears to be Plato's view in the later *Phaedrus*: 'if a man comes to the door of poetry untouched by the madness of the Muses, believing that *technē* alone will make him a good poet, he and his sane compositions never reach perfection, but are utterly eclipsed by the performances of the inspired madman.'[42] The point is: *technē* is not sufficient. But it is not necessary to *lack* it in order to be a good poet or, for that matter, a good eulogist of a good poet.

Some have doubted the extent to which Ion is supposed to be genuinely inspired.[43] But this is not very troubling. His acquisition of the epithet 'divine' at the end of the dialogue is ironic in tone, but need not be insincere in substance. Ion is touched, relatively remotely, by the divine chain of inspiration—he is 'divine' by proxy. What he produces is genuinely fine and admirable, and it is these qualities in particular which Plato wishes to explain as having a divine source. But just for this reason Ion cannot take the credit by attributing the fineness of his performances to his own agency. If the gods may choose Tynnichus as their direct mouthpiece, their power may light—at further remove —upon a pretentious fool. We do not have to find *him* particularly admirable, for the 'divine dispensation' thesis to be literally believed by Plato.

What then of the inspiration of poets? Although Plato says that his doctrine of inspiration corresponds with what 'the poets inform us', scholars have recently suggested that the view of inspiration as an irrational state in which one is 'out of one's senses' is simply Plato's own.[44] Poets traditionally called on the Muses (the invocations at the beginning of the *Iliad* and *Odyssey* are probably the best known examples) for assistance in exercising their craft, in getting their story right, in having sufficient powers of memory, and in conveying the truth

---

[42] *Phdr*. 245a5–8, slightly adapted from the translation by Hamilton. For more discussion, see below, Ch. 7.
[43] See Flashar, 72–3, 88.   [44] See Tigerstedt (1970); Murray.

about their subject-matter. Skill, craft, knowledge, and moral wisdom are all assigned to poets with no suggestion that inspiration would rob them of such qualities. Plato's notion, however, is a new one at odds with this. For him craft-knowledge and poetic inspiration exclude one another: the inspired are in a state of mind in which they do not understand what they are doing and are even not full agents, merely mouthpieces for higher beings who speak through them. According to W. J. Verdenius, inspiration takes on a problematic character once this change to the traditional notion has been made. 'The old collaboration of the poet and his Muse breaks down', he writes,[45] 'because the poet, in his ecstasy, is no longer himself. . . . The same inspiration which establishes his contact with the Muse mars his understanding of her intentions.' In Verdenius' view the poet is like an over-excited messenger who can pass on only a garbled version of an important piece of news. What rings untrue in Verdenius' reading is the implication that inspiration for Plato consists of two separable components: (*a*) receiving some message from a higher authority, and (*b*) being in an irrational frenzy. If only—we are supposed to think—one could receive the message whilst in a fit state of mind to make rational use of it.

But there is no clue from the *Ion* that this is possible, because Plato is not looking to the divine source of poetry as an explanation of its truth or wisdom—rather as an explanation of its fineness as poetry, which he identifies as a distinct question. There is a tension throughout the dialogue between two senses of 'speaking finely'.[46] Only the fisherman can judge if Homer speaks finely—correctly—of the fisherman's craft, or whether Ion in his eulogizing lectures 'speaks finely'— correctly—of these same matters. But in these very lectures Ion is said to 'speak many fine things' about the poet, and what the poet himself says in his art is of a dazzling beauty. Plato thinks that the ability to speak correctly, truly, or wisely stems from knowledge or *technē*, to possess which is to apply rational principles of which one is fully conscious. By contrast, to speak finely or beautifully, as poet, performer, or eulogist, so as to bring about pleasure and emotional involvement in an audience, is not a matter of knowledge or *technē*, but of inspiration. The older notion of inspiration has the poet fully in control of his mind, yet aided by the Muse in delivering truth and wisdom. In Verdenius' view inspiration is both the Muse's delivery of truth and wisdom, and the poet's being in a state of unknowing passivity.

[45] Verdenius (1983), 44.   [46] As pointed out by Dorter, 75.

But Plato is further away from the older notion than that. There is in his account no divine 'truth' to be interpreted rightly or wrongly—only a power which enables the production of beauty. Through the mediation of a human mouthpiece the gods speak beautifully, as Socrates says at 534e. The 'interpreter of the poet's thought' moves us simply because he is a channel for the transmission of inspiration.[47]

So is this twist of the inspiration doctrine designed to belittle poets? The difficulty of taking the 'passive possession' view literally may force us to construe it as remaining at the level of metaphor. Then we are pushed in one of two directions: either the account is meant not seriously, but as an ironic demolition of the poets' own pretensions; or Plato's metaphorical flights offer serious praise of poetry by essentially poetic means.[48] The dialogue as a whole cannot be read as praising poetry unequivocally; but its obvious irony belittles not so much poetry as one character's ill-thought-out claim to a kind of knowledge and expertise he does not have. Good poets produce a species of beauty or fineness, and it is quite in order to say that we should admire them for this, while insisting that they do not do so from the rational application of readily explicable principles, as in a standard *technē*.[49] Read in this way, the *Ion* does not devalue poetry itself, but puts forward a theory of what makes good poetry good. And it makes fun of those who do not accept that theory and take themselves to have gained an enormous amount of knowledge from poetry. These are the same *epaineteis* of Homer who in the *Republic* (606e1 ff.) claim that their poet is the chief educator of Greece. They rely on the premiss that to make poetry finely (*kalōs*), the good poet must do so with knowledge, and from this they conclude that Homer, who makes poetry finely about a panoramic range of subjects, has knowledge of all the crafts, and of all matters concerning the human and the divine.[50] But the premiss is false, and so is the

---

[47] Moravcsik states the correct view succinctly: 'At no point . . . is inspiration construed as a special kind of insight; the inspired poet . . . lacks what Plato would regard as genuine knowledge or understanding' (1982, 35). Ferrari (1989, 99) also sees that Plato contrasts 'inspiration with understanding and verbal performance with genuine communication'.

[48] Tigerstedt (1969), 26, who cites Goethe and Marsilio Ficino as exemplary authorities for the 'ironic' and 'praising' readings respectively.

[49] Thus 'Plato's attitude toward inspiration mixes sweet with sour' (Woodruff (1982*b*), 138), though this need not betoken the ineptness implied by Else: 'He sets out to hold [poetry] up to mockery . . . But somehow in the doing he is carried away and paints so glowing a picture of the poetic afflatus that we almost believe it *is* divine' (1986, 8).

[50] *Rep.* 598d8–e5. See below, Ch. 6, and Janaway (1991).

conclusion—as Plato shows (or comes near to showing) when he approaches the topic in serious mood.

Shelley approaches Plato's view in saying that poetry 'acts in a divine and unapprehended manner, beyond and above consciousness',[51] though really, as we saw in the passage quoted at the outset, he thinks that the 'power' of the mind in creation 'arises from within', from, presumably, a portion of our own nature of which we are not conscious. This too is a mere gesture, as undeveloped, if also as evocative, as Plato's: it is unclear what such a 'power' is going to be. But there is a core position common to Shelley and Plato: that when poetry is good, it does not owe its goodness to any exercise of rational principles by its author, and that its author can offer no explanation, from within the conscious apprehension of his or her own psychology, for the fineness of the product. I have not said that this view of the nature of good poetry is true. Deciding the extent of its truth is, however, a task which Plato sets for the philosophy of art, and one which will remain with us in this book.

[51] Shelley, 116.

2

Arts, Crafts, and the Production of Pleasure

PLATO alleges that the performing arts of music and tragic drama aim solely to produce pleasure in their audiences, and that to do so they employ a sophisticated kind of guesswork. They do not—as he would prefer—aim at what is good for the audience, nor do they pursue their ends by adhering to general, rational principles. Their practitioners cannot, then, claim knowledge, nor any genuinely beneficial effect on the community. In these ways they are unlike medicine and should instead be classed with public rhetoric, of which Plato cannot approve. Rhetoric is massively persuasive, and dangerous because its speaker (*rhētōr*) seeks merely to gratify the audience, who then cannot distinguish gratification from learning and improvement. Knowledge and genuine excellence are lost, but their loss is masked by the presence of a beguiling counterfeit which more than satisfies its recipients. We shall see these allegations made in the *Gorgias*, where Plato again uses the concept of *technē*, though this time in a more strongly theoretical manner. By the criteria Plato uses here neither rhetoric nor the pleasure-giving performing arts which he discusses qualify as *technai* at all.

There is a misapprehension which some historians of aesthetics have fallen into—that it is safe to treat *technē* as the central positive concept in Plato's philosophy of the arts. The picture is this: first an all-embracing theory of what *technē* is, then a division of 'the arts' (*technai*) into various classes and subclasses (such as the productive and the 'imitative'), where what applies to *technē* as a whole applies to each species, including poetry and the other 'fine arts' of modern times.[1] I think this picture is misguided. In his later works Plato is interested in a systematic account of *technē* by the method of division, and for the purposes

---

[1] Examples: Bosanquet, 38; Grey, 303–10; Lodge, 52–63; Hofstadter and Kuhns, 3; Beardsley, 32–3. Sometimes *technē* is rendered 'art', with the acknowledgement that 'art' includes both fine arts and crafts. However, Lodge (62) repeats Collingwood's claim (discussed below), saying that 'poetry is an outstanding example of human craftsmanship' for Plato.

of such classifications various art activities will belong under the heading of *technē*.[2] But in earlier writings the story is quite different. We have looked at the *Ion*, where poetry's artistic success (as we would call it) stems from inspiration, and mentioned the *Apology*, where Socrates complains that poets cannot explain what they have written about. In the *Gorgias*, as we shall see, tragedy and some kinds of music are explicitly denied the status of a *technē*. The trend culminates in *Republic* Book 10, where it is argued that poets lack knowledge, and where they are contrasted unfavourably with ordinary craftsmen. It would be fanciful to treat all these passages as aberrations from some preconceived system of classification in which poetry is neatly subordinated to the concept of *technē*.

R. G. Collingwood provides an interesting example of the aesthetician's mistake about *technē*. While in his own theory 'art' and 'craft' are mutually exclusive categories,[3] he attributes to Plato the view that poetry is simply a craft. Craft, he claims, is what in Latin was called *ars*, and in Greek *technē*. He glosses it as 'the power to produce a preconceived result by means of consciously controlled and directed action'.[4] Collingwood sees that *technē* cannot properly be translated as 'art' and is somewhat closer to his own conception of 'craft'. Yet he announces boldly that his own conception was 'expounded once for all' in the writings of the Greek philosophers, and that Plato and Aristotle 'took it for granted that poetry, the only art which they discussed in detail, was a kind of craft, and spoke of this craft as *poiētikē technē*, poet-craft'.[5] In the Greek conception, he continues, the poet 'is a kind of skilled producer; he produces for consumers; and the effect of his skill is to bring about in them certain states of mind, which are conceived in advance as desirable states. The poet, like any other kind of craftsman, must know what effect he is aiming at, and must learn by experience and precept . . . how to produce it.'

We may note two of the characteristics Collingwood himself assigns to craft, and which he claims are lacking in the case of art (or 'art proper'). Firstly, the distinction between means and end—a craft always has an end-product, to which certain actions are means. Characteristic of such

---

[2] See *Soph.* 219a–d, 233d–236c, 264c–267d; *Pol.* 284e, 288c; *Phil.* 55d–56c. These passages are discussed in Ch. 7 below.

[3] Collingwood recognizes the importance of hard-won technique for artists (1938, 26–9), and allows that a work of art *can* also be a work of craft. But, for him, something's being an exercise of craft-technique is never part of what makes it art.

[4] Ibid. 15.   [5] Ibid. 17, 18.

actions is that they 'are passed through or traversed in order to reach the end, and are left behind when the end is reached'. Secondly, the distinction between planning and execution—

The result to be obtained is preconceived or thought out before being arrived at. The craftsman knows what he wants to make before he makes it. This foreknowledge is absolutely indispensable to craft: if something, for example stainless steel, is made without such foreknowledge, the making of it is not a case of craft but an accident. ... If a person sets out to make a table, but conceives the table only vaguely, as somewhere between two by four feet and three by six, and between two and three feet high, and so forth, he is no craftsman.[6]

Collingwood argues that what is 'properly' called art shares none of the features of craft. According to Shelley, 'A man cannot say "I will compose poetry"'. Collingwood agrees. In his view, all art including poetry is an act in which the artist expresses his or her emotion in a moment of authentic self-realization. Prior to the completion of a poem, there can be no accurate specification of the finished product. There may be planning and execution of a kind, but there is no foreknowledge such as the practitioner of a craft must have. The idea is that if I could tell you what I wanted to express in a poem prior to its completion, it would be redundant to complete the poem—or, contrary to hypothesis, it would already be complete, because I would already have expressed my emotion in telling you. For the same reason, the means–end distinction is lacking. The 'end' is not specifiable until it is reached, and the 'means' are not discarded as mere instruments once an 'end' is reached— for, according to Collingwood, the process of expressing one's emotion really is the work of art itself.

Now Collingwood thinks Plato had the correct conception of craft, but confusedly made poetry into a species of craft which worked as a means to the end of arousing emotions. What Plato objects to, on this story, is poetry's craft-like manipulation of its audience into the frivolous emotional states of 'mere entertainment'. It is true that Plato criticizes some of the arts, including some poetry, for aiming at the production of pleasure. But, contrary to what Collingwood says, this is part of the argument that such arts are in the strict sense not instances of *technē* at all. In fact, Plato's views are closer to Collingwood's own than he appreciates. It is precisely poetry's unprincipled, un-craft-like

[6] Ibid. 15–16.

nature which makes it so suspicious to him. In the sense of 'skill' that matters to Plato, poets are not skilled producers.

We should be wary of making too many assumptions about 'craft' and '*technē*'. Although it is common to talk of a Socratic 'craft-analogy', it has been doubted recently whether 'craft' is an appropriate translation of *technē* at all. Some *technai*, such as medicine, are too theoretical to be called crafts; others, such as arithmetic, lack any separable end-product.[7] 'Expert knowledge' or 'expertise' are probably the terms which best match the range of *technē*. On the other hand, activities which we do call crafts are usually included under *technē*. Thus if poetry turned out to be a kind of skilled making analogous to building or weaving, then it would be a *technē* too.

To what extent should we agree with Collingwood in divorcing art from crafts such as these? His view that true art must occur wholly without preconception or the deliberate application of means to an end is undoubtedly a myth. But there is a less hard-line view which permeates a great deal of modern thinking about art. This is the view that art involves an exercise of craft as a necessary condition, but is not exhausted by it. Kant provides a clear instance. The production of works of fine art, Kant claims, requires 'a *talent* for producing that for which no definite rule can be given: and not an aptitude in the way of cleverness for what can be learned according to some rule';[8] but nevertheless 'there is . . . no fine art in which something mechanical, capable of being at once comprehended and followed in obedience to rules, and consequently something *academic* does not constitute the essential condition of the art'.[9] Even though without craftsmanship there would be no art at all, the criterion of 'fineness' in fine art always exceeds the requirement that a craft has been exercised properly. We shall see that in some respects Plato's denial of the status of *technē* to musical performance and tragedy is parallel, except that, as with the case of inspiration, his evaluation is reversed: if a performer is not *technikos*, that is a ground for disapproval.

Plato deploys the concept of *technē* in the early dialogues for

---

[7] The translation 'craft' may wrongly suggest an activity whose end-product is identifiable independently of the activity itself. (As Critias asks in the *Charmides*, 'What is the product [*ergon*] of the art of arithmetic or geometry, in the way that a house is the product of building, a cloak of the art of weaving, or many other such products of many arts which one could point to?' (*Char*. 165e6–166a1, trans. Watt). See Roochnik, who argues against the view of Irwin (1977*a*); and Nussbaum (1986), 97, 445.

[8] Kant, §46, 168.   [9] Ibid. §47, 171.

different purposes to suit different dialectical contexts.[10] He often uses the ordinary, familiar *technai* as examples when refuting claims to knowledge, or illustrating the difference between knowledge and mere opinion. Each such *technē* must embrace some body of knowledge that is teachable, it must have a clearly identifiable subject-matter of its own, and it must be sufficiently based on generalizable principles that it can claim knowledge of the whole of its subject-matter.[11] The other, narrower conception is that of the single, higher-level *technē*, the 'ruling' or 'adequate' *technē*. None of the ordinary specialized *technai* amounts to a totally self-sufficient expertise: each lacks an account of what, overall, counts as its *good* exercise. The adequate or ruling *technē*, by contrast, would always aim at the good, guided by principles which enabled it to give an account of what the good is.[12]

In the early dialogues Plato shows us a Socrates for whom goodness and knowledge are closely linked. 'Goodness' or 'being good' is the condition called *aretē* in Greek, the excellence or virtue of something or somebody. Socrates seeks the *aretē* of a human being as such—what it is for someone to be excellent, or possess virtue as a human being. That being good is equivalent to knowing what is good and evil is one of the main planks of Socratic ethics. It is a strong and paradoxical claim, embracing both the thought that knowledge of good and evil is necessary for being good, and the thought that in order for someone to be good, it is sufficient that they know what is good and what is evil.[13] Now possessors of *technē* are experts in a specified field of knowledge, whose judgements are superior to the run-of-the-mill judgements of the many, and who are in a position to transmit knowledge through teaching to others. Success is predictable and objectively ascertainable: 'there is a right method, and answers do not depend on the prejudices of particular people.'[14] Whether something is a good table or chariot is not

---

[10] I am indebted here to Woodruff (1990), and to Roochnik.

[11] Nussbaum (1986, 94–6, with 442 ff.) gives a succinct account of the features of *technē* in Greek thinking from the fifth century down to Aristotle, drawing particularly on medical literature. The chief features of *technē* in her account are: (1) having universal principles that apply to a group of similar cases and yield predictions about future cases; (2) being teachable to an individual prior to that individual's direct experience; (3) having precision—a notion frequently linked with that of a measure or standard; (4) being able to give an explanation of why procedures adopted are successful.

[12] In spelling out this contrast, Woodruff has written that Socrates 'allows the term [*technē*] for crafts that are plainly subordinate, and withholds it from those that might masquerade as a Ruling *Technē*', the latter being the supposedly authoritative activities of 'poets, politicians and the like' (1990, 69–70).

[13] This account is influenced by Irwin (1977*a*), chs. III and IV.

[14] Ibid. 75.

just a matter of opinion, but requires reference to principles stating that if a chariot has certain specific features it will be a good chariot. In many of Plato's prime cases the presence of these features will be objectively measurable.

The production of excellence by a *technē* is not haphazard, then. It is regular, reliable, predictable, transmissible, and explicable in terms of general and impersonal principles possessed by its practitioners. If one believes that knowledge of good and evil is necessary and sufficient for human excellence, and observes that excellence in many special fields is brought by *technē*, then it is tempting to suppose that possession of a kind of supreme *technē* will be equivalent to human excellence. In a much-discussed part of the *Protagoras* Socrates goes to the extreme of advocating a moral *technē* which would accurately measure all goods and evils on a single scale of value, determining them as 'more or less, greater or smaller, nearer or more distant' (357a5– b4). This would be achieved if there were a single desirable standard of measurement, which Socrates here (but nowhere else) suggests is pleasure. In the *Gorgias* he holds that any true *technē* aims always at the good, which is distinct from pleasure. What persists is the drive to show that having or transmitting moral excellence consists in possessing genuine expertise of a certain kind.

The dramatic context of the *Gorgias* is Socrates' conversation with the great practitioner and teacher of rhetoric, Gorgias, and with Polus, his younger colleague. Gorgias of Leontini is usually treated as one of the sophists.[15] He travelled widely and displayed his talents for rhetoric, though it appears that, unlike other sophists, he did not profess to teach excellence via the medium of persuasive speaking.[16] His rhetorical style, which Plato sometimes parodies, is calculated for impressive effect, using repetition of sound-patterns and deliberately piling up redundant parallels or opposites for almost any word or idea. It comes across as ponderous and artificial—but bears out the fact that Gorgias was also a theorist about language and its effects. The best source for Gorgias' views about the nature of speech is his *Encomium of Helen*, in which he exercises his rhetorical powers in arguing that Helen, who ran off adulterously with Paris, should be absolved of blame, whatever caused

---

[15] Dodds dissents (1959, 7), but is criticized for taking the term 'sophist' too narrowly by Kerferd, 45. Kerferd gives a clear account of Gorgias' doctrines (78–82), including a paraphrase of the most important passages in the *Encomium of Helen*. See also Guthrie (1971), 20, 25, 44–5, 50–1, 168, 180–1, 269–74.

[16] Cf. *Meno* 95b9–c4: Gorgias laughs at the other sophists who claim to teach *aretē*— his task is to make clever speakers.

her to act as she did. Particularly interesting is the section in which he argues that if speech (*logos*) influenced her actions, she is not to be blamed. Speech is a 'powerful lord' with an overwhelming ability to persuade.[17] Speech 'constrains',[18] and leaves the persuaded one without responsibility for what she does. In so doing, it operates on the human capacity for belief or opinion, rather than knowledge of the truth. Indeed knowledge is impossible.[19] All we can have at our disposal are opinions, together with speech, which is an irresistible tool for persuading people to adopt opinions, provided we capture our hearers by giving them pleasure. A speech for Gorgias 'delights and persuades a vast audience by the skilfulness of its composition, not by the accuracy of its statements' (*technēi grapheis, ouk alētheiai lechtheis*); at work is a power 'which by its witchery enchants, persuades and changes the souls of men'.[20] Because truth is not its aim, and knowledge supposedly could not be its outcome, all persuasion by speech is a deception of opinion, a deception of the soul,[21] which Gorgias classes as a form of witchery (*goēteia*). Speech works in the same way as a drug works on the body, except that rather than curing or killing, it affects the soul with a whole panoply of emotions.

For just as different drugs dispel different secretions from the body, and some bring an end to disease and others to life, so also in the case of speeches, some distress, others delight, some cause fear, others make the hearers bold, and some drug and bewitch the soul with a kind of evil persuasion.[22]

We know that Gorgias applied his notion of deception in particular to tragedy:

Tragedy bloomed and was celebrated, a marvellous sound and spectacle for the men of that time, and one which by means of myth and suffering produced 'a deception [*apatē*]', as Gorgias says, in which the deceiver is more justly esteemed than the non-deceiver and the deceived is wiser than the undeceived.[23]

As with speech in general, poetry's 'deception' goes along with its emotional effect. The *Encomium of Helen* again:

[17] *Helen* (Diels–Kranz 82 B 11), §8—trans. G. Kennedy in Sprague (ed.), unless otherwise stated.
[18] Ibid. §12. The Greek here is *anankazein*, which can also mean 'forces' or 'necessitates'.
[19] In *On What is Not*, or *On Nature* (Diels–Kranz 82 B 3), and in *Defence of Palamedes* (Diels–Kranz 82 B 11a). See Sprague (ed.), 42–6, 54–63.
[20] *Helen*, §§13, 10—trans. Dodds (1959), 8–9.
[21] *Helen*, §8: *tēn psuchēn apatēsas*, and §10: *doxēs apatēmata*.
[22] *Helen*, §14.
[23] Plutarch, *de audiendis poetis* 15D (Diels–Kranz 82 B 23)—see Sprague (ed.), 65.

I both deem and define all poetry as speech with metre. Fearful shuddering and tearful pity and grievous longing come upon its hearers, and at the actions and physical sufferings of others in good fortunes and in evil fortunes, through the agency of words, the soul is wont to experience a suffering of its own.[24]

In Gorgias' view persuasion induces beliefs and other attitudes ('speech constrained the soul, persuading that which it persuaded, both to believe the things said and to approve the things done').[25] Such persuasion occurs because of the emotions speech produces in its hearers —or it is perhaps the production of emotions which is the process of persuasion itself. The 'drugging and bewitching' of the soul is both its having emotions produced in it by an external agency and its coming to be persuaded, i.e. to hold beliefs and other attitudes. Clearly there is deception if the beliefs are false and the other attitudes in some way wrong. What Gorgias means by the deception of poetry is then the complex of someone's acquiring beliefs and other attitudes, all of which are erroneous, by undergoing the emotional effects of hearing speech with metre.

We shall have occasion to refer back to Gorgias, not least in discussing *Republic* Book 10.[26] Here I pose one final speculative question about the 'deception' doctrine: Was it the view that poetic fiction is the production of illusions which we take for real things? Jonathan Barnes, who attributes to Gorgias a rather grandiose 'theory of art' which says that it 'essentially strives for illusion',[27] has constructed for Gorgias the following argument: 'poetry arouses genuine emotions, genuine emotions require genuine beliefs, therefore poetry arouses genuine beliefs; however, beliefs in fictional situations are false, so poetry arouses genuine false beliefs—or, in other words, is deception.'[28] We may wonder, however, whether this ingenious construction is necessary. The *fictionality* of poetry is not really the issue for Gorgias, because he finds the same power to deceive in all speech, putting forward poetry's deception as one instance.[29] No doubt Gorgias believes that poetry arouses real emotions. But someone's thinking this does not, of itself, settle the question whether they hold that fiction is believed to be reality. There

[24] *Helen*, §9.   [25] Ibid. §12.   [26] See below, Ch. 6.
[27] Barnes, 464.   [28] Ibid. 465–6 (my paraphrase).
[29] I am not convinced by the suggestion of Pohlenz (470) that 'for the dramatic poet *apatē* (deception) meant something entirely different from what it meant for the public speaker . . . in the case of drama it was, as illusion, the constitutive feature, since it made what was represented appear as real to the spectator . . . and indeed it had the effect of making him go along with the fictive events as experiences of his own, and feel the sufferings and joys of the people in action as his own' (my translation).

is an intermediate (if perhaps unstable) position, according to which the emotion is genuine, but does not involve falsely taking a fiction for a reality. Finally, if poetry is held to deceive us illusionistically into the opinion that we see Achilles kill Hector, or Helen really commit adultery, why do those who have been deceived count, for Gorgias, as 'wiser than the undeceived'? It does not seem plausible to describe as 'wiser' the (extremely rare) person who has taken the fictional situation for a reality.

On a different reading the 'deceived' would be those whose minds had been altered by poetry's enchantment. Just as in public oratory the crowd that undergoes the emotional effects of hearing speech thereby acquires new beliefs and attitudes, so poetry, with its powerfully convincing (but not illusionistic) picture of events, may persuade us into some belief or attitude of our own about adultery, for example, or about love, responsibility, death, or heroism, about the rights and wrongs of a particular incident or a general way of behaving. We may speculate that it is those who come away from a tragedy with such opinions changed or influenced who count as 'wiser than the undeceived'. Thus poetry's 'deception' for Gorgias need be only, like that of rhetoric, its bewitching persuasion of the mind. This kind of deception is at any rate closer to the heart of Plato's concerns than any preoccupation with illusion as such. With all this in mind we turn to Plato's *Gorgias*.

Appropriately enough, the nature of rhetoric is the subject that leads into the discussion of *technē* at *Gorgias* 462b. When Gorgias himself fails to give an acceptable definition of rhetoric, Socrates offers one: rhetoric is 'no *technē*', he says, but rather 'the knack of producing a certain gratification and pleasure' (462b8–c7). Socrates proceeds to elaborate a distinction between the two mutually exclusive categories, craft (*technē*) and knack (*empeiria*), into which various activities fall. A 'knack' is also referred to as a mere 'procedure' (*tribē*, 463b4)—an activity that can be repeated on many occasions, which happens to work, but for which the agent has no explanation. A knack goes after pleasure

entirely without a craft, not at all considering the nature or the explanation of the pleasure, and altogether without reason, making practically no distinctions. By habit and experience it keeps only memory of what usually happens, by which it produces its pleasures. (501a4–b1.)

Cookery and cosmetics provide pleasure and gratification to the body in this way; sophistry and rhetoric do so for the soul. Socrates proposes calling all these activities part of 'something not at all fine'—namely 'flattery', which is best understood as a tendency to ingratiate oneself with others by pandering indiscriminately to their tastes.[30] No part of 'flattery', Socrates argues, is a genuine *technē*.

Today we make a distinction between 'knowing how' and 'knowing that'. There seems little reason to deny that a habitually successful exercise of rhetorical ability is a case of knowing how to do something. But this is not sufficient to make it a *technē* for Plato. A true craft must indeed be a kind of 'knowing how' (someone who knew many propositions about disease and cure but could never apply them in action would not have mastered the medical *technē*), but it must also involve a particular kind of 'knowing that'. In addition, it must have a characteristic end towards which it works. From the discussion in the *Gorgias* it is possible to pick out the following essential contrasts between craft and flattery: (1) A *technē* aims at the good, or the best; flattery aims at what is pleasant, 'without the best', or 'caring not a bit for the best' (464c4, 465a2, 464d1). (2) A *technē* knows 'what is good and bad'; flattery succeeds by knack and procedure, hence by guessing rather than knowing (500b2–5; 463a2–b1). (3) *Technē* has an account (*logos*), by which it operates, so that it can say what is the explanation of each thing; flattery has no such account (465a2–6). Cookery, for example, aims not at what is a good for the body, but at pleasure. Any success its practitioner has in producing pleasure results not from following any principle, rather from what Plato calls 'guessing'—hitting the right result without being able to explain why.[31] Medicine, by contrast, not only aims at the good (almost always to the exclusion of pleasure, in the short term[32]), but administers to the body what it knows is for its good, because it can give a principled explanation of why its actions achieve

---

[30] 'Flattery': *kolakeia*, a highly disparaging term, as Dodds's memorable gloss tells us: 'The *kolax* is what the eighteenth century called a toad-eater or lickspittle and schoolboys call a bumsucker' (1959, 225).

[31] Cf. the famous passages at *Meno* 97e6–98a8, 99c1–100b4. An inexplicable 'divine dispensation' (*theia moira*, the same expression as was applied to Ion) may enable some people, including statesmen, priests, prophets, and poets, to have the right beliefs; but this is not the same as genuine knowledge. Knowledge is having a belief which is 'tied down' by a 'working out of the reason'. This working out (*logismos*) marks the crucial difference between merely getting things right, and knowing.

[32] At *Prot.* 354a5–7, 'doctors' treatment involving cautery or the knife [amputation] or drugs or starvation diet' is an example of something 'good but painful' (though the argument as a whole pronounces such things 'good' only in that they bring greater long-term pleasure). At *Rep.* 357c6 ff., being treated when ill is something good not for its own sake, but for its consequences.

what they do. In the process medicine introduces order (*kosmos*) and structure (*taxis*) into the body, which makes for its excellence (*aretē*) (504a2–c9).

The close connection Plato makes between good, knowledge, and an account can perhaps be elucidated thus. In order to aim at the achievement of the best state of something of some kind (*K*), one must have a conception of what a good thing of that kind (a good *K* thing) is. In a *technē* this conception must reliably guide action to a successful outcome. One's conception of a *K* thing must be correct and one must not attain the outcome by chance whilst happening to have the right conception. One must, then, have knowledge or understanding of what a good *K* thing is—hence knowledge of the true nature of a *K* thing—and be able to give a rational account of the procedures undertaken to reach one's goal. 'I don't call anything a *technē* which is without an account (*alogon*)', says Socrates (465a5–6). The person with a true *technē* is in possession of the principles which he or she has followed in order to produce the desired outcome in any particular case. He or she is able to give a *logos*—an account, explanation, reason. Any *alogon pragma* (thing without an account) is not a *technē*.

The activities which Socrates calls 'flattery' aim at pleasure, treating their direct product—say, a meal, or a speech—as purely instrumental towards the bringing about of pleasure in a recipient. Provided that the thing I produce causes pleasure, my end is attained. Any conception of 'the best' product is therefore irrelevant—I need only observe carefully what has caused pleasure in the past, and repeat that. Success depends on whether what I produce is to the recipient's liking. Thus, though I may be able to recognize a good meal or speech when I see it, I lack any generalizable explanation of how to succeed, or any criteria for the assessment of meals or speeches in general, which can predict, according to the features they possess, whether they will be good or bad.

Plato makes each instance of 'flattery' the false image (*eidōlon*) of an instance of craft. Cookery is the image of medicine, cosmetics that of gymnastics. In each case an apparent good condition mimics a genuine one: medicine produces the genuine good condition of the body, cookery a merely apparently good condition which mimics it. Likewise rhetoric, in producing gratification by the persuasion of public speaking, merely mimics justice; and sophistry is the false image of genuine law making. Hence activities which are not genuine exercises of *technē* can seem to be genuine to those who are not on their guard. 'If a doctor and a cook had to compete among children, or among men as foolish

as children, to decide which of them understands more about worthy
and base food . . . then the doctor would die of starvation' (464d5–e2).
The *rhētōr*'s position is the same

> about the just and the unjust, the fine and the shameful, and the good and the
> bad . . . —he doesn't know the things themselves, what is good or bad, what
> is fine or shameful or just or unjust, but has devised persuasion about them so
> that though he doesn't know, among those who don't know he appears to
> know, rather than the man who knows. (459d1–e1.)[33]

So Plato sets out to show that rhetoric is not an adequate *technē*. In
ordinary usage it will continue to be classed as a *technē*, as it is at the
start of the *Gorgias*. But in Plato's stricter philosophical sense a truly
adequate *technē* both aims at the good and is a form of knowledge.
Because good and pleasure can diverge, as is argued later (495e–500a),
a *technē* is not concerned to produce what pleases. Pleasure may be a
consequence of its application, but it will eschew what pleases if that
is incompatible with the good. It will not, however, eschew the good
if that is incompatible with what pleases. The practitioners of activities
which aim solely at pleasure, meanwhile, are unable to discriminate
good from bad pleasures—it needs a craftsman (*technikos*) to do that
(500a4–6).

Now what is the position of the arts going to be? In the opening part
of the dialogue the arts figure prominently as examples of craft or
expertise.[34] But this tells us little of substance. At this stage in the
dialectic the argument is governed by the assumption that rhetoric too
is a craft. Painting, sculpture, and music are brought forward as at least
having a clear subject-matter, in contrast to rhetoric, which has no
clearly definable subject that it is 'about'. This is the first move in the
campaign to oust rhetoric from the strict category of *technē*. But painting and sculpture might also fail to qualify once 'aiming at the good
by applying known principles' is made constitutive of *technē*. Plato
produces no argument to this effect in the *Gorgias*. But some of the
performing arts decidedly do not qualify.

In conversation with Callicles Socrates discusses a number of musical practices which he puts under the heading of 'gratifying souls all in
a crowd at the same time':

---

[33] This and the previously cited passage are closely echoed at *Rep.* 598b8–c4 and
600e4–601b1, in the discussion of poetry. Poets make *eidōla*—false images—of excellence, which take in children and fools.

[34] See 448b11–c1, 453c6, 449d3–4, 450c10 for mentions of painting, music, sculpture.

First of all, let's consider flute-playing. Don't you think it is the kind of practice we mentioned, Callicles, pursuing only our pleasure, and concerned with nothing else? . . . And aren't all of this kind similar—such as lyre-playing before large audiences? . . . And what about the teaching of choruses, and the making of dithyrambs? Isn't it apparently something of the same kind? Or do you think Cinesias the son of Meles cares at all about saying the kind of thing to make the audience better? Or does he care about what will gratify the mob of spectators? . . . But consider: don't you think that all singing to the lyre and composition of dithyrambs has been discovered for the sake of pleasure? (501e1–502a8.)

The discussion concerns those arts designed, like rhetoric, for public performance which gives pleasure to a large mass of people. A dithyramb was a poem written to be sung by a chorus at one of the regular Athenian festivals. As this practice developed, the works apparently became highly elaborate, the musical element predominating over the text.[35] Cinesias was a dithyrambic poet active during Plato's early life, a somewhat controversial figure who has been called a leading representative of the 'new music' of the day.[36] The lyre (in fact, its larger relative the *kithara*) figures twice here: in straightforward lyre-playing, and in singing accompanied by the lyre. Both were practised in public competitions at Athens. Aristotle agrees that such performances aimed only at the pleasure of the audience and resulted in a tendency towards impressive technical 'fireworks'.[37] In 'flute-playing', the instrument is the *aulos*, which was a reed-instrument rather than a flute. By reputation it was not wholly respectable. It was used as an accompaniment in the theatre, but was also associated with 'the wilder sort of evening parties',[38] and with ecstatic dancing at Dionysiac and other cults. We may infer that the *aulos* was also used as a solo instrument in public performances involving a high degree of exciting virtuoso display. Its reedy timbre was in itself no doubt a thrilling sound. In some respects, the nearest twentieth-century equivalent is the saxophone.[39]

[35] 'The making (*poiēsis*) of dithyrambs' refers to the composition of the poem of which the dithyrambic performance was a setting, 'the teaching of choruses' obviously to the element of musical preparation and performance itself—see Dodds (1959), 323.

[36] Ibid. Cf. Aristophanes' caricature of Cinesias in *Birds* 1373–1404, which ridicules his 'multiplication of meaningless epithets' (Pickard-Cambridge, 60).

[37] *Politics* 1341a9, b10, as discussed by Dodds (1959), 323.

[38] Dodds (1959), 322, on whose account I rely. Dodds notes that Aristotle calls the instrument 'not *ēthikon*, but rather *orgiastikon*', and that the Pythagoreans condemned it as vulgar.

[39] Urmson writes: 'Much about the *aulos* is uncertain; one of the few certainties is that it is not a flute. English musical writers refer always to the aulos; even "shawm" is better than "flute", and "tenor saxophone", while appalling, is not as bad' (1984, 210).

So Plato is discussing specific practices, not music as a whole. Elsewhere he has room for the thought that music does more than aim at pleasure, as witness the view he gives to Protagoras (*Prot.* 326a4–b6): music in education can 'instil self-control and deter the young from evil-doing'. The young are taught the lyre, and then progress to singing poetry accompanied by the lyre. By the process of familiarization with different forms of rhythm and *harmonia*, they 'become more civilized, more balanced, and better adjusted [*euarmostoteroi*—more well-in-tune] in themselves and so more capable in whatever they say or do'. This is a view of the educational role of music which Plato will himself endorse in the *Republic* and later in the *Laws*.[40] But it is not incompatible with what is said in the *Gorgias*. Some musical performances are aimed solely at gratification rather than at what is good. But singing and the playing of instruments are not necessarily to be used in this way, and can also constitute a valuable part of one's moral education. Plato does not here give us a theory of music as such, nor does he say that all music is a bad or a worthless thing—merely that the music of pleasure-giving public display should be classed as a form of 'flattery', not as *technē*.[41] Pandering to their tastes in an ingratiating way, music thus performed does not do the audience any good, Plato thinks, but masquerades as something which does.

Now the discussion moves on to another art: 'Then what about this august and wonderful pursuit, the composition of tragedy, and its concern?' (*Gorg.* 502b1–2). The epithets are clearly ironic,[42] but reflect the importance Plato attaches to classifying tragedy correctly. Socrates argues that tragedy's concern too is to gratify the mass of spectators at its performance, and that therefore it is a species of flattery. It is even a species of rhetoric:

SOCRATES. Is its undertaking and concern, in your opinion, just to gratify the spectators? Or does it struggle, if anything is pleasant and gratifying to them, but base, to avoid saying it, and if something is without pleasure but beneficial, to say and sing this, whether they enjoy it or not? Which way do you think the composition of tragedies is equipped?

CALLICLES. This much is clear, Socrates, that it concentrates on pleasure and on gratifying spectators.

SOCRATES. And didn't we say just now that this sort of thing is flattery, Callicles?

CALLICLES. Quite.

SOCRATES. Well now, if someone took away from all poetic composition the

---

[40] *Rep.* 398c–401d, discussed in Ch. 4 below; *Laws* 809a–813a, discussed in Ch. 7.
[41] See Irwin (1979), 211.   [42] Dodds (1959), 324.

melody, the rhythm, and the metre, doesn't what is left turn out to be speech
[*logoi*]? . . . And isn't this speech addressed to a large mob of the people?
. . . Then poetic composition [*poiētikē*] is a kind of public oratory. . . . And
surely public oratory is rhetoric. Or don't you think the poets practise rhetoric in the theatres?

CALLICLES. Yes, I think so.

SOCRATES. And so we've found a kind of rhetoric addressed to the people,
including children and women and men all together, and slaves and free. And
we can't altogether admire it; for we say it's flattering. (502b2–d8.)

These few highly disparaging remarks are not Plato's final word on
tragedy, nor do they really say anything about poetry more generally.
(The conclusion that *poiētikē* is a kind of public oratory need not be
taken to apply across the board.) The discussion is limited by its subordination to the themes of rhetoric, pleasure, and good. In Gorgias'
own writings tragedy (and indeed all poetry in his case) is made con-
ceptually subordinate to speech in general, the great power to persuade
and deceive human opinion. With Gorgias present, Socrates is thus
bringing out a further consequence of his account of rhetoric for someone who thinks as Gorgias does. But is Plato's subsumption of tragedy
under rhetoric at all plausible? Tragedians portray persuasive dialogue
and sometimes 'set debates, with formal speeches arguing for and against
a thesis'.[43] But it would be short-sighted to call this the essence of
tragedy, forgetting the great lyric choruses, the reflective monologues,
the messengers' speeches reporting the worst, or the lament of the hero
or heroine after the inevitable reversal of fortune. Tragedy as a whole
can count as 'rhetoric' only on the grounds that it employs speech to
gratify a mass of spectators. (Playing the *aulos* is, it seems, not be
classified as rhetoric. Is this just because tragedy gratifies with speeches,
aulos-playing with melodies?) That would make the claim 'tragedy is a
species of rhetoric' relatively uninformative—tautologous with 'tragedy
gratifies in the medium of speech'.

However, the core of Plato's claim is that tragedy aims at gratifying
a mass of spectators, not at what is good. The circumstances of the
performance of tragedy in Athens, at the festivals of the Great Dionysia
and others, are well known, and we need have no quarrel with Plato's
description of the audience. We should also remember that tragedies
were written for a single occasion of performance, which was a com-
petition. In the *Theaetetus* Plato celebrates with relief the contrasting

[43] Dodds (1959), 325.

circumstances of philosophical discussion: 'We have no jury, and no audience (as the dramatic poets have), sitting in control over us, ready to criticize and give orders.' (*Tht.* 173c4–5.) Tragedians were perforce concerned to aim at pleasing both masters—nor were the verdicts of the two always independent.[44] In this light, the notion of the tragedian trying to 'persuade' or 'win over' a mass audience—in a way *analogous* to the *rhētōr*—is fully intelligible.

In classing tragedy as a form of flattery, aiming at pleasure not the good, Plato comes down firmly against the tragedian's exercising a *technē* in the strict sense. Tragedy will lack any rational principle by which to explain its activity, and will succeed by something akin to guesswork. If any artistic practice is aimed at pleasure or gratification as an end, precisely this distances it from the strict philosophical category of *technē*. Poets, composers, actors, singers, instrumentalists may produce fine works, but it is not from knowledge that they do so. They can give no account which explains why the product of their activities turned out to be a fine one. They can say what they did, and have enough experience to have picked up the 'knack' of getting things right nearly all the time (since practice makes perfect). But they cannot point to general principles which link their actions with the right outcome. Performance and composition in these arts is an *alogon pragma*, a thing without an account, a business without a rational principle. With this goes the claim that the 'rightness' aimed for in poetry and music, and the criterion of success, is that of pleasing an audience, whereas with a true *technē* the criterion of success is irrespective of pleasurable reaction (sometimes at odds with it) and consists in the production of an object or outcome which is measurable against an objective standard of goodness.

Is not this view a travesty of the arts? That depends on what is true concerning the arts. There are two main questions: (1) Is poetry or music indeed an *alogon pragma*, or is either after all the domain of a *technikos*? (2) Is the aim of poetic and musical performance, and the criterion by which they are judged to have succeeded, the giving of pleasure? It is difficult to answer these questions in isolation from one another, and without importing many other notions. They eventually lead deeper into the philosophy of art than present space will accommodate. Nevertheless, an argument can be constructed to support answers

---

[44] As we may infer from Plato's later insistence that judges really should not take their lead from the crowd (*Laws* 659a–b).

compatible with Plato's account. In outline it is as follows. For tragedy *not* to be an *alogon pragma*, its author must work according to generalizable principles which explain a successful dramatic outcome. But it is arguable that the aim of tragedy, and its criterion of success, is pleasure—of some sort. And there are no generalizable principles which reliably specify that pleasure will be felt in an object of a certain kind. So tragedy, given its characteristic aim and mode of evaluation, cannot work according to generalizable principles of the right kind. It is therefore not a *technē*, but an *alogon pragma*. To make this argument plausible, we need some backing for two claims, namely the claim that tragedy aims at and is judged by pleasure, and the claim that there are no generalizable principles of pleasure.

Does tragedy aim at pleasure? Is the criterion of its success that of producing (or being such as to produce) pleasure? At a very broad level, we must surely answer: Yes. The idea of an excellent drama which fails to give pleasure at all is an odd one—assuming that it has not met the fate of being wrongly understood or not properly staged. Imagine a dramatist, like Collingwood's carpenter, successfully fashioning a piece which corresponds with an intricate set of preconceptions and rules: still, he or she has scarcely 'succeeded' in producing a good drama, unless it is the case that pleasure would result from a performance of the piece in appropriate circumstances to people who understand it. The idea that the bringing about of pleasure might be a purely incidental aim of the tragedian is one we should also reject. Even if, contrary to what Plato thinks, tragedians do aim to educate us, make us wiser or more pious, their way of pursuing these aims is, unlike the way of many another educator, essentially via a kind of pleasure.

However, before acquiescing in the claim that tragedians aim at pleasure, we should be circumspect. Plato imposes on the performing arts a dubious polarity, between, on the one hand, an activity's aiming at the good (or the best) outcome and, on the other, its aiming at pleasure via a product which is merely instrumental towards producing that pleasure—as if the artist's product is not aimed at on its own account and is not itself 'good' in any sense. We could read into this the dubious implication that the tragedian is simply out to please the audience, and does not care at all what he or she produces, provided it brings about pleasure. Calling tragedy 'flattering' already carries this implication.

Against this, we may first note an important sense in which embracing pleasure as an aim does not exclude aiming at the best, or at the good, in the object that is to bring about pleasure. We may want to say that the tragedian aims indeed at pleasing the audience, but that he or she wants to please them by putting before them a *good* tragedy, and having them be pleased by apprehending just those features in virtue of which it is a good tragedy. Pleasures are distinguished by their intentional objects—the objects they are directed towards. So there is such a thing as pleasure in a good play, which can be distinguished from other pleasures experienced while present at the performance of a play, caused by that performance, but not really having the play itself as intentional object. An example of Aristotle's makes the point. A tragedy, on his account, should make us feel a pleasure associated with our response of pity and fear, but

those who employ spectacular means to create a sense not of the terrible but only of the monstrous, are strangers to the purpose of tragedy; for we must not demand of tragedy any and every kind of pleasure, but only that which is proper to it. And since the pleasure which the poet should afford is that which comes from pity and fear through *mimēsis*, it is evident that this quality must be impressed upon the incidents.[45]

Spectacular stage-machinery and breath-taking turns of events can give pleasure. So, no doubt, can the sheer diction of a superb actor or the beauty of a sequence of gestures. It would be possible to enjoy a tragedy in the way transient Western tourists today might enjoy an Indonesian epic drama.[46] But there is also a pleasure 'proper to tragedy', to have which one must apprehend as fearful and pitiful the connected series of depicted incidents, the plot. Plato's polarity of good and pleasure falsifies, because it disguises the fact that aiming at pleasure does not exclude aiming at a good product. And to experience pleasure in something does not exclude either its being good or the apprehension of it as good.

The notion of something's being a good tragedy or a good musical performance—which Plato appears to ignore in the *Gorgias*—remains totally unexplained here. So does Plato recognize that there are such things as good poems, good musical compositions, or good performances? Recalling the *Apology* and *Ion*, we can say that he does. In the former, poets 'say many fine [*kala*] things' but cannot explain 'their most perfect works'.[47] In the *Ion* Socrates talks of good epic poets,

---

[45] *Poetics* 1453b8–14.

[46] See Scruton (1974), 163–4, for essentially the same example.

[47] *Apol.* 22c2–3, 22b3–4. In the latter passage Socrates talks of the poems *ha moi edokei malista pepragmateusthai autois*—perhaps 'which seemed to me their most accomplished efforts'.

good lyric poets, and a bad poet who nevertheless produced the finest lyric; he talks of works which are *kalos*—fine, splendid, beautiful—and questions the rhapsode about what it is like when he is performing well in public. Plato omits the notion of a good tragedy or musical perform-ance in the *Gorgias* because he is concerned with the good *of the souls* that consume them. Cinesias and the tragedians do not intend to make their audiences better people, but to please them. Yet they may never-theless care whether their performances are good performances, or their works good works. A base action may be depicted because, in the context of the plot, it gives pleasure; but a dramatically inept depiction will be avoided, even if it would give pleasure of some kind. Take a modern parallel: a film-maker might debate whether to include an explicitly sexual scene in a film. Let us take it for granted that this particular scene would give the majority of viewers pleasure. Despite this pleasure, the scene might be excluded either because it was judged base and corrupting or because the film would be a better film without it. Plato laments that artists fail to make the former, ethical, type of decision. But his description allows for—without mentioning—'artis-tic' decisions of the latter type. So we can agree to the broad claim that tragedy aims at pleasure without having to accept the implication that tragedians are bent on causing pleasure irrespective of the fineness of their dramatic productions.

Now we turn to the other claim which needed some support: that there are no principles of pleasure. For Plato the tragedian's or musi-cian's aiming at pleasure and being judged on the basis of bringing it about is linked with the idea that they can give no explanation. They have the knack of producing pleasure, but can give no explanation 'of the pleasure', or of 'what they do' (501a1–b1). This may look straight-forwardly false. We can easily imagine the director of a dithyrambic chorus explaining to the ensemble why one performance worked better than another: 'In this performance the lines of the poem were articu-lated properly because your breathing was better co-ordinated', or 'hav-ing slowed down the tempo, there is now room for all the ornamentation'. These are straightforward reasons for the success of a performance (even if 'success' equates with giving pleasure to a mass audience). Aristotle's detailed remarks about what makes a good tragedy good are still exemplary pieces of the same kind of reason-giving. So this looks like a clear sense in which these artistic practices are not 'without a *logos*'. However, there is a big difference between critical reasons and principles of taste or composition. What we have described is the reason-

giving of criticism: reasons for artistic success or failure given after
the event. When it is clear whether the performance worked or not, the
experienced critic can often explain why by citing observed features.
Plato, by contrast, emphasizes knowledge which produces desired out-
comes with a reliability not simply gained by approximation or repetition of what has worked in the past: he is thinking of the situation of
the composer or performer *vis-à-vis* the work not yet executed. For
Plato to be wrong, there must be principles of composition or performance which the tragedian or performer can rationally follow in order to
ensure success. Still agreeing that the relevant 'success' is some suitably qualified pleasure, are there such principles?

To support the claim that there are no 'principles of pleasure', let us
return somewhat abruptly to Kant. A central plank of Kant's argument
concerning judgements of beauty (what he calls 'judgements of taste')
is that they can never be arrived at by use of a rule or principle. 'There
can', he writes, 'be no rule according to which anyone is to be compelled to recognize anything as beautiful. Whether a dress, a house, or
a flower is beautiful is a matter upon which one declines to allow one's
judgement to be swayed by any . . . principles.'[48] The compulsion or
swaying he refers to is that of deductive inference. An object's possessing certain features, combined with a general rule or principle that any
object possessing those features is F, allows one to deduce the conclusion that the particular object is F.[49] (An example might be the judgement 'This poem is a sonnet'. This could be supported by the observation
that the poem has fourteen lines of a certain metre and a certain rhyme
scheme, together with the principle that anything with those features is
a sonnet.) But, according to Kant, such a model does not apply when
we judge something beautiful, or aesthetically good. No list of an object's features can ever be sufficient for us to deduce its beauty by
means of a principle. A judgement that something is beautiful has as its
basis a feeling of pleasure of a particular kind: a disinterested pleasure
in the object's perceptual form.

Now Plato never gives an analysis of the kind of judgement which
is at the heart of Kant's problematic.[50] However, when Kant comes to

[48] Kant, §8, 56.

[49] See ibid. §34, 141. My discussion is influenced by Mothersill, chs. 3–5. Mothersill
argues persuasively that there are no 'principles of taste', and also that no one really
believes there are any. Later (197) she explicitly links rule-governedness with Plato's
conception of *technē*.

[50] On Plato's 'missing concept of [Kantian] taste', cf. Moravscik (1982), 41–2.

discuss the *production* of works of beauty, we discover a point germane to Plato's notion of the *alogon pragma*. Kant claims, as we saw, that the production of fine art requires 'a talent for producing that for which no definite rule can be given'.[51] He is sensible enough to realize that the execution of the arts involves a basis of craft-like rule-following. But the fact that rules have been followed is never sufficient for us to be able to deduce that a beautiful object will ensue.[52] Hence there are no genuine principles for the artist of the form: 'Produce an object with properties F, G, and H, and you will produce a successful work of art.' I say 'genuine principles', meaning by that principles which really work. One might compose poetry always with some rule in mind, and doing so might, by some means, help one to compose exceptionally good poetry. But one would be using a genuine rule or principle of taste only if, prior to the poem's execution, one could deduce that a poem composed in accordance with it would be exceptionally good. One might be able to guarantee thus that the product would be (in our revealing phrase) a workmanlike sonnet, or a sonnet that was correct after some specified style. But, for all that, it might still not be judged beautiful, or a true success.

The point I wish to make is that if tragedy is not to be an *alogon pragma* in Plato's sense, then the Kantian denial of principles of composition must be false. One of the necessary conditions for tragedy to count as an adequate *technē* is that there be something like principles of taste (at least principles of good composition), known to the poet. Here then is the argument which lends some measure of support to Plato: the tragedian aims at pleasure, and successful composition is closely linked to the bringing about of pleasure; but since there are no generalizable principles of pleasure, there will be no proper principles of successful composition. The glaring omission, once we juxtapose Plato with Kant in this way, seems to be any conception of aesthetic value: Plato forces the tragedian, the *aulos*-player, and the dithyrambic chorus to compete in the arenas of rational expertise and moral improvement, only to mock them for achieving nothing. Why not allow that there is aesthetically good music, drama, or poetry, and set these other questions (at least temporarily) aside?

It is artistic practices, not works *per se*, which Plato is examining for

---

[51] Kant, §46, 168.

[52] A rule which enjoined the making of an indistinguishable copy of an object already judged beautiful might be urged as the trivial exception; but this is a tricky issue. See Janaway (1993).

benefit or the lack of it. And he is aware of the common view that poetry plays a beneficial role in education—witness the speech by Protagoras considered earlier, in which teachers not only teach music, but set 'the works of good poets' before boys, precisely on account of their improving content (*Prot.* 325e4–326a4). In the *Republic* too, as we shall see, the positive role of poetry in education is debated at length. Plato knew, therefore, that the question whether the arts are beneficial to the soul cannot be answered with a straightforward No. He makes a division between practices of learning to recite and perform, which can in the right conditions be beneficial to the reciter or performer, and the practice of public performance or display, which he thinks is never genuinely concerned for the good of the audience. The *Iliad* when learned by heart by the young, and the *Iliad* when enacted to rapturous acclaim by the rhapsode (for Ion would surely come under the same strictures as tragedy and the *aulos*-player) need have no common value. This said, there remains a worry about the work itself, because Plato seems inclined to call Homer's works fine poems. What makes them fine?

A number of the claims we have seen so far—that the arts aim at a pleasure which is divorced from knowledge and ethical benefit, that they are not crafts, that there are no principles of composition, and that the fineness of the artist's product is inexplicable except by some power of 'inspiration' or 'genius'—cohere into an intelligible whole, which is far from alien to us. The surprise again for the modern reader is that Plato should be so ready to disparage the arts he discusses for having these very 'artistic' features. The question now facing us is whether Plato fails to understand the idea that the fineness of a work or performance may be aesthetic (concerned with a kind of fulfilling experiential encounter which cannot be netted in the search for truth, wisdom, accuracy, or moral effect)—or whether he has recognized the claim of aesthetic value and is out to reject it.

3

The Fine and the Beautiful

So far we have seen Plato interested in what the arts contribute to knowledge or goodness. The modern reader, however, will tend to think that a poem can be fine in another way, irrespective of its beneficial effect on someone or its imparting knowledge, and some would say that a kind of pleasure is an essential factor in this. Not all pleasures are intrinsically valuable—some are perhaps not valuable at all—but we may wonder whether Plato acknowledges 'aesthetic pleasure' as something of value which an *alogon pragma* such as poetry or music might afford. There are three questions of interpretation here: (1) Does Plato recognize (under whatever name) something that we would call aesthetic pleasure? (2) Is there room for him to think of it as something valuable? (3) Does he associate aesthetic pleasure or its equivalent particularly with the arts—as opposed to, say, the human body or the multifarious forms of nature?

I shall suggest a qualified affirmative answer to all three questions. But that will still leave philosophical work to do. Even if Plato recognizes the arts as principal providers of aesthetic pleasure, we do not know to what extent that will furnish any defence of them as valuable activities. If 'aesthetic pleasure' in the arts turns out to have a value of its own, it might nevertheless be like the pleasures of playing backgammon or smelling roses. These, I assume, are valuable in themselves, but are not essential components of the best kind of life for a human being. Indeed, a life largely organized around attaining these pleasures could seem perversely mis-directed. I shall argue that Plato recognizes the arts as providing aesthetic pleasure, but does not regard their doing so as giving them a prominent place in the best of human lives.

'Plato wants to cut art off from beauty, because he regards beauty as too serious a matter to be commandeered by art. . . . Kant, on the other hand, wants to cut beauty off from morals. Kant restricts beauty for the same reason for which Plato restricts art, to get it cleanly out of the way of something more important.'[1] 'He [Plato] never denied the beauty of

[1] Murdoch, 17–18.

art. But he asserted that it was less than that of the phenomenal world, and far inferior to that of the world of the intellect.'[2] These statements reflect the truth that for Plato the arts at best occupy a low rung of something that is the ultimate object of human aspiration, what he calls *to kalon*, or *auto to kalon*, phrases traditionally rendered as 'the beautiful' or 'beauty', 'the beautiful itself' or 'beauty itself'. Many salient examples of things that are *kalos* are indeed beautiful things, and the word in ordinary Greek when applied to people and physical things has a central meaning to do with visual attractiveness.[3] Nevertheless *kalos* is a term with a much wider use as well, and is more like 'noble', 'admirable', or 'fine'.[4] It will pay to remember this, otherwise we run the risk of over-aestheticizing Plato. Inadvertency must not lead us to construe Plato's ultimate aspiration as purely aesthetic;[5] the highest value is located for him in something more all-embracing, which for now we may call 'fineness itself'. The aesthetic quality which we call 'beauty' is one aspect of fineness, although it is not always separately noticed or valued.

But before we ask whether Plato shares 'our' concept of beauty— what do we think beauty is? Collingwood is helpful again for his clarity. He suggests that phrases of the form 'a beautiful *X*' express 'an attitude of admiration for a thing well done, irrespective of whether that thing is an aesthetic activity, an intellectual activity, or a bodily activity'.[6] If

---

[2] Grube (1927), 287.

[3] See the survey of uses by Dover (1974), 69–73. Whether a thing has or lacks fine *appearance* is commonly a central question in whether it is *kalos*. Sexual intercourse and superficial personal appearance provide different examples in the *Hippias Major*: the one of something that cannot be fine because it is not fine *to see*, the other of something which possibly is fine just because it *looks* fine (*HiMa*. 299a3–b1 and 293e7 ff.). Mothersill (263) is perceptive about a puzzle the second passage raises: in effect, What is the difference between being beautiful and looking beautiful? The ridiculous man may look beautiful in sufficient garb, though he is not beautiful. Alcibiades is beautiful—but what is that? He too is beautiful in that he looks, appears, is seen to be beautiful. All beauty depends on appearance. ('True beauty is what matters, but the appearance of beauty is not flatly a fraud.')

[4] Paul Woodruff writes: 'Like beauty, *to kalon* is something splendid and exciting; and in women or boys it is the loveliness that excites carnal desire. But the use of *kalos* for that quality is embraced by its use as a quite general term of commendation in Greek. "Noble," "admirable," and "fine" are better translations, and of these "fine" is best of all in virtue of its great range' (1982*a*, 110). See also Moravcsik (1982), 30–2 and 43, for a helpful discussion of the fine and its relation to beauty.

[5] Cf. Irwin (1979), 154: 'There is no reason to believe that the use of "*kalon*" for what we call moral properties indicates that the Greeks have a particularly "aesthetic" attitude to morality, as the translation "beautiful" might suggest.'

[6] Collingwood (1938), 39.

we adopt Collingwood's view, then *to kalon* is very like beauty, and it
makes sense to maintain that 'Plato has a lot to say about beauty, in
which he is only systematizing what we find implied in the ordinary
Greek use of the word':

> To call a thing beautiful in Greek . . . is simply to call it admirable or excellent
> or desirable. A poem or painting may certainly receive the epithet, but only by
> the same kind of right as a boot or any other simple artifact. The sandals of
> Hermes, for example, are regularly called beautiful by Homer, not because they
> are conceived as elegantly designed or decorated, but because they are con-
> ceived as jolly good sandals which enable him to fly as well as walk.[7]

This captures some of the truth about calling a thing *kalos*. But why
follow Collingwood and say that the English 'beautiful' is substantially
the same? We cannot just stipulate out of existence the understanding
of 'beautiful' which gives it a peculiarly aesthetic significance.

It is Kant who has here provided the clearest paradigm for recent
aesthetics. Kantian beauty (*das Schöne*) is something we may predicate
of any kind of object (it is pointedly not restricted to the arts), but in
doing so we always make an evaluation which is expressly neither
moral nor utilitarian. The attribution of Kantian beauty depends on the
occurrence of a distinct kind of pleasure, which for present purposes we
may simply call 'aesthetic pleasure'. In her recent discussion of beauty,
written within this Kantian tradition, Mary Mothersill[8] has argued that
the term 'beauty' picks out a concept of aesthetic value of the most
general nature, which is a 'standing concept', or one which we could
not do without. Beauty, according to her, is a kind of good, which may
be found in objects of any sort, and 'is causally linked with pleasure
and inspires love'.[9] Plato pervades Mothersill's discussion, for she thinks
that this standing concept of beauty is also his: 'if Plato characterizes
as *kalos* such disparate items as youths and maidens, goddesses, horses,
lyres, codes of law, this suggests that *kalos* is a *good* match for the
English "beautiful" which has an analogously wide range.'[10] This is not
to agree with Collingwood, whose view is that 'beautiful' has this same
wide range *and does not pick out an aesthetic concept*. Mothersill's
view is that beauty is *the* aesthetic concept *and* has a range analogous
to that of *kalos*.

The view I develop will be at odds with both Collingwood and
Mothersill. I do not accept the bald ruling that 'beautiful' has no aesthetic

---

[7] Collingwood (1938), 38.   [8] Mothersill, 247 ff.
[9] Ibid. 271.   [10] Ibid. 251.

connotation, and will, for now, retain it as the term picking out a generic, standing concept of aesthetic value.[11] But if this is what our 'beautiful' means, I do not believe that Plato's *kalos* is its straight equivalent. *Kalos* is a much wider term. There are things which are *kalos* because they give aesthetic pleasure—but that is only one species of *kalos*. Mothersill says that poems and sculptures are 'cited as clear ... instances of beauty' by Plato.[12] Yes, but poems and sculptures may only belong to the sub-species of what is *kalos*-by-giving-aesthetic-pleasure. *Kalos* as such cannot be equated with 'beautiful' in its aesthetic sense.[13] When in the *Symposium* Plato talks of *to kalon* as the supreme object of love, to which we make a transition from first loving a particular human body that is *kalos*, it is then, I admit, hard to resist using the word 'beauty'. To say that we first love a particular person's physical fineness and ascend to loving fineness itself loses the resonance of Plato's language in that extraordinary passage, and also its sense for us. Yet this does not overturn the view that *kalos* in general is a much wider term than 'beautiful' when the latter is taken as the generic aesthetic predicate.

Returning briefly to the *Gorgias*, we find that Socrates addresses part of our first question—is there aesthetic fineness?—by offering the following account of what is fine:

All fine things, such as bodies, colours, shapes, sounds, practices—do you not call them each fine with reference to something? First of all, for instance, don't you say that fine bodies are fine either because of use, for whatever each of them is useful for, or because of some pleasure, if they give onlookers enjoyment when they look on? ... And don't you call all the other things fine too in this way—shapes and colours—either because of some pleasure or because of some benefit or because of both? ... And don't you call sounds and everything to do with music fine in the same way? (474d3–e5.)

There is a case for saying that Plato here acknowledges the existence of aesthetic pleasure in a limited way. The point may be elucidated thus. Colours, shapes, and sounds seem to have been selected as the simplest objects of straightforward sensation or perception, and Plato appears happy to say that there is pleasure in the mere seeing or hearing of them. He recognizes that fineness may be a matter of benefit, or a

---

[11] I argue elsewhere that Mothersill's account of beauty will not stretch to cover natural and artistic beauty univocally (see Janaway (1993)).

[12] Mothersill, 251.

[13] Here I follow Moravcsik (1982), 31: 'what we call beautiful is for the Greeks "fine in appearance"', a species of what is fine.

matter of both benefit and enjoyment. It may please us to see an object which also is of some use or benefit to us—a well-wrought urn could be fine because of its pleasing contour and also because we usefully store things in it; or (elaborating Plato's example) think of a man with a strong physique who is a fine man because he can help us in adversity, and fine because we enjoy seeing him when he is throwing the discus. (The linkage of 'bodies' with 'giving onlookers enjoyment' suggests an athletic context.) But there is also a pleasure in seeing or hearing things where we may discount benefit altogether. Such things have the kind of fineness which Aquinas (defining beauty) calls 'id cujus apprehensio ipsa placet' ('that of which the apprehension in itself pleases').[14] Such things do not just please us when we apprehend them; rather it is the *very* apprehension of them which pleases. It is this pleasure in seeing or hearing that, in the most minimal sense, we could call an 'aesthetic' pleasure.

This brief passage arguably shows that Plato recognizes aesthetic pleasure in a limited but informative sense. It also suggests answers to the other questions we have raised. Firstly, some of the arts are included among the providers of this kind of pleasure—explicitly 'everything to do with music' (though note that music's fineness may also reside in its being beneficial or of use to us). Secondly, Plato is prepared to include things which give such pleasure among things that are fine. The two points combined allow us to construct the thought that artistic products which give aesthetic pleasure are a species of fine things. We have discovered that Plato comprehends the idea of a positive value in some pleasing works of art, independently of any further use or benefit they may have.

The dialogue of Plato's which takes the fine as its central topic is the *Hippias Major*.[15] Socrates is here in conversation with the sophist Hippias of Elis, who is satirized as superficial, unthinking and self-satisfied. The description of his multi-talented achievements is peppered with

---

[14] *Summa Theologiae* 1a. 2ae. 27, 1 (76–7). The definition is of the beautiful (*pulchrum*). Mothersill (323 ff.) argues that Aquinas' formulation encapsulates a truth which stands up to philosophical scrutiny.

[15] If it is by Plato: the dialogue's authenticity, though broadly accepted, remains a subject for argument. See Waterfield's discussion in Saunders (ed.), 217–28, for a start on the debate. Woodruff (1982*a*) provides an extensive case for authenticity; Kahn a forthright argument against, but note his comment (269) that 'no serious philosophical harm will be done to scholars and students who take the work for Platonic, so cleverly has the author done his job'. I treat the *Hippias Major* as a work by Plato, written before the *Republic* and the *Symposium*, making no other assumptions.

references to his being 'fine', his doing things 'finely' (*kalōs*), and so on ('You're putting fine thoughts in fine words, Hippias', says Socrates at 282b1). Thus his inability to say what fineness is seems all the more calamitous, though he shares with Ion (who also cuts a fine figure in public) an unawareness of the direction the Socratic manoeuvres are taking. Hippias and Ion each make a claim to 'speak finely' about a compendious list of subject-matters, and both claims are coupled with astounding ignorance. There is also an underlying continuity with Gorgias, who is mentioned in *Hippias Major* as 'the well-known sophist' (282b4–5), and seems to have provided Hippias with the model for his pompous rhetorical style.[16] With Plato's *Gorgias* in mind, we can see that Hippias' early claim to 'know most finely of men how to pass virtue [*aretē*] on to other people' (284a2–3) is an obvious target for demolition.[17]

When aesthetic pleasure emerges at the end of the dialogue, it is only after many different angles on fineness have been tried. Socrates makes it crystal-clear to us (if not to Hippias) that he seeks an answer to the question 'what the fine is itself',[18] and that this is to be distinguished from the question 'What is a fine thing?' What Socrates wants is that which *makes* all fine things fine, understood in a constitutive rather than a causal sense: What constitutes the fineness which all fine things have?[19] The dialogue puts the same point by asking for 'that because of which fine things are fine' or 'that by which fine things are fine'. The answers Hippias first gives confirm the range of the term *kalos*: 'A fine girl is a fine thing' (287e4); 'the fine is just gold' (289e3); and 'it is always finest . . . to be rich, healthy, and honoured by the Greeks, to arrive at old age, to make a fine memorial to his parents when they die, and to have a fine, grand burial from his own children' (291d9–e2). The last of these is clearly not an aesthetic fineness. The first is probably not, if 'a fine girl' is fine because she is desired (or is human beauty *always* aesthetic?). In the example of gold the claim that 'wherever that is added, even if it was seen to be foul before, it will be seen to be fine when it has been adorned with gold' (289e4–6) may more readily

---

[16] See Woodruff (1982*a*), 116–17, 123–35.

[17] I make no assumptions about the chronological ordering of *Gorg.* and *HiMa*. Woodruff regards the issue as 'too close to call' (1982*a*, 102). Dodds argues that *Gorg.* 474d–475a is probably later than the parallel passage *HiMa*. 298a–b (1959, 250).

[18] *auto to kalon hoti esti*, *HiMa*. 286d8–e1.

[19] Woodruff refers to the fine as the 'logical cause' of fineness in things (see 1982*a*, 151 ff.), borrowing the term from Vlastos (1969), 91 ff. The fine is referred to as 'what *makes* things fine' at 290d2, 294a1, 294d6–7, 300a9–10, 302d1–2.

suggest that Hippias has an aesthetic value in mind—though even here nothing necessitates an exclusively aesthetic reading.

The example Socrates throws back at him is Pheidias' monumental statue of Athena inside the Parthenon. If gold is truly that which, by being 'added', makes all fine things fine, the great Pheidias must have been ignorant of fineness, and hence a 'bad craftsman [*dēmiourgos*]'. Why? 'The point is . . . that Pheidias didn't make Athena's eyes out of gold, nor the rest of her face, nor her feet, nor her hands—as he would have done if gold would really have made them be seen to be finest— but he made them out of ivory' (290b2–5). Hippias, unruffled, replies that ivory is fine too. But if it is gold *and* ivory that are fine and make things fine, why did the sculptor construct the middles of Athena's eyes out of stone? The truth is that properties which make something fine can equally make something else foul. (The same properties could make something else simply lack fineness—a distinct way of failing. An Athena with golden eyes and ivory robes might have been an abomination, but it might simply have been a flop.) Any of the properties mentioned makes things fine, then, only when it is appropriate. Another example of the same kind is the stirring spoon for a bean soup: should it be made of gold or of figwood? If the figwood spoon is finer, then once again gold is not what makes all fine things fine. Hippias' surprise at the demeaning turn the conversation suddenly takes here is a well-worked piece of comedy (290d7–e1). But the same transition may have its point for us too: splendid aesthetic fineness is not the exclusive topic of discussion. Fine pots and spoons are fine things, even though among fine things they are not especially fine, as Hippias recognizes in an earlier remark.[20]

This discussion has come nowhere near defining *auto to kalon*. Hippias has merely given examples of things which are fine, and has chosen things each of which can in some way be seen to lack fineness: a fine girl is not fine in comparison with a goddess, not all applications of gold produce fine objects, and the supposedly fine life Hippias describes, including burying one's parents, would not be fine for someone like Achilles whose father was immortal.[21] We shall not discover what

---

[20] 288e6–9. A girl and a horse are finer than a fine pot. The only other fine thing in the immediate context is a lyre. None of these need be taken as exhibiting a particularly 'aesthetic' fineness.

[21] 'The first fails because it is not fine in every comparison; the second because it is not fine in every use, and the third because it is not fine in every instance' (Woodruff (1982*a*), 48).

the fine itself is until we can locate something strictly or completely fine, something for which there is no comparison, use, instance—in short, no way at all—in which it can be seen *not* to be fine.[22] In pursuit of this, Socrates and Hippias try out other evaluative notions: the appropriate, the useful, and the beneficial—but each fails in turn to provide a definition of the fine itself, whereupon Socrates proclaims himself 'stuck', in a state of *aporia*.

It is now that aesthetic fineness seems to provide a way out: is the fine after all 'what is pleasant through sight and hearing'?

If whatever makes us be glad, not with all the pleasures, but just those through hearing and sight—if we call *that* fine, how do you suppose we'd do in the contest?

Men [i.e. people: *anthrōpoi*] when they're fine anyway—and everything decorative, pictures and sculptures—these all delight us when we see them, if they're fine. Fine sounds and music altogether, and speeches and storytelling have the same effect. (297e5–298a5.)

Obviously we are treading the same terrain as in *Gorgias* 474d, discussed above. But music is the only art mentioned by name in the *Gorgias* passage—now alongside music we find two species of visual art, and story-telling. This passage in *Hippias Major* is thus significant for uniting disparate arts under a single conception of fineness whose defining feature is pleasure through sight and hearing. Paintings, sculptures, speeches (if that is the correct translation of *logoi*[23]), story-telling (*muthologiai*), and all of that general class of human artefacts which count as 'decorations'[24] are put together with music as fine in the same way. We may note further that *mousikē*, translated above as 'music', often means just music, but in some contexts, such as the extended discussion of education in *Republic* Books 2 and 3, it is a seamless whole which includes music among a larger group of arts that have to

---

[22] See ibid. 153–5 on the conception of what is *strictly* fine. *Symp.* 211a (discussed below) elaborates on this conception.

[23] Dodds (1959, 250) places *logoi* parallel with the *Gorgias*' 'branches of learning' (*mathēmata*). But do the latter please 'by sight and hearing'? There is surely little to suggest that for Plato the pleasures of listening to the spoken word are the same as the pleasures of learning. It is rhetoric and tragedy that aim at pleasure in the medium of *logoi*, and it would be odd for Plato to call these 'branches of learning'.

[24] *Poikilmata*. Dodds (loc. cit.) treats *poikilmata* as simply 'patterns', no different in principle from the colours and shapes of the *Gorgias* passage. But the word connotes embroidery or ornamentation resulting from human agency, and its association in the text with painting and sculpting suggests that the patterns are those of artefacts. (When Plato elsewhere (*Rep.* 529c7–8) uses the same word to describe the heavenly bodies as 'ornaments which brighten the sky . . . embroidered in the visible world', it is a metaphor.)

do with sound, rhythm, song, and speech. The concatenation of 'fine sounds and music altogether, and speeches and storytelling' suggests this sense here. Some of the things listed are not art products ('people', recalling the 'bodies' in the *Gorgias*, and 'sounds', which perhaps embrace more than the artistic *mousikē*). Yet the passage shows that the products and practices of the arts are things Plato finds it natural to associate with aesthetic pleasure, and that for this purpose they form a cohesive group.

Placing the unified branch of 'music altogether' side by side with the other obvious grouping of all decoration, painting, and sculpture, we have arts pleasing to the sense of hearing, and arts pleasing through sight. But that these *two* groups of arts are expected to cohere stores up trouble, and allows the definition of the fine as 'what is pleasant through hearing and sight' to fail on a technicality. For what, according to this definition, is the *one* characteristic which all fine things share in, and which makes them fine? It is not the sheer characteristic of giving rise to pleasure, since there are pleasures which the definition excludes: 'what is pleasant to the other senses . . . food and drink, what goes with making love, and all the rest of that sort of thing' (298d8–e2). These are undeniably pleasant things, but

anyone in the world would laugh at us if we called it not *pleasant to eat* but *fine*, or if we called a pleasant smell not *pleasant* but *fine*. And as for making love [*ta peri ta aphrodisia*], everybody would fight us; they'd say it is most pleasant, but that one should do it, if he does it at all, where no one will see, because it is the foulest thing to be seen. (299a1–6.)

Eating and smelling involve lowly pleasures which are just not admirable or interesting enough to be judged 'fine'. Things to do with *ta aphrodisia* are refused the title because they are foul to be seen, confirming again that a thing's having an admirable outward appearance will always be relevant to whether it is *kalos*.

Not everything pleasant is fine. So, if it is not being pleasant *per se* that provides the single definition of the fine, what is it? Here is the difficulty. What is it that is common between, say, a painting the seeing of which pleases us, and a melody the hearing of which pleases us? It is not that both please through sight, nor that both please through hearing (299e2–300a3). Nor is it true of each that it is pleasant through sight and hearing. Yet what is true of both of two things, Socrates insists, really must be true of each: if both the painting and the melody please by being F, then the painting is F and the melody is F. On these grounds the definition fails. Socrates seems to become more interested in a tortuous piece of logical theorizing then in pursuing fineness, even though something akin to Aquinas' definition beckons: the fine is what pleases in the very apprehension of it—with some suitable qualification on what counts as 'apprehension', if one can be found.

Stuck with 'pleasure through sight' and 'pleasure through hearing', Socrates at least asks whether there is any overarching common feature, and he answers that 'they are the most harmless pleasures and the best' (303e1–5). He then strangely interprets his own remark as saying that 'beneficial pleasure' is the fine (303e9). 'Beneficial pleasure' excludes (*contra Gorgias* 474d) both the merely pleasing and the merely useful, leaving only the category of things which are called fine because of pleasure and benefit. It would rule out the fineness of 'purely aesthetic pleasure'. However, this interesting final development is curtailed because of the problems encountered earlier over defining the fine in terms of the beneficial. The dialogue ends with Hippias re-asserting his Gorgianic claim that one should stick to 'presenting a speech well and finely, in court or council or any other authority' (304a7–b1) and walk off with the rewards. Socrates counters with the traditional Socratic worry, addressed first and foremost to himself: 'How will you know whose speech—or any other action—is finely presented or not, when you are ignorant of the fine? And when you're in a state like that, do you think it's any better for you to live than die?' (304d8–e3.)

Having acknowledged the existence of aesthetic pleasure, and having located it substantially within the group of activities which we call 'the arts', Socrates has at last confronted the question: What is it about just these pleasures that is peculiarly fine? It is disappointing that he rejects the only answer he thinks of—but his formulation of that answer itself is perplexing. For it would be stretching things to the point of incredulity if we were expected to equate 'most harmless' (or 'least harmful') with 'most beneficial'. My examples of smelling a rose or playing backgammon show this: they may well provide pleasures which are among the most harmless, but it is still an open question whether these pleasures are among the most beneficial, or are beneficial at all. In the *Gorgias* Plato presented the line that public performance of instrumental music, dithyrambs, and tragedy does the audience no good whatever, but *merely* serves to give them pleasure. Which is the more plausible defence against this line: that the pleasure provided by the arts is fine because it is harmless, or that it is fine because it is beneficial?[25]

We have so far met no evidence that Plato considers aesthetic pleasure—to the extent that he recognizes it—a harmful thing. Reflect, however, that a sweet-smelling plant can be poisonous. Its smell would not be a bad thing, but its being poisonous *and* sweet-smelling would make it all the more dangerous. This, I think, is how Plato comes to view some of the arts. Good poetry which pleases us when we hear it is *eo ipso* a fine thing—no need to deny that. But until we have asked how it stands with relation to knowledge, learning, and human excellence, we have not said anything particularly important. In the same vein, it is doubtful whether a friend of the arts would wish to take a stand on the 'pleasure through sight and hearing' which Plato acknowledges, for it is a pretty flimsy affair. Is the value of attending a recital of Homer or a Sophocles drama to be found in the pleasure of sight and hearing? It is still unclear what the question means, but what is good about these occasions—if anything is—cannot be just that they look and sound pleasant. How could we ignore the thoughts with which the poet engages our imaginations and our emotions, seeming to teach us something about life and about ourselves? These are surely where a friend of the arts would begin.[26] Thus it becomes plausible that the kind of 'aesthetic pleasure' Plato recognizes is indeed only a small portion of fineness, which in itself is insufficient to make the arts worthy of our highest aspirations.

In the much later dialogue *Philebus* Plato comes close to a positive notion of aesthetic pleasure, but very little that is 'artistic' appears to be covered by it. The great distinction which divides the pleasures here is that of the pure and the mixed. Mixed pleasures contain, or depend on, some form of pain or distress, while pure pleasures do not. The pleasures to be taken in some kinds of beauty are 'quite unlike those of scratching', for instance (*Phil.* 51d1). Pleasure in scratching depends

---

[25] The claim in *Rep.* 10 (595b5–6) that mimetic poetry is ruinous to the intellect could be countered by according it the fineness of harmless pleasure. But this would be playing into Plato's hands, for by the end of *Rep.* 10 (607d8–9), he demands a defence of poetry 'as not only pleasant [*hēdeia*], but also beneficial [*ōphelimē*] to cities and to human life' (my translation).

[26] 'The traditional defence of poetry has been founded on the consideration that the finest works of poetry can help us to better our lives. They provide us with a particularly important means of enriching our awareness of human experience, and they enable us to give to our feelings greater precision, purity, strength and depth. Poetry is a means of increasing our intelligence and strengthening our moral temper' (Budd (1983), 155).

on the distress of the itch that is relieved. But some pleasures in colour, shape, and sound are not at all of this nature:

> By 'beauty of shape' I don't mean what most people would understand by it—I am not thinking of animals or certain pictures, but, so the thesis goes, a straight line or a circle and resultant planes and solids produced on a lathe or with ruler and square. . . . On my view these things are not, as other things are, beautiful (*kala*) in a relative way, but are always beautiful in themselves, and yield their own special pleasures quite unlike those of scratching. I include colours, too, that have the same characteristic. . . . With sounds, it is the smooth clear ones I am thinking of, ones that produce a single pure tune (*melos*), and are beautiful not just in a certain context but in themselves—these and their attendant pleasures. (51c1–d9.)

As elsewhere, a particular kind of fineness is to be equated with what gives pleasure to sight and hearing.[27] But Plato takes a step nearer to a modern notion of 'aesthetic' pleasure when he rules out any admixture of distress. For this, by implication, rules out any admixture of desire. A sound might give pleasure if it was the voice of one's beloved that one had longed to hear, or the bell ringing at the end of a tedious school day—but such pleasures in sounds are conditional on a prior lack. If the perception of a sound or shape satisfies a particular desire, and is pleasurable because of its so doing, Plato will count the pleasure not as 'pure', but as the replenishment of a prior deprivation. This is, I think, the best interpretation of what Plato intends by saying that shapes and sounds are 'beautiful not in a relative way', 'not just in a certain context but in themselves', and that they 'yield their own special pleasures'.[28]

[27] Pleasures of smell also tend to be 'pure' in that they require no admixture of distress. But they are 'less divine' (51e1) than those of shape, colour, and sound—presumably because delight in the latter is 'the beginning of delight in numbers, whereas smells lead nowhere' (Gosling (1975), 122).

[28] Cf. Gosling (1975), 122. I am aware of two other views: Hackforth (1958), 98–9: 'their beauty does not depend on contrast with something less beautiful, or positively ugly', as opposed to things that are 'relatively beautiful in the sense that they come at some point on a scale of greater and less aesthetic satisfaction'. Hackforth also sees an affinity here with the way in which the Form *auto to kalon* is absolutely, and not relatively, *kalon*. But I agree with Gosling (1975), 121, and Murphy, 244, in finding these views not clearly supported by the text. Murphy's view is that what is being ruled out is something beautiful only in relation to something else (against a background, for example), and not in itself—the most natural reading of *ouk einai pros ti kala . . . all' aei kala kath' hauta* (51c6–7)—but he faces the problem that this does not explain either the examples excluded or those included. However, Murphy's reference (245) to a pleasure in 'beauty alone without any adventitious appeal to other human interests' seems right.

Plato also rules out of consideration 'what most people would understand' by beauty of shape, namely animals (living things, humans included, presumably), and pictures. Why is this? A painting which depicts something is liable to give pleasure—so why not a 'pure' pleasure? Schopenhauer complains of over-naturalistic nudes and paintings of oysters and herrings which engage the appetites, saying that when this happens 'purely aesthetic contemplation is at once abolished'.[29] Can Plato be thinking that all depiction engages desires or emotions concerning the depicted object? The pleasure in the picture would then not be a pleasure 'all of its own', and the picture would be a fine one only relative to our attitudes towards things of the kind depicted. The reference to the beauty of living things may also trade on the same idea: living things are like pictures in that they excite desires and emotions, so that we cannot appreciate their beauty 'pure', as we can that of a geometrical construction.[30]

It is hard to know where Plato thinks of his examples of 'pure' pleasure in the beautiful occurring. They seem to apply to human ventures that are artistic in the broad sense: his geometrical figures, for example, are 'produced' (though in fact, as far as the argument goes, they might just as well be discovered in nature). But a vast volume of artistic productions will be excluded from this category. No representation will give 'pure' pleasure. Nor, we assume, will 'expressive' modes, rhythms, and texts, which will be beautiful because of the emotional character which they 'imitate' and which they are liable eventually to set up in the listener.[31] Plato is seeking visible and audible forms which are objects of pleasure not because they are parts of an artistic structure, but because of what they are, regardless of context. Very little of what is fine in the arts, in his understanding or in ours, will therefore be included under the heading of pure pleasure.

Plato has already claimed earlier in the *Philebus* that the pleasure we take in tragedy and comedy is 'mixed'. It does not, however, have exactly the same analysis as the pleasure in scratching. There, a state was pleasurable only because it brought the cessation of a prior distressing state. In watching a tragedy, it is rather that *at the same time*

---

[29] Schopenhauer, i. 208.

[30] The alternative explanation is that Plato is criticizing *mimēsis* as an 'inferior reduplication' of 'commonplace reality' (Hackforth (1958), 99). But that gives no clue as to why the non-representational, non-artistic beauty of living things should also be excluded from the 'pure' category.

[31] Cf. the explanation by Gosling (1975), 122.

we feel distress and pleasure. 'The audience at a tragedy actually enjoy their tears' (48a5–6). Plato continues to assume that distress in the audience is genuine. Given that premiss, no one would enjoy tragedy in the same way if the events were depicted so as to *avoid* distress! The whole point of a tragedy—and of why we enjoy it—would be lost. Our liking for portrayals of the painful is puzzling.[32] Plato offers a hint of a general explanation when he says that many emotions which are forms of distress—anger, fear, yearning, sorrow, love, envy, malice— turn out to be 'imbued with an unexpected degree of enjoyment' (47e5). If sorrow and fear in real life can be tinged with pleasure, perhaps pleasure in a depiction of the fearful and sorrowful is only what psychology would predict, after all. But there is clearly no likelihood of tragedy's proving an object of 'pure' pleasure in the sense which Plato goes on to delineate. Pleasure in comedy, too, depends on our having certain emotions. Plato argues that we must feel malice towards a character whom we laugh at as an object of ridicule, and (less convincingly) that malice is in itself a distressing emotion. Therefore, our pleasure in laughing at a comedy is also mixed with distress (48a8–50a9). Indeed, wherever emotions are involved, pure pleasure is not to be found. 'In dirges, tragedies, and comedies, not only on the stage, but in the whole tragi-comedy of life, distress and pleasure are blended with each another' (50b1–4). We might observe that this idea of a 'pure' pleasure embodies something of a flight from life itself.

Well, as Socrates might say, all that is fine . . . but aren't we forgetting something else that someone once said about *to kalon*? At the climax of his literary masterpiece, the *Symposium*, Plato has Socrates relate the wise words which Diotima, a woman of Mantinea, supposedly addressed to him, revealing an absolute beauty as the supreme object of love. The whole dialogue is devoted to love, evoking and portraying it as well as attempting to define it. What is loved is what is *kalos*, and in this context, as I have conceded, we can scarcely help thinking of beauty. Because love is the topic, we meet no soup-ladles, pots, or sandals, however fine. Perhaps more surprising is that in Diotima's account of the lover's ascent to beauty itself, the fine objects of love encountered on the way include no paintings, sculptures, music, story-telling—nothing artistic. Despite Plato's poetic writing in this work, and the inclusion in the cast-list of a comic and a tragic poet— Aristophanes and Agathon, each of whom speaks with eloquence—we

---

[32] The discussion of this familiar point by Schier (1989) is stimulating.

learn little concerning the arts from the explicit content of the *Symposium*. Rhetoric is given full rein but then put in its place: when Socrates is called upon to take his turn at speaking about love, he first subjects the previous speaker, Agathon, to a cross-examination. It is agreed that Agathon spoke finely, in a spectacular rhetorical style which reminded Socrates of Gorgias.[33] But Socrates draws a sharp contrast between two activities, namely speaking finely (*kalōs*) and speaking the truth (the former possible on Gorgias' theory, the latter not). He purportedly refutes one of Agathon's statements—so what Agathon said was not the truth, and he did not know what he was talking about—'still, you did speak finely, Agathon' (201c1). Fineness masks falsity: rhetoric is, once again, a mere image in words.

Once launched into his retelling of Diotima's teachings, Socrates brings forward the new definition of love as 'desire for the perpetual possession of the good' (206a11–12). The argument requires the replacement of 'beautiful' by 'good', which is simply achieved by Diotima's saying we may 'change terms and substitute *agathos* for *kalos*' (204e1–3). This makes the class of things that are *agathos* and the class of things that are *kalos* coincident, the terms being 'interchangeable . . . but not synonymous'.[34] Being fine is one thing, being good another, but still all and only good things are fine things. So if a poem or a painting is fine (perhaps by being pleasing to see or hear), then it cannot help being in the class of good things. But we should not assume that this settles very much about the value of the arts. Agathon's speech was fine. It was beautiful. But for whom and in what way would Plato regard it as good? It appealed to (persuaded? deceived?) the gathering, but was based on a falsehood. Agathon's or anyone's tragedies, similarly, according to the *Gorgias*, may be as fine as they like, but in fact benefit no one in the respects that matter to Plato. Both

---

[33] *Symp.* 198c1–5. Dover (1980, 123–4) explains some features of Plato's extended parody of Gorgias, and shows by metrical analysis how 'Plato has taken considerable trouble to give Agathon's peroration [197d1–e5] a poetic character in addition to caricaturing its "Gorgianic" structure'.

[34] Price, 16, following Dover (1980), 136: 'Anything which is *kalon*, i.e. which looks or sounds good (or is good to contemplate), is also *agathon*, i.e. it serves a desirable purpose or performs a desirable function, and vice versa.' 'Contemplation' has to be taken pretty widely to make this explanation stick, and we also have to be careful about desirable functions and purposes. Someone's life could be fine and good without *looking* particularly interesting, and without subserving any function or purpose *outside itself*. Price's more cautious gloss brings out both points: 'The *kalon* is what presents itself appealingly (though not only to the senses); the *agathon* is good for someone in some way (though not only instrumentally).'

before and after[35] the *Symposium* Plato thinks that what presents itself appealingly may fail to be good in important ways and may even be harmful to those whom it charms.

Have we in Diotima's speech at last struck an account which will place artistic products firmly among the good things towards which human beings should aspire? Diotima assigns a role to poets and poetry when she talks of the offspring of the soul rather than the body. The motivation of all *erōs* is procreative, it desires to generate something new. This is woven in with the notion that all humans desire immortality, and the original strand which says that love is love of the beautiful. ('From fairest creatures we desire increase,| That thereby beauty's Rose might never die.') The aim of love is 'to procreate and bring forth in beauty'. Thus the happiness we seek in possessing beauty is the kind of immortality we think may be provided by producing offspring—'the nearest thing to perpetuity and immortality that a mortal being can attain'. It is only 'in' beauty that we wish to procreate.[36] While physical intercourse and procreation provide the context for the ordinary understanding of *erōs*, Diotima's account uses the physical as a metaphor for something more general. The same impulse to generate can show itself in spiritual form, and is in Plato's eyes clearly superior when it does so. Without having to have 'recourse to women' one can seek out a beautiful companion with a beautiful soul and with him generate 'children of the soul' which really can last forever. What is the offspring of the soul?

It is wisdom and virtue [*aretē*] in general; of this poets and such craftsmen [*dēmiourgoi*] as have found out some new thing may be said to be begetters; but far the greatest and fairest branch of wisdom is that which is concerned with the due ordering of states and families, whose name is moderation and justice. (209a3–8.)

Poets rank only with inventive producers in general, and can claim to do nothing so fine as lawgivers—that said, Diotima is prepared to give

---

[35] Tragic poetry is again called *kalos* but harmful overall in *Rep.* 10 (595b3–c2, where the context—conceding admiration to Homer—makes *kalos* (c1) unlikely to be merely ironic).

[36] 206e5–8. The imagery is thoroughly sexual, based on a particular assumption about why males desire sexual intercourse with beautiful females, and also on the common ancient assumption that it is the male who 'generates', with the female serving as the place or receptacle where generation occurs. Plato also offers no argument for the ideas that heterosexual intercourse is essentially motivated by reproductive ends, or that reproduction manifests the desire for immortality.

poets credit as begetters of wisdom and virtue (or excellence). Homer and Hesiod feature prominently, alongside the lawgivers of Sparta and Athens, Lycurgus and Solon, in a resounding defence of the superiority of non-physical generation, whose children

surpass human children by being immortal as well as more beautiful. Everyone would prefer children such as these to children after the flesh. Take Homer, for example, and Hesiod, and the other good poets; who would not envy them the children that they left behind them, children whose qualities have won immortal fame and glory for their parents? . . . and so it is in many other places with other men . . . who by their many fine actions have brought forth good fruit of all kinds; not a few of them have even won men's worship on account of their spiritual children, a thing which has never yet happened to anyone by reason of his human progeny. (209c6–e4.)

Something is seriously awry here. The depreciation of children as merely 'human' is startling. The pretension to know that the *Iliad* and *Works and Days* are finer than any human child is unexplained. If fathers are not worshipped for producing their offspring, the reason is surely not that the product is generally shoddy and liable to die. A further problem is this: How do the poets fit into the rest of Diotima's picture? 'In' what beauty did Homer generate his long-lived children?[37] Even if the aim of his making poetry was to seek a kind of immortality, what was the beautiful object he loved and from which he desired increase? We are given no clue to this. The speech concurs with the standard admiration of good poets for their production of works which are fine and can endure far longer than a human life. ('So long as men can breathe, or eyes can see,| So long lives this . . .'.) Being a poet ranks higher than having children. But Diotima's positive role for poetry does not attach to it on account of 'aesthetic pleasure'. Poetry is fine here because it gives rise to wisdom and excellence—a highly conventional thought which has been challenged by the Socrates of earlier dialogues, and which the Socrates of the *Republic* will deny outright. The thought is not explained or developed further in the *Symposium*.

Later there is another slight hint of a new view about poetry, but arguably it turns out to be spurious. After Socrates' speech, and after the speech of his lover, Alcibiades, comes a brief evocative picture of the dying hours of the all-night party, with Socrates still trying to

---

[37] Dover (1980, 151–2) speculates that 'it can only be the virtuous character of the [society] for which Homer sang', which seems somewhat lame. Plato's text gives no hint of an answer. Price (27) brings out the unsatisfactory nature of this passage.

persuade his poetic co-symposiasts of some point about tragedy, comedy, and *technē*. ('They were giving way to his arguments, which they didn't follow very well, and nodding. Aristophanes fell asleep first, and when it was fully light Agathon followed him' (223d6–8).) Here is what was going on in the small hours:

The main point was that Socrates was compelling them to admit that the man who knew how to write a comedy could also write a tragedy, and that someone who by *technē* was a tragic writer was capable of being also a comic writer. (223d2–6.)

Now if there were after all a genuine all-embracing poetic *technē*, we could begin to imagine how poetry might be what Diotima said, something genuinely productive of excellence and wisdom, something more like medicine or lawgiving. Dover remarks: 'the argument, strikingly unlike what is said by Socrates in *Ion* 531e–534e, is not developed elsewhere in Plato, and reconstruction of the form it might take is a useful exercise for students of ancient philosophy.'[38] Well, first we must think how Socrates would compel someone to admit that a tragedian must also be able to be a comedian. Surely only by some assumption about the nature of things done 'by *technē*', such as the assumption that a *technē* must succeed by reliable, generalizable principles. Assuming that there were a poetic or dramatic *technē* which enabled both Aristophanes and Agathon to do well, we must conclude that each could master both genres. But it is easiest to imagine Socrates arguing *against* the assumption of a poetic *technē*, precisely as a way of accounting for their lack of generality as poets—just the same argument, in fact, which accounted for Ion's exclusive leaning towards Homeric poetry.[39]

In the famous culmination of Socrates' Diotima-speech, the account of the upward progress of the initiate of love, there is no explicit reference to poetry or any of the arts. Choosing the path on which the generation of children is not even possible as an incidental distraction, the ideal lover must start by loving one boy's body for its beauty, then generalize this love to all beautiful bodies, ascend to love of a single

---

[38] Dover (1980), 177.

[39] This is the beautifully simple reading offered by Grube (1935), 184 n. 1, and by Taylor, 234. See also Flashar, 44; Woodruff (1982*b*), 149 n. 11. For a different view of the passage, linking it to a unity between tragic and comic views of *erōs* presented in the dialogue, see Nussbaum (1986), 194, and 469 n. 55; a similar suggestion is made by Else (1986), 11–12. Clay argues for a connection with the figure of Socrates himself, seen as a fusion of the tragic and the comic.

soul, then generalize to a love of what is common to all souls. From then on, in company with a beloved, he should move on to love practices, laws, and sciences (*epistēmai*: branches of knowledge), opening up a 'vast ocean of beauty' which will make it seem narrow-minded simply to love one person or object. At all stages he will generate fine discourse, brought to birth by union with beauty. Some of this discourse, in the early stages, may be poetry, though Plato does not say so. But, apart from that, the arts do not figure here—why not? Decoration and music are not mentioned, says Dodds, 'since they are not objects of *erōs*'.[40] In the restricted sense of *erōs*, of course, they are not. But Plato is labouring mightily to replace that sense with another. If something called *erōs* is transferable from human love-objects to branches of knowledge and the Spartan constitution, why not to music and the visual arts? And why does the ideal lover not produce such arts in response to the higher objects of *erōs*? Is Plato studiously silent about the arts here, or just silent because it does not occur to him that they should play a role? There is another view: 'Strangely enough, Diotima and Socrates do not assign a role to the arts in this process of reawakening to Beauty, though it takes but a short step to do so, and this stopping on the verge has not prevented the *Symposium* from luring numerous readers . . . to press on.'[41] But the lure is to be resisted. We have no right to assume that Plato has waiting before him a smooth train of thought leading to a positive, quasi-modern account of the arts. (Besides, he was 'on the verge' of writing the *Republic*.)

   Diotima's ascent continues, and so it is that

The man who has been guided thus far in the mysteries of love, and who has directed his thoughts towards examples of beauty in due and orderly succession, will suddenly have revealed to him as he approaches the end of his initiation a beauty whose nature is marvellous indeed, the final goal, Socrates, of all his previous efforts. This beauty is first of all eternal; it neither comes into being nor passes away, neither waxes not wanes; next, it is not beautiful in part and ugly in part, nor beautiful at one time and ugly at another, nor beautiful in this relation and ugly in that, nor beautiful here and ugly there, as varying according to its beholders; nor again will this beauty appear to him like the beauty of a face or hands or anything else corporeal, or like the beauty of a thought or a science, or like beauty which has its seat in something other than itself, be it a living thing or the earth or the sky or anything else whatever; he

---

[40] Dodds (1959), 250.
[41] Beardsley, 41. Lucas (260) also sees Plato taking 'a step along the path' to exaltation of the artist.

will see it as absolute, existing alone with itself, unique, eternal, and all other beautiful things as partaking of it, yet in such a manner that, while they come into being and pass away, it neither undergoes any increase or diminution nor suffers any change. (210e2–211b5.)

The lover attains to the Form, *auto to kalon*: the beautiful, or the fine, *itself*, which is set in contrast with the multiplicity of mere beautiful things. They participate in it, and, as we learn elsewhere, it is this relation of participation in the Form of the beautiful that makes anything beautiful.[42] Socrates tried to cajole Hippias into seeking that one single characteristic, the presence of which constituted something's being *kalos*. Plato now tells us how fineness itself must be conceived. It is single, eternal and unchanging, dependent on nothing for its existence, and distinct from any particular thing (or class of things) that is *kalos*. This passage has commonly been read as saying that the beautiful itself simply and strictly *is* beautiful, in the sense that it itself is a beautiful thing.[43] Plato lists many ways in which an ordinary beautiful thing could also be the opposite of beautiful, in order to show that, in contrast, the beautiful itself suffers none of these admixtures of the ugly or the foul; this invites the interpretation that the Form itself is *kalos*. Furthermore, unless the Form is itself beautiful or fine, Plato's extravagant claims for its effect on the lover's life make no sense. The Form, once known, must strike the human mind in such an overwhelming way that it diminishes all other objects of love. It must *be* completely and overwhelmingly beautiful. Then we can explain why Plato can speak with such moment of 'the region where, if anywhere . . . a human life is liveable, contemplating absolute beauty'.[44] To fulfil this exalted role, the beautiful itself (arguably) has to be measured on the same scale as familiar beautiful things, and be superior to them in value on that scale.

---

[42] *Phdo.* 100b3–e3.

[43] The classic statement of this interpretation is in Vlastos (1965). In a recent challenge to it, Penner has argued that 'the aim in the upward path is *not* to ascend from less fully beautiful to most fully beautiful objects. Rather it's to ascend from inferior (nominalist) candidates for being *what beauty is* to the best of all candidates' (1987, 139). Penner argues (see 127 ff.) (i) that Plato is not committed to the claim that the Form is itself a beautiful thing by his talk of 'the beautiful itself', (ii) that he is not so committed by the contrasts between the Form and other things which are and are not beautiful, (iii) that he is not so committed by the talk of the beautiful itself as a supreme object of *erōs*. One might agree with (i) and (ii) while finding (iii) unconvincing. Price (43 n. 49) writes: 'if [Beauty itself] is to gratify the lover in a manner analogous to beautiful sights . . . it must itself, supremely, be beautiful to contemplate. Nowhere else does "self-predication" (or better, self-participation) have such clear point.'

[44] *Symp.* 211d1–3: my translation, influenced partly by Nussbaum (1986), 467 n. 34.

The beauty of former treasures such as boys, clothing, and gold becomes, from this vantage point, something to disdain. It is 'beauty tainted by human flesh and colour and a mass of perishable [mortal] rubbish'—while the eternal, untainted fineness itself is 'divine', and the lover who has intercourse with it will be the most nearly immortal of humans (211e2–212a7). Plato has not given up his sexual imagery, and he does not forget to mention the offspring generated by the lover who lays hold of the Form: 'he will beget not images of excellence [*eidōla aretēs*], in that he will not grasp an image, but true excellence, in that he grasps the truth' (212a3–5). To be capable of bringing genuine excellence into the world is to know and love the eternal, divine, logical cause of things' being fine, and nothing short of that. Could the supreme lover of *auto to kalon* be a poet? Poets were earlier said to be among the 'begetters of wisdom and excellence'. But a Homer, in order to have engendered true excellence, must have grasped the eternal Form of the beautiful, not a mere image of it. Could a Homer do that? Perhaps Diotima's teachings are mysteries too mysterious to contain a definite answer. On the other hand, in a more sober passage in the *Republic* Plato chooses the same words to give a resounding No: all poets, starting with Homer, make only images of excellence; they never rise to, or know, the real thing, they never grasp the truth.[45]

It is only when the lover is at the earliest level of loving the beauty of bodies that poetry is seriously in consideration. The 'beautiful discourse' generated at this early stage possibly includes poetry,[46] though Plato does not say so explicitly. Perhaps it would have been misleading to say so. Since tragedy, comedy, and epic are not likely to spring from such a context, the poetry engendered by the love of a beautiful body is hardly representative of what Plato usually discusses under that heading. More importantly, such discourse is only a beginning. At higher levels non-poetic discourse takes over: a moral discourse 'that improves the youths', and then 'much fine and noble discourse and thoughts contained in abundant philosophy'. In Diotima's final vision poets quietly slip out of view. Beautiful poems last a long time, but could never be an exchange for beauty itself.

Surely, however, the aesthetic is lauded as a self-standing value in this whole passage? And, since the aesthetic will have something to do with the arts, surely Plato cannot be seen as excluding them from the

---

[45] *Rep.* 600e4–6. The same phrase, *eidōla aretēs*—'images of excellence'—is used here and at *Symp.* 212a4. *Tou alēthous ephaptomenōi* at 212a5 is also echoed by *tēs de alētheias ouch haptesthai* in the *Rep.* passage.

[46] For this view of 210a7–8, see Moravcsik (1971), 292–3, and Price, 41, 47.

highest human life? Care is required. It is unclear how much of Diotima's teachings are really concerned with an aesthetic fineness, or even an aesthetic beauty. At the first stage, again, where the lover loves the beauty of bodies, Plato talks of *to ep' eidei kalon*, the fine in appearance or outward form. Do we then have, as has been suggested, 'love of bodies for the sake of bodily beauty that can be abstracted and contemplated on a general level', followed by a 'move from mere sexual interest to some sort of aspiration, presumably aesthetic'?[47] A sharp distinction cannot always be made between 'erotic' and 'aesthetic' contemplation of human beauty, and it would be wrong to try to force such a distinction upon Diotima. However, it is fairly clear that for her the contemplation of human bodies is never purely aesthetic. The lover is not one to whom pleasure occurs merely in the looking (unlike the 'onlookers' of *Gorg.* 474d8–9), and his aspiration, whatever it ends up generating, is always erotic. And is there a move in the direction of the aesthetic? Higher up the ladder towards the ideal we find the contemplation of laws, sciences, and excellences, and it is not clear that we should describe these as the objects of an aesthetic aspiration.

Although Plato is talking about value, about fineness, and about beauty, there is little indication that artistic practices or an exclusively aesthetic form of value have any special place in the *Symposium*'s vision of the best of lives. And yet one reason remains why it is strange to say this. For *Symposium* 210a–212a is among the most elevated and beautiful stretches of writing ever composed. To be moved by it to any degree is to allow ourselves the thought of a standpoint from which the fair products of the arts count for little and the complexion of all human institutions is dimmed by contrast with the Forms. But what has been capable of making the aspiration to this 'higher' region live in our minds is the offspring of Plato the literary artist, who has brought us to this point scarcely by argument—rather by extended, subtly modulated rhetoric, layers of fictional narrators, and beguiling persuasion.[48] I have argued so far that Plato is not blind to the beauty which poetry has to offer, but that he does not place any very great value upon it. His own poetic achievements, I shall eventually suggest, do not conflict with his opposition to the poetry which he actively rejects. But it is to the *Republic* that we must first turn, to see what the reasons for that rejection are.

---

[47] Moravcsik (1971), 291. For criticism, see Price, 37–8.

[48] Socrates tries to *persuade* others of what Diotima said to him, having been *persuaded* himself (212b1–3). At one point she convinces him 'like a perfect sophist' (208b7–c1). See Nussbaum (1986), 176–7.

4

The Formation of Character

IN his treatment of the arts in Books 2–3 of the *Republic* Plato's concerns are moral and political. He wants to build a model of the best-organized community and of the healthiest type of human being, founded on a system of education which would enable both to exist. His question is always: What do the arts contribute to these endeavours? Now there is a point of view—I call it aestheticism—for which such an exercise is simply a mistake. Aestheticism would say that the real value of art *as art* is solely aesthetic, concerned with a kind of pleasure taken in an object 'for its own sake' and independently of any moral or political considerations. On this view, aesthetic value itself transcends moral or political value; moreover, any beneficial effect an aesthetic work has on a community's morality or an individual's education is extraneous to the question of its 'real' value. Now aestheticism's claim may not be obviously false; but it is not obviously true, even if in the past it has seemed so. Writing in 1944, Jaeger could comment that Plato's assumptions were difficult because 'modern "art" has painfully and victoriously torn itself away from the "moralizing" tendency of the eighteenth and early nineteenth centuries. We feel absolutely certain that the enjoyment of a work of "art" has nothing to do with morality.'[1] Whether or not this certainty (or this 'we') is still there, Plato's opposed view, that *nothing* about an artistic product can be discounted as ethically or politically neutral, succeeds in making aestheticism seem at best a partial view.[2]

For Plato, pleasure plays a leading role in deciding which poetry is the most 'poetic', but he pointedly refuses to equate the most 'poetic' poetry with the most valuable. In fact, he argues that the greater the pleasure, the greater the danger of corruption. If a poem is morally or politically dubious in its depiction of events, its detrimental effect will be all the greater the more 'poetic' it is. There is surely some plausibility in this. I recall a recent newspaper article concerning anti-Semitic films made under the Third Reich, which addressed the question: Should

[1] Jaeger, 214.   [2] Cf. Halliwell (1991), 335, for this verdict.

they now be released for general viewing? Most of the films were poor *as films*, but one in particular (entitled *Jud Süss*, and 'highly recommended' by Goebbels) was thought probably worthy of suppression *because of its artistic superiority*. This judgement parallels the many which Plato makes about Homer and his colleagues. It is essential to see past our likely disagreement with Plato about what is morally dubious: we understand in principle an argument that the 'artistic' can be more worthy of suppression than the crude and inept.[3]

Having mentioned film, let us note another point which a number of commentators have made. Plato's censorship of poetry is an attempt to influence a medium of mass communication, in which, as he sees it, ethical judgement about what is portrayed has been subordinated to the end of gratifying the audience. He engages with poetry in the way recent critics have engaged with television, cinema, and video: 'the endless proliferation of senseless images', 'ubiquitous and intrusive purveyors of bad taste, deformed paradigms, and questionable values', from which children and others nevertheless learn.[4] If we think that such products of our culture should be answerable to obligations of a moral or political nature, especially when children are at the forefront of the debate, as they are for Plato, then we should not find Plato's approach alien.

The *Republic* begins with scrutiny of the question 'What is justice?' In a way that is sometimes overlooked,[5] poetry and myth enter the discussion near the start of Book 2. Socrates proposes that justice is something good in itself, irrespective of consequences (though he thinks it also has beneficial consequences), and that it is better than being unjust. But Plato is at pains to emphasize how popular thinking is at odds with the Socratic line, and he has Glaucon and Adeimantus present a rhetorical defence of the view that people should be just only to the extent that it brings greater reward and reputation—being just is as such a mere chore, and if one could escape detection and punishment, the unjust life would be much better. In support of this line, Glaucon uses the traditional tale of Gyges, whose ring made him invisible and so able to commit injustice on a grand scale. Adeimantus cites Hesiod and

---

[3] *Lady Chatterley's Lover* was defended on the grounds that it had literary merit, and that it was not liable to corrupt. The first defence would cut no ice with Plato if the second failed.

[4] Quotes from Murdoch, 65; Nehamas (1982), 51. In more recent articles (1988), (1991), Nehamas makes an extended parallel between Plato and recent critics of television.

[5] Exceptions are Gadamer, 51; Ferrari (1989), 111; Else (1986), 17–18.

Homer who present lines of thought congenial to the anti-Socratic view of justice, such as

> you can choose to have evil, and heaps of it, too,
> for its house lies near and the path to it is smooth.
> But the immortals decreed that man must sweat
> to attain virtue; the road to it is steep and long
> and rough at first.[6]

A sprinkling of passages is brought forward from which can be gleaned the following sentiments: justice is a troublesome business, injustice easy; the good aspect of justice is merely some reward in the future; those who are unjust can always appease the gods by prayers and sacrifices.

Adeimantus asks 'When all such sayings about the attitudes of men and gods towards virtue and vice are so often repeated, what effect . . . do we think they have upon the minds of our youth?' Imagine someone 'who is naturally talented and able, like a bee flitting from flower to flower gathering honey, to flit over these sayings and to gather from them an impression of what kind of man he should be and of how best to travel along the road of life' (*Rep.* 365a4–b1; recall the winged, bee-like poets of *Ion* 534b1–3). From such reading someone might fashion a view of his own life: that he should act unjustly behind a mere façade of justice, drawing round himself what Plato calls a painted illusion of virtue or excellence (*skiagraphia aretēs*). He might express the moral choice facing him in terms of a quote from Pindar or compare himself to the crafty fox in the poetic fable by Archilochus (*Rep.* 365b2–4, c4–6). Here is moral thinking soaked in poetry, constructed by something akin to an inspirational talent, and committed to living out a mere artificial picture of a just life. Socrates' task is that of setting up an alternative account of justice. We already glimpse why part of that account will take on the question of how moral beliefs are acquired by way of poetry. Nor would a contemporary reader have been surprised: it has been rightly said that 'we cannot understand Plato's criticisms of poetry unless we remember that the Greeks thought it was the epitome of all knowledge and culture'.[7]

Socrates' competing account of justice gets underway with the idea of approaching the question on the large scale, in a city (368e8–369a3). Thus begins the parallel investigation of city and soul which dominates

---

[6] Hesiod, *Works and Days*, 287–91.

[7] Jaeger, 214. Plato 'follows the traditional affective and emotional training accepted by Protagoras'—Irwin (1977*a*, 201). Cf. *Prot.* 325e1–326a4.

the *Republic*. There is room for discussion about how Plato intends the city–soul analogy. Later Socrates will say that it is not important whether such a city as he describes could ever come about, and he compares himself with a painter: 'Do you think that someone is a worse painter if, having painted a model [*paradeigma*] of what the finest and most beautiful human being would be like and having rendered every detail of his picture adequately, he could not prove that such a man could come into being?'[8] Right at the end of Book 9, using the same word *paradeigma*, he speaks of 'the city which we were founding and described, our city of words' as 'perhaps . . . a model laid up in heaven, for him who wishes to look upon, and as he looks, set up the government of his soul' (592a10–b3). We are certainly meant to learn from the paradigm city how to approximate to an ideal of individual justice in ourselves. And part of the point of driving the poets from the city in Book 10 is that each individual should keep poetry beyond the margins of his or her soul.[9] But Plato spends so long on the details of his model city (many of them without analogues in the individual) that he must regard them as of independent interest.

Among the roles that Plato initially accepts must be carried out in any truly human city are those of what he calls *mimētai*—mimetic artists—'many of whom are concerned with shapes and colours, many with music: poets and their auxiliaries, rhapsodes, actors, choral dancers.'[10] The list of arts here comprises essentially the same as we saw in the *Hippias Major*, but what differs is the description of all these practitioners as *mimētai*. We may gain some guidance as to how to take this from the accounts of *mimēsis* given later in Books 3 and 10.[11] But it is safest to render the term as 'mimetic artists'. As an approximation we may think of this as including people who produce performances, representations, images, or fictions, in whatever medium.[12]

The mention of the mimetic artists in the same breath as 'all kinds

---

[8] 472d4–7, Reeve's revised version of Grube.

[9] See *Rep.* 605b2–c4, 608a6–b2.

[10] *Rep.* 373b5–8. Both Grube's translation and Reeve's revision omit 'rhapsodes'.

[11] On Book 10, see Chs. 5–6 below; Book 3 on *mimēsis* is dealt with later in the present chapter. Having admitted mimetic artists, including actors, it might seem surprising that Plato should later consider it an open question whether to have tragedy and comedy in the city (394d1–6). But there is no inconsistency: starting from the 'luxurious' city, Socrates can progressively 'purge' it (cf. 399e5–6). (See Adam, i. 147.)

[12] To translate *mimētai* as 'imitators' (as do Jowett and Shorey, for example) risks begging too many questions: we do not yet know in what sense, if any, the arts provide 'imitation'. 'Performers' (Annas (1981), 77) excludes painters and sculptors, and does not obviously include poets. Grube's alternative 'artists' is wide enough and less prejudicial, but may wrongly implicate Plato in some modern conception of art.

of hunters', and 'the makers of various kinds of equipment, including those to do with the adornment of women' puts them in no very privileged position in the community. Just before this Socrates has stated (373a4–8) that the city will have to include not only necessities—houses, clothes, shoes—but also painting and embroidery, and things made from gold and ivory. In the same category come 'couches, tables, . . . all sorts of delicacies, perfumed oils, incense, prostitutes, and pastries'.[13] He is setting up what he calls a 'luxurious' or 'feverish' city, which recognizes that once basic needs for food, habitation, and clothing have been satisfied, human desires for comfort and pleasure will (unlike those of pigs[14]) continue to proliferate. Socrates prefers the minimal city which does not cater for other than necessary desires—it is lean and healthy where the luxurious city is swollen (372e6–8, 373b2–4). Nevertheless he concedes that all the characteristic human desires must be acknowledged, so luxuries and entertainments must be provided, the various arts among them. Later the city's fever abates to some degree and the arts are 'purged' extensively—but they are never completely removed.

Even before admitting luxuries, Plato introduces a principle which he applies throughout with momentous consequences. This is the so-called Principle of Specialization,[15] most simply stated as the principle that each citizen shall have one and only one role or function within the city. Behind it are essentially three complementary thoughts. Firstly, each citizen's role must be exercised for the benefit of the community of citizens. They do not live in parallel, each fending for themselves and satisfying the whole range of their desires by their individual labour; rather each depends on the labour of others within the city, and correspondingly what each does by way of work must be answerable to the desires of all. The ground for this is that the communal way of satisfying desires is 'easier' than that involving all individuals acting in parallel (369e2–370a6). Secondly, Plato makes the assumption that 'each one of us is born somewhat different from the others, one more apt for one task, one for another' (370a7–b2). Some diversity of tasks is thus 'naturally' suited to any collection of human beings. Thirdly, it is in the nature of a *technē* that it can be exercised more finely by someone who has mastered it alone, rather than many *technai* (370b4–6). Two general consequences of the Principle of Specialization are that

---

[13] 373a2–4, Reeve's version.
[14] See the reference to a 'city of pigs' at *Rep.* 372d4.
[15] So called by Annas (1981), 73 and *passim*.

each citizen can be required not to diversify in the roles he or she carries out, and that any proposed activity must be justified in terms of a benefit which it brings to the community.

Plato moves on to discuss the arts in the context of designing a programme of education for the model city. But the prime recipients of this education emerge from a specific application of the Principle of Specialization: the city must have an army, because it must be able to secure and extend its territory, if it is to support a body of citizens of sufficient size and diversity. And by an obvious argument it must be a specialized army of what Plato calls guardians. Fighting a war is a matter of *technē*, not an ability casually picked up. It requires knowledge and practice. 'Therefore . . . as the task of the guardian is most important, so he should have the most freedom from all other pursuits, for he requires *technē* and the greatest diligence' (374d5–e2). Plato thus secures his specialist class of guardians, who are 'most important' because on them depends the continued existence of the whole city. His concern for their education is precisely defined by the need to bring up people whose character fits them well to the single role of guardians of the city; a delicate balance must be struck, since this class must be fierce and high-spirited towards the world outside, but gentle and supportive towards the city itself. Even if there exist people with characters naturally suited to such a role, they also require an education, which Plato now seeks in a judicious mix of gymnastics and *mousikē*: the description of the latter including not only technical matters of rhythm and mode in music, but also poetry, drama, and fiction or story-telling, and eventually widening out into a discussion of the arts in general. Altogether this discussion of the arts stretches from 376e in Book 2 through to 403c in Book 3—a little less than one tenth of the whole *Republic*. Although much of it is the repeated exemplification of points through quoted passages of poetry, we are clearly dealing with issues of substantial importance to Plato.[16]

In his examination of the content of poetry and myth Plato advocates state censorship of some of the finest works of his culture with a full-blooded passion and an attention to detail which are surely hard to stomach for most readers in the late twentieth century. Lists are drawn up of scenes which may not be portrayed, and the city will order its poets and story-tellers to comply. The prohibitions concern the portrayal of

---

[16] Discussion of the arts in Books 2, 3, and 10 together takes up roughly one seventh of Plato's space.

gods and heroes. No one is to show gods committing crimes, as do Cronos and Zeus against their fathers in the traditional myths. Other prohibited themes are battles and quarrels between gods, gods transforming themselves into other shapes, deceiving or lying, the terrors for human heroes of death and the underworld, lamentation over someone's death by a god or a hero, indulgence in violent laughter, undisciplined abuse, gluttony, over-powering sexual desire, greed for money and possessions, resentment or disobedience towards a god, atrocities of war. Heroes must be shown as better than ordinary human beings, and gods must never be shown to be anything but perfect, unchanging, and the cause of good. Many of the most powerful scenes in Homer will be proscribed. Plato shrinks from having to say so 'out of respect for Homer' (391a3), but nevertheless spells out the kind of lines which he will have cut by law from the *Iliad* and *Odyssey*. Tragedy too will be curtailed: god-induced sufferings (such as those of Niobe or the house of Pelops) contravene the principle that the divine is cause only of good, unless it can be shown that the sufferings are deserved as a punishment which after all 'benefits' its recipient (380a5–b6).[17]

We should not lightly assume that all censorship is bad; furthermore, many different reasons may be urged for it. Plato is concerned initially with the education of the young, and works under the assumption that when anything is young and tender 'it takes shape, and any mould one may want can be impressed upon it' (377b1–3). He thinks that beliefs may be 'taken into the soul' (377b7–8) at this impressionable stage (as we still say). So it matters, right from the nursery on, what stories (*muthoi*) are told to the young guardians. All tellers of stories, including nurses and mothers, play an important role in 'fashioning their souls'. It is in this context that we must consider the worst of the crimes of the mythical gods, such as Cronos' treatment of his father Ouranos, in Hesiod's *Theogony*. Plato is too sensitive to name the crime or quote the passage, which (as his audience would know) contains these lines:

> Great Ouranos came, bringing on night, and upon Gaia
> he lay, wanting love and fully extended;
> his son, from ambush, reached out with his left hand
> and with his right hand took the huge sickle,
> long with jagged teeth, and quickly severed

---

[17] The banned 'sufferings' here are *pathē*. Gould links this term with a traditional (especially tragic) conception of undeserved catastrophes caused by the gods (see Gould, pp. xvii–xviii, 21, and *passim*).

his own father's genitals, and threw them to fall behind.[18]

Later in the story Cronos swallows his own children, except Zeus who defeats him by force. Plato says: 'I do not think this should be told to foolish and young people . . . If there were some necessity to tell it, only a very few people should hear it, and in secret.'[19] Many will surely sympathize (however significant they may find the poet's imagery).

Plato sees a continuity, however, not only between childhood story-tellers and all poets who 'put together fictitious stories' (377d4–6), but also in the audience, for he is prepared to regulate consumption of poetry by the middle-aged and the old as well.[20] This makes for an obvious difficulty in his argument. From the point of view of the child's acquisition of beliefs, it is plausible to say that the distinction between a nursery tale and an epic poem is immaterial. (At one point, Plato considers the objection that the stories of the gods in Homer are allegorical, but he remarks that the young cannot distinguish what is allegorical from what is not, and may still acquire deep-seated beliefs from a literal interpretation of a story (378d6–e1).) But if the argument for censorship turns on the malleability and lack of sophistication of the young, we should expect there to be, at least in principle, some point at which a person's character and beliefs become fixed enough not to require such care. The idea that no one in a community should witness what a child should not witness does not immediately recommend itself.[21] If Plato gives no reason for extending his prohibition to mature adults, that is a serious weakness in his case. Plato has an answer to this challenge, but it comes later in the *Republic* after he has argued for the division of the soul and (in Book 10) explained how there is in all of us a childish 'part' which is engaged by dramatic representation. Although we may calmly recognize dramatic action as fictional and

[18] Hesiod, *Theogony*, 176–82, trans. Caldwell.

[19] *Rep.* 378a2–5. In the *Euthyphro* we meet a character who prosecutes his own father for murder, citing as a justification the behaviour of Zeus and Cronos in punishing their fathers (*Euth.* 5e5–6a5). This shows us the kind of impression Plato is worried about making on young souls. (See Adam, i. 112.)

[20] *Rep.* 378c8–d2. Cf. 387b4–5: 'the less they should be heard by children and by men . . .' (also 380c1). Halliwell (1991) suggests that the intention throughout is to describe 'a kind of model of an aesthetic environment', 'a complete *culture*', not limited by a purely educational context (329–30). See Irwin (1977*a*), 330–1, for a list of passages in which Plato seems to direct education more widely to *everyone* in the city—though, by Irwin's own lights, the guardians are singled out in eighteen passages.

[21] Annas comments: 'This is . . . paternalism, treating adults as though they were children' (1981, 85).

explain its significance as allegorical, this is not the whole story. A 'lower' part of everyone's soul craves emotional expression and likes to indulge its craving in a welter of powerful images without the intervention of thoughts about the worthiness or rationality of doing so. If we acknowledge such a 'child within' we shall be less likely to find Plato's extension of censorship to adults lacking in support.[22]

The guardians are required by the Principle of Specialization to fulfil one and only one role in the city. If their moral character is faulty, then the whole city will be endangered. So, if this moral character is moulded by beliefs acquired in early education, and if such beliefs can be acquired from fiction, Plato has good reason to hold that the young guardians should not be exposed to everything that fiction is able to offer. The guardians must be brave, self-controlled, disciplined, not prone to deception, crime, or sacrilege. Beliefs acquired early about modes of behaviour among the superhuman gods and heroes could interfere with their attaining these qualities. More specifically, they must 'fear slavery more than death' (387b4–6) if they are to be free, and must believe 'that no citizen has ever hated another and that this is impious' (378c7–8). Hence the ban on depicting misery and terror in the afterlife or conflict among the gods. Plato's attack on the traditional Olympian theology is noteworthy. He seeks to replace it with a view of 'the god' or 'the gods' as unchanging, in no way deficient in fineness or virtue, and as the cause only of good (379a–381e). Only conceived thus will the divine, as an absolute standard, be worthy of belief. If the guardians are going to have anything like a religion, it had better be one which sets before them an appropriate moral paradigm.[23]

I have used the term 'fiction'. Plato classifies the myths and epic scenes he discusses as *pseudeis logoi*, or false discourses. The precise role which this conception plays in the argument is not always easy to discern. Plato says that the young guardians should be educated first in the *pseudeis logoi*, and later in the species of discourse which is true (376e11–377a2). So 'falsehood' must be merely a way of classifying discourses, not in itself a reason for objecting to them,[24] otherwise all

---

[22] Ferrari (1989, 114) is excellent here. The Book 10 argument is dealt with in ch. 6 below.

[23] Commentators often locate Plato in a tradition of philosophical criticism of early poetic theology going back to Xenophanes (Diels–Kranz, 21 A1, B11, B12). Later poets such as Pindar and the tragedians shared these criticisms of Homer. (Gadamer, 43–4; Jaeger, 213–14; Ferrari (1989), 110.)

[24] Guthrie (1975, 457) agrees that this is a 'neutral' use of *pseudos*, and suggests that 'fiction', 'fictitious', and 'invented' convey the sense.

such stories would be banned without the long exercise in selecting specific themes and passages. Plato does not, however, think of stories as 'fiction' in any sense which would assign them an autonomous value.[25] It soon becomes clear that within the class of stories defined by their being false some approximate more to truth, and this is the issue that most concerns Plato. His statement of the point occurs at 377d7–e3:

Which stories do you mean . . . and why do you object to them?
— Because of what one should object to first and most, especially if the fictitious is not well told.
— As for instance?
— Whenever any story gives a bad likeness of the nature of the gods and heroes, like a painter drawing a bad picture, unlike what he is wanting to portray.

Whether a likeness has been made badly (*kakōs*) or finely (*kalōs*) is thus a discriminating factor within the class of *pseudeis logoi*, or what I shall call fictions. A discourse which is literally false, in being a fiction, can nevertheless be a more or less accurate portrayal of something. If a fiction does not make a good likeness it is a falsification: 'the greatest *pseudos* about the most important matters was that of the man who told a *pseudos* badly (*ou kalōs epseusato*) when he said that Ouranos did what Hesiod tells us he did.'[26] What Plato means here is that a fiction was not finely told, in that it was a falsification, a bad likeness of the truth.

Obviously there is a distinction between the question whether a poetic discourse is fitting or beneficial and the question whether it is true.[27] Plato sometimes makes use of the distinction—for example, the tales of Cronos and Ouranos should not be told to the young, even if they were true, he says.[28] On the other hand later, when discussing falsehoods which can be useful or beneficial, he says: 'because of our ignorance of what truly happened of old, we then make the fiction [*pseudos*] as like the truth as we can, and so make it useful' (382d1–3). Here moral benefit seems to depend on correctness of representation. So how do

---

[25] On this see Ferrari (1989), 113.
[26] Cf. Halliwell (1992), 58, for a similar explanation of *pseudos* here.
[27] 'A distinction is drawn between mere lies and the lie which is in itself *ou kalon*, unbeautiful and immoral in tendency, e.g. the story of Uranus and Cronos . . . Such legends not merely misrepresent the gods, but also corrupt mankind' (Adam, i. 112).
[28] *Rep.* 378a1–3. The issues of veracity and moral effect are separated at 381e4–6 (stories slander the gods and at the same time make children more cowardly) and 386b10–c1 (stories are neither true nor beneficial).

faithful representation and moral appropriateness relate to one another? The issue is one of substance, for if we understand misrepresentation and impressing a bad character on the young as two distinct faults, then we must face Plato with the possibility of a fiction's failing on one count while succeeding on the other. Would Plato be content with any fiction—misrepresentation or not—provided it had a beneficial effect on the character of his young guardians? Would he ban the most accurate fictional representation if it was morally corrupting? Or, for the sake of the truth, would he allow the guardians to hear things that would jeopardize their character? The dilemma does not become explicit for Plato because he is confident that the most accurate representation of the gods and heroes will also be the one that is conducive to moulding souls of the right kind. But consider, for example, the rival tragic view that the supernatural plays the leading role in ensuring human suffering: if this could somehow be shown to be nearer the truth, where would it leave Plato? If the tragic view were less conducive to the production of courageous and obedient citizens, Plato must either modify his picture of the character-traits required by his guardians, or accept that a fiction which misrepresents these fundamental matters is after all a beneficial educational instrument.

If there are no strictly true stories about the divine and the supposed distant past, what standard of correctness of representation can there be? Aristotle remarks that poetry tends to express the universal—'how a person of a certain type will on occasion speak or act, according to probability or necessity',[29] and for Plato too this is what is required. The heroes ought to function as true paradigms of human behaviour, and the gods as a universal supernatural expression of general truths about the world and the place of human beings within it. Plato thinks that poets are trying to represent these basic features of humanity, and that one way they can be criticized, like a painter who tries to paint a particular subject, is for failure to produce a good likeness. (Internal plausibility of the story might be another standard of correctness—but is it more or less plausible in the story that Achilles behaves insultingly towards his dead opponent rather than honourably, or that he weeps out of all measure at the death of his beloved comrade, rather than bearing his loss moderately?)

A similar interpretation has recently been put forward by Julius Moravcsik: 'if a poet represents humans or gods, he will have to have

---

[29] *Poetics* 1451b8–9. Adapted from the translation by Butcher.

a certain conception of the natures of these entities. This conception, implicit or explicit, is subject to the same rational criticism as such conceptions in any other context'; it tells us 'not only what . . . a human does, but also what it—under ideal circumstances and conditions—should do'.[30] Thus we can demand of a poet what his or her picture of the ideal functioning of the human agent is, say, in terms of how beliefs, desires, and emotions enter into rational decision-making. There are really two claims about poetry here. One is that poetry can be required to put forward some discernible paradigm of human (and divine) agency—that 'insight into important aspects of human nature is essential to any successful literary work of art'.[31] The second is that such paradigms can be judged correct or incorrect from a point of view external to poetry itself. Neither claim is obviously false. Furthermore, if one accepts the first, it is hard to resist the second. We evade the idea that poetry or fiction can be judged correct or incorrect only if we free it from the restriction of the first claim and allow it to be valuable in educational terms without putting forward any paradigms of human agency at all—something Plato does not consider at this point.[32]

We may disagree with Plato's moral paradigm. Martha Nussbaum[33] has criticized Plato here on the grounds that he 'assumes the standpoint of perfection' and asks, looking down from there, about the value of what are peculiarly human emotions. In particular, she claims, Plato wants to teach that the genuinely good person is self-sufficient (not feeling grief, passionate love, or fear) and not vulnerable to suffering. With this paradigm before us, we are to emulate 'beings who are completely without merely human needs and interests'. Now Plato says the following about the vulnerability of the 'good man':

[he] does not think death to be a dreadful thing for another good man, his friend. . . . And he will not mourn for him as for one who has suffered a terrible thing . . . [he] is most self-sufficient in living the good life and, above all others, has least need of another person. . . . Then it is less dreadful for him than for another to be deprived of a son or a brother, of possessions and any other such things. . . . He will therefore give least way to lamentations, and bear it most quietly when such a misfortune hits him. (387d5–e7.)

---

[30] Moravcsik (1986), 40–1. See also Halliwell's discussion of the paradigmatic force of mimetic works (1992, 56 ff.).

[31] Moravcsik (1986), 43.

[32] Though implicitly he allows something like this later in discussing 'gracefulness' (400c–403c).

[33] Nussbaum (1986), 157–8.

Although Plato seems confident that his 'good man' will not mourn in the circumstances he describes, the passage asserts only a comparative self-sufficiency, not the absolute 'perfection' Nussbaum discerns.[34] Nevertheless, there is a problem: given that we are human, with all our vulnerabilities, how can a higher standpoint—even one of comparative self-sufficiency—illuminate what is of value for us? Plato's reply would surely be that, as a model to aspire towards in early education, the self-sufficient, non-lamenting agent is preferable. But the integrity of this reply depends on his having located the correct moral paradigm. We may wish to argue for a rival paradigm such as the tragic view of humanity, or we may wish to argue that there is no single true account of the ideal human agent. If either line were successful, Plato's position would be seriously compromised: he is certain that only his choice of subject-matter will produce expert guardians, but if the truth about humanity is different, a very different curriculum would be demanded. And if the model city can achieve its caste of specialized, morally pure guardians only by feeding them a tailor-made falsification of human nature, then the model is bankrupt.

In Book 3 of the *Republic* we are not yet in a position to establish what is and what is not a falsification of human nature. At 392a Socrates leaves behind the realms of gods, heroes, spirits, and things in the underworld, and proposes to move on to tales about human beings.[35] The suspicion is that the poets and other writers go wrong in saying that injustice can bring happiness, that justice is a burden, and so on—but clearly this brings us back to the point at issue in the *Republic* as a whole. We started with a collection of such sayings from the poets, and were promised an account of justice in the individual by analogy with the model city. We have not completed that account, so the discussion is here postponed: 'we shall agree what tales must be told about humans when we have discovered the nature of justice, that it is by nature beneficial to its possessor' (392c1–3). Plato is right: if poetry is answerable to moral philosophy, then we need to have done our moral philosophy properly first.

Plato's discussion now moves on to matters other than poetry's subject-matter. But let us pause to take stock. There are many points where we may disagree with Plato about politics, education, or moral psychology. To what extent should a state have responsibility for educating its

---

[34] See Irwin (1988), 376 n. 1.

[35] Adam's view is that these are the 'true *logoi*' that were distinguished from the false at 376e (see Adam, i. 110; Belfiore (1985), 49).

citizens? Plato assigns the state total responsibility, but clearly arguments might be advanced in favour of no control by the state, or only some. To what extent should poetry and story-telling play a role in education? It is less likely that we shall disagree with Plato here. Like him we neither countenance an education wholly taken up with poetry and myth, nor one from which they are wholly absent. Is there a single correct account of human nature? If so, is Plato's version of it correct? Here, as I have said, we may reserve the right to disagree. But what has Plato said *about poetry* to which we may object? Perhaps it is what he has not said that will strike the reader. He has not said that the young should be exposed to 'good poetry'. Nor has he said that hearing all these tales of the gods and heroes brings us a pleasure or fulfilment of its own, and is therefore a valuable activity to include in the life of the young. Rather, he says this:

We shall ask Homer and the other poets not to be angry if we delete these and all similar passages [concerning the pitiful souls of the dead]: not because they are not poetic [*poiētikos*] and pleasing to the majority of hearers, but the more poetic they are the less they should be heard by children and by men who must be free and fear slavery more than death. (387b1–6.)

Plato claims that people acquire from poetry beliefs, desires, and emotions which can have a significant effect on the development of their ethical character. He thinks that the greater the poetry's pleasure-giving potential, the more pronounced the effect on one's character is likely to be. He assumes that poetry is answerable to the question whether what it portrays gives a true likeness of human life, and that this question may take precedence over the question whether it gives pleasure. These four claims offend against the view that art's value in education is its giving pleasure, irrespective of its relation to 'life'—but that is merely a form of the questionable view I have called aestheticism. Artists and critics have frequently sided with Plato. For Iris Murdoch, 'Bad art is a lie about the world'.[36] For Ruskin, good novels well read (as they rarely are, he thinks) are 'nothing less than treatises on moral anatomy and chemistry; studies of human nature in the elements of it'.[37] And Ezra Pound, who also compares artist to scientist, manages to sound more severe than Plato himself:

If an artist falsifies his report as to the nature of man, as to his own nature, as to the nature of his ideal of the perfect . . . of god, if god exist, of the life force,

---

[36] Murdoch, 83.   [37] Ruskin, 65–6.

of the nature or good and evil, if good and evil exist ... If he lies out of deliberate will to lie, if he lies out of carelessness, out of laziness, out of cowardice, out of any sort of negligence whatsoever, he nevertheless lies and he should be punished or despised in proportion to the seriousness of his offence.[38]

The rest of Plato's discussion of *mousikē* falls into three parts: the first deals with poetry's mode of diction or *lexis* (dealing in particular with the conception of *mimēsis*) (392c–398b), and the second with lyric odes and songs (398c–400c), while the third is an eloquent description of the way all the arts impart gracefulness to the soul (400c–403c). The question of *lexis* or 'mode of diction' receives an explanation so long-winded that we may suspect Plato regards the point as a new one.[39] But what is at issue is a straightforward distinction between two forms of narration: narration which uses dramatic characterization, and narration which does not. Plato's word for dramatic characterization is *mimēsis*. His word for narration is *diēgēsis*. It has sometimes been thought that Plato makes a clean dichotomy between narration and characterization, but in fact he states clearly that the choice is between simple narration and narration brought about by way of characterization.[40] In the *Iliad* it is narration both when Agamemnon or some other character speaks and 'between the speeches' (393b7–8). What happens between the speeches in Homer is that 'the poet himself is speaking and does not attempt to turn our attention elsewhere as if the speaker were someone other than himself' (393a6–7). But when the poet has written a speaking character such as Chryses 'he speaks as if he were Chryses and tries as far as possible to make us think that the speaker is not Homer, but the priest, an old man', in which case 'he makes his language as like as possible to that of whatever person he has told us is about to speak' (393a8–b2, c1–3). Later this is described as the poet 'hiding himself' (393c11). Plato makes his distinction clear by translating a chunk of the *Iliad* into (dull) non-dramatic narration, and by spelling out the genres in which the different forms of narration are used: narration in the poet's voice, without *mimēsis*, is found mostly in dithyrambic poetry; tragedy and comedy are narration entirely through *mimēsis*; and epic poetry is an example of narration partly with and partly without *mimēsis*.

---

[38] Pound, 43–4.
[39] Ferrari (1989, 114–15) thinks the terms may not be 'Platonic neologisms', just ones with 'a technical air' which the dialogue's characters, especially Adeimantus, would not be used to.
[40] *Rep.* 392d5–6: *haplē diēgēsis*, as against *diēgēsis* which is *dia mimēseōs gignomenē*.

Plato also feels the need for a brief argument that '*mimēsis*' is the natural term to apply to those passages where the poet 'makes his speech like that of another'. To 'imitate' (*mimeisthai*) someone is to 'make oneself like somebody else in voice or form' (393c5–6). Outside poetry or the arts *mimēsis* often means simply 'acting like' someone else, in the sense of doing as they do—which would include emulating as well as mimicking someone.[41] Plato seems to be arguing that the activity of writing words spoken by a dramatic character should be called *mimēsis* because it is an instance of the more general phenomenon of 'making oneself like' someone. Within the poetic sphere *mimēsis* is here applied not just to the activity of the poet. For clearly it is an actor or rhapsode, rather than Homer, who makes himself like Agamemnon *in voice*. Homer writes words which the audience is to take, within the story, to be the words of the character, Agamemnon; these words must resemble those the character would use, which, loosely perhaps, is for Homer to make himself like the character in voice. But there is not even a loose sense in which Homer makes himself like Agamemnon *in form*. Plato rolls into one the poet's writing a dramatic character and the actor's or rhapsode's acting it out. So three different things are combined in this discussion of *mimēsis*: the poet's use of dramatic characterization (narration through *mimēsis*), poetic *mimēsis* which embraces the activity of both poet and performer, and the still wider category of 'doing as someone does', in or out of drama. The gap between merely behaving as someone else does and acting out a dramatic character might seem small if one thinks of the latter in terms of *resemblance* to a kind of person or action, as Plato does.[42]

After this, the discussion of *mimēsis* becomes harder to follow, at least on a superficial level. In quick succession, Socrates asks two questions about the role of *mimēsis* in the model city:

We need to agree whether we will allow the poets to make narrations to us using *mimēsis*, or to make some using *mimēsis* and others not, and what kind of things in each case, or whether they are not to use *mimēsis*.

---

[41] This is suggested by Nehamas (1982, 56–7) as the key sense of *mimēsis* in passages before Plato—though note that a number of different views have been put forward (e.g. Koller; Else (1958); Keuls, ch. 1; Sörbom). The account by Halliwell (1986), ch. 4, is illuminating here. On Plato's usage, I agree with Halliwell (1992, 60) that Plato wants features of the ordinary 'imitation' or 'emulation' to carry over into the sphere of poetic enactment, in particular its 'character-forming power'.

[42] At *Rep.* 395b6, e.g., *mimēmata* are said to be *aphomoiōmata* (likenesses) of actions.

I presume, he said, that you are examining whether we shall accept tragedy and comedy into our city, or whether we shall not.

Perhaps so, I said, or perhaps even more than that, but we must follow the argument wherever, like a wind, it may lead us. . . .

Consider this point, Adeimantus, whether our guardians should be mimetic or not. (394d1–e2.)

More than the acceptance of tragedy and comedy is at stake because Plato will try to establish some more profound truths about the way in which enacting a dramatic part moulds the young soul. But why does he move from the initial question about the poets to the seemingly distinct question whether the guardians should be mimetic or not? This reminds us, firstly, that the dominant concern at this point is what the poets provide for the education of the guardians. But there is also the assumption that if the young guardians make use of mimetic poetry in their learning, their learning will itself be mimetic. This is because, as many writers have pointed out, in Plato's culture contact with poetry would always be by way of performance, either recitation or singing. You would take in Homer's depiction of Achilles either by seeing a rhapsode declaim the part on stage, or by reciting and thereby enacting the part yourself.[43] So the question whether poetic educational material will be mimetic amounts to the question whether the recipients of education will themselves indulge in *mimēsis*.

Two principles feature as assumptions in the ensuing argument. Firstly, the Principle of Specialization enunciated earlier; secondly, what I shall call the Principle of Assimilation, which states that people come to resemble whatever they enact. This is supposedly an empirical truth: 'Have you not noticed', Socrates asks, 'that imitations [*mimēseis*], if they last from youth for some time, become part of one's nature and settle into habits of gesture, voice and thought?' (395d1–3). This is not wholly implausible, especially if we think of the way in which these days various forms of therapy and training (of teachers, doctors, or army officers) are liable to involve dramatic role-playing. We too seem to believe that this may enable one to become what one acts out.

The Principle of Specialization states that any role of expertise is best carried out by someone who has no other role in the city. It is simply an instance of this that they imitate X best who do not also imitate Y: undertaking *mimēsis* of more than one thing takes away the ability to perform a *mimēsis* of any one thing as well as one might

---

[43] See Havelock, esp. chs. 3, 9; Annas (1981), 94–6.

(394e8–395b6). There is empirical evidence of this, too. Poets are either tragedians or comedians, professional performers are either rhapsodes or actors, actors are either tragic or comic actors, and human nature is 'fragmented by even smaller differences than this' as regards mimetic abilities just as much as abilities in 'real life' (recall again how Ion specializes in Homeric poetry). If this is true, it tells us that, just as the guardians must not undertake a plurality of real-life activities, so they must not engage in *mimēsis* of a multiplicity of character-types. At most they must play one kind of role. According to the Principle of Assimilation, engaging in *mimēsis* of any character-type that differs from the ideal guardian will tend to make them less like the ideal guardian and more like something else. The conclusion Plato reaches by applying his two principles is that the objects of *mimēsis* for the guardians should be only the kind of people they themselves are or are being trained to be, namely 'brave, self-controlled, pious, and free men and all their actions' (395c4–5). He says that this is the *mimēsis* they should indulge in, if they imitate at all.[44] Nowhere does he say that they should wholly abstain from *mimēsis*.[45] Thus he does not take the option left open at 394d of forbidding the poets in the model city to practise any *mimēsis*.

In the final part of the discussion of *mimēsis* Socrates asks Adeimantus to choose between three styles of poetry for inclusion in the education of the guardians. Commentators have sometimes expected that this threefold division will be the same as that made at 394c—i.e. narration through *mimēsis*, narration without *mimēsis*, and narration through both— or that the latter division is the former 'modified'.[46] But this is not the case: Plato has substituted another threefold division. He accepts that the guardians will use some *mimēsis*; therefore, in terms of the earlier distinction, they will narrate through both *mimēsis* and simple narration, a point which Plato goes out of his way to emphasize.[47] Yet their style will involve imitation only of one kind of person, avoiding other models, and hence will have to use a large measure of simple narration,

---

[44] *ean de mimōntai*, 395c3.

[45] Cross and Woozley (272) state Plato's position thus: 'they should play no other role *nor should they imitate*' (my emphasis)—presumably based on 395c2–3, *ouden dē deoi an autous allo prattein oude mimeisthai*. However, this surely means: 'they should neither do nor imitate anything else', particularly since the next sentence begins 'And *if they do* imitate . . .'

[46] The view of Tate (1928), 18.

[47] At 396e5–7: '*estai . . . hē lexis metechousa . . . amphoterōn, mimēseōs te kai tēs allēs diēgēseōs*'—a *lexis* sharing in both *mimēsis* and the other kind of narration.

not adopting any other voice which departs from the one noble manner of diction that is the guardians' own. Plato is interested in defining the narrative style of someone *kalos kagathos*—'fine and good', the standard designation for a superior person of noble class. (Grube's translation 'the true gentleman' hits the right note in this respect.[48]) Such a person is also called 'a moderate man'.[49] In narrating, this person will fall quite naturally into *mimēsis* of the actions and language of a good man, but will draw the line at enacting scenes in which a good man is less than perfect (when overcome by disease, sexual passion, or drunkenness, for example). Nor will he wish to 'make himself like' someone inferior to himself, except if that person happens to be performing a good deed, or, Plato adds, perhaps for the sake of play (*paidias charin*, 396d5–e2). Just for a joke, one might portray a member of the lower orders doing something disreputable, presumably out of a desire to ridicule that person. Then one would not be departing from one's 'noble' character but in a way reinforcing it.[50]

Plato's list of 'inferior' subjects which his guardians must be ashamed to enact is class-specific—many lowly occupations are expressly excluded from their mimetic training, along with the role of slaves, and what Plato thinks of as slavish behaviour, such as cowardice and other moral error, ridicule, or bad language. It is also gender-specific. Despite Plato's later idea (454b–457a) that women should be included in ruling and military tasks according to their ability, he appears to assume here that the guardians will be male, and as such will not be allowed 'to imitate a young or older woman who is railing at a man, or quarrelling with the gods, or bragging while thinking herself happy, or one in misfortune and sorrows and lamentations, even less one in illness or in love or in labour' (395d5–e3). It seems obsessively anti-female to think of including this last example. It is, however, reminiscent of the charge made by Aristophanes that Euripides showed the public, among other things, 'women giving birth in temples'.[51] Euripidean heroines may be a particular target for Plato,[52] though clearly they will not be the only casualties in tragedy and comedy to fall before Plato's restriction of *mimēsis* to the model of the 'good man'.

All these exclusions fix the first style in the list from which

---

[48] Dover (1974), 41–5, catalogues some uses of the term, which he asserts to be often descriptive of a social class.

[49] Or 'measured', *metrios*, *Rep.* 396c5.

[50] For this view cf. Ferrari (1989), 119; Nehamas (1988), 215; Halliwell (1992), 64 n. 24.

[51] *Frogs*, 1080.   [52] As suggested by Adam, i. 150.

Adeimantus must choose. It narrates using both simple narration and *mimēsis*, but keeps *mimēsis* to the minimum because 'the good man' is the only character it enacts dramatically. The second style is said to be its antithesis, that of someone who thinks nothing unworthy of himself and will enact or imitate anything 'in earnest [not to make fun of it] and before a large audience' (397a1–4). To show the comprehensive range of this style Plato mentions a panoply of sound-effects and animal noises, whose relevance to the argument is puzzling.[53] But the essential point is that all the kinds of person and action prohibited in the first style will be open to this kind of speaker. With so much to imitate, this style 'will consist entirely of *mimēsis* in voice and gesture, or at least have very little straight narration' (397b1–2). It will also need to employ a great variety of musical modes and rhythms, while the style that enacts only the words and deeds of the good man will be homogeneous in these respects as well (397b6–c6). Which do we choose for the guardians: the first style, which has *mimēsis* at a minimum because only one kind of character is enacted, the second with its maximum *mimēsis* of diverse subjects, or a third style resulting from the 'mixture' of these two? Adeimantus, of course, opts for the 'unmixed imitator [*mimētēs*] of the good man'. Commentators have found the idea of a third, mixed style here difficult.[54] But Plato is not confused. A mixture between the

[53] Adam (i. 151) finds a reference to the use of stage-machinery and musical effects in drama, although the style is supposed to be totally *dia mimēseōs phōnais te kai schēmasin*, which is probably 'by voice and gesture (or posture)'. Adam also mentions the degenerate form of dithyramb—but this is not mimetic in the right sense. Else (1986, 36) suggests that this imitator of dogs, birds, and thunder is a *thaumatopoios* or magic-show man, a 'seedy music hall character' who 'has little or nothing in common with any serious Greek poet'.

[54] Julia Annas writes of this passage: 'there is uncertainty over whether Plato does in the end allow there to be any good, imitative poetry in the ideally just state. His muddle here is irritating, but understandable . . . he is very sure what is bad, but less sure about what is good. He is caught between the idea that imitation is all right as long as only morally certified models are imitated, and the idea that there is something morally fishy about imitation as such' (1981, 99). Annas says that all is well (without 'muddle'), if one keeps the twofold division between the good man's style and its opposite apart from the earlier threefold division between pure *mimēsis*, simple narration, and narration using both modes of diction. But the only reason she gives for thinking that Plato fails to keep the two divisions apart is that 'at 397d, Socrates asks which style we shall have in the city—one of the pure ones or the mixed one?' It is a common assumption that the threefold division of 394b–c must play a role in the choice of Adeimantus at 397d. Else for some reason thinks that a threefold distinction between *diēgēsis*, *mimēsis*, and 'their mixture' would be 'more consistent' or 'logical' than what is in the text (1986, 29). That Plato is not confused is brought out well by Ferrari (1989), 118; Gaudreault, 80–83; and Grube (1981), 75–6, n. 23.

good man's and the versatile style is not identical with the *lexis* which uses both *mimēsis* and simple narration. It does use both, but, as we saw earlier, this may be true of the good man's style and the versatile mimetic style, although the proportions of *mimēsis* to simple narration are not equal in those two cases.

What differentiates the good man's style from that of someone who 'thinks nothing unworthy of himself' is its governing aim or motivation. The good man's style is governed by a normative conception of how one should behave and speak. The extent to which it uses *mimēsis* is merely secondary to this consideration. Perhaps someone with this motivation will use no dramatic enactment and narrate everything in his own voice, but not because *mimēsis* as such is bad: he will use *mimēsis* if it conforms to his overall aim of assimilating himself to the preferred way of acting and speaking. On the other hand, the versatile mimetic style is governed by the aim of indulging in *mimēsis*, and the more of it the better. Any considerations about how one should look and sound will be subordinated to the goal of producing dramatic effect.[55] Now we can see what the 'mixture' of these two approaches is: it is a style governed by both these motivations, in which one seeks to accommodate one's poetic narration to a conception of the good person, but also values dramatic impersonation of many characters simply for the sake of doing it. Socrates emphasizes that the 'mixed' style brings pleasure, while 'the opposite to the one you have chosen is by far the most pleasing to children and their tutors and to the majority of the mob'.[56] Children are not yet in a position to be guided by the normative conception of the good man, and 'the mob', Plato presumably thinks, never will be. They seek only the maximum of pleasure. But the mixed style might be thought a good compromise: why not allow the guardians to indulge in *mimēsis* for the sake of its own peculiar pleasures, provided that we also train them towards the good character demanded by their role in the city?

In rejecting anything but the style of the good man as 'not fitting in'

[55] 'Plato forbids not imitation ... but imitativeness, the desire and ability to imitate anything independently of its moral quality and without the proper attitude of praise or blame toward it' (Nehamas (1988), 215). Belfiore (1984) coins the term 'versatile imitation' for what Plato objects to. Cf. also Ferrari (1989), 117.

[56] *Rep.* 397d6–8, my translation of *hēdus ge kai ho kekramenos, polu de hēdistos ... ho enantios hou su hairēi*, which makes a distinction between the mixed style which is *hēdus*, and the style of the inferior man which is *polu hēdistos*.

to the model city,[57] Plato shows that the root of his position is a fear of *diversity* or *plurality* within the individual: 'with us a man is not double or multiple'. By the Principle of Assimilation, anyone who imitates many things becomes like each of them, hence becoming, in a sense, a multiple person. Someone who sought to emulate the good man, but who also enjoyed *mimēsis* for its own sake, would be 'multiple' to a lesser extent, but would at least be 'double' in being ruled by two motivations which may conflict. The more models he permitted himself to imitate, the less single he would be in his commitment to developing the one character he regarded as his ideal.

We may suggest another sense in which fostering *mimēsis* for its own sake might breed diversity. In tragedy, or in the *Iliad*, a number of different characters are presented to us. In dramatic interchanges between protagonists, conflicting points of view are given voice, without necessarily any single assessment which we can call the poet's own; the characters each have an equal claim on our attention and emotional engagement.[58] *Mimēsis* as such brings with it a pleasure and an exciting stirring of the emotions. But to pursue *mimēsis* as an end in itself, for the sake of this emotional involvement, even 'mixed' with the pursuit of the good man's style, is to risk assimilating oneself to diverse characters with diverse points of view. Plato concludes his discussion of *mimēsis* with his first image of banishment, amid ironic praise (recalling the *Ion*) of the virtuoso dramatic artist as 'sweet' and 'holy':

If a man who in his cleverness can become many persons and imitate all things should arrive in our city and want to give a performance of his poems, we should bow down before him as being holy, wondrous and pleasing, but we should tell him that there is no such man in our city and that it is not lawful that there should be. We would pour myrrh on his head and crown him with wreaths, and send him away to another city. We ourselves would employ a more austere and less pleasure-giving poet and storyteller for our own good, one who would imitate the speech of a good man.[59]

---

[57] *Rep.* 397d10–e2. In 'you would say that it does not fit in to our city' (d10–e1), the 'it' seems to refer only to the extreme style of the inferior man, the opposite of the style chosen by Adeimantus. But the reason given for rejecting this is surely also a reason for rejecting the 'mixed' style.

[58] Cf. Annas (1981), 98. Plato makes the point explicitly at *Laws* 719c5–d1.

[59] *Rep.* 398a1–b2. The crowning and anointing may allude to the practice of adorning statues of the gods. Another evocative view, reported by Adam (i. 154) sees an allusion to the anointing of swallows by Greek women.

If his argument so far is persuasive, Plato is entitled to send away the mimetic poet who tries to infiltrate the education system. Given the Principle of Specialization, the Principle of Assimilation, the assumed educational value of poetry, and the interventionist role he conceives for the state, he has no choice. The pleasure of *mimēsis* weighs little against the cumulative power of these considerations. And if the soul remains liable to radical 'moulding' throughout life, or always retains a childish part, then there are grounds for the complete dismissal of the poet who is dedicated to *mimēsis* as an end.

The next section of Plato's discussion of *mousikē* concerns music proper, though still in connection with lyric poetry. We need not speculate about the details of the musical modes, which Socrates claims not to know properly. Let us instead look at the philosophical principles that underlie his prescriptions. Song has three elements: words, mode, and rhythm.[60] As far as the words go, what was said above about the content of speech without music is sufficient. And mode and rhythm ought to be appropriate to the words. Lamenting modes or scales (*harmoniai*) and soft, relaxed ones will not be required in the city because there will be no narrations of events to which they are appropriate. Socrates wants to have just two musical modes, one robust and warlike, the other peaceful but self-controlled and 'willing'—they turn out to be the established Dorian and Phrygian modes. Note that the rationale behind this invokes *mimēsis* in a very broad sense: 'Leave me those two modes,' says Socrates, 'which will best imitate [*mimēsontai*] the accents of brave and moderate men both in misfortune and in prosperity' (399c1–4). Clearly *mimēsis* here is not dramatic impersonation. We might talk of music 'expressing' a mood or character, of its 'being expressive of courage', or even 'being courageous'—terms for a phenomenon which philosophers to this day have been unable to unravel with any great conviction.[61] Plato calls the phenomenon *mimēsis*, presumably because he thinks of the music as *resembling* a character or mood. If the music I perform is warlike or self-controlled, Plato thinks that in performing it I 'make myself like' the typical warlike or self-controlled individual. From the same idea come prescriptions about which instruments the model city should make and use, the *aulos* once again falling foul of Plato's preferences, along with complicated stringed instruments designed to be versatile in playing an exotic range of modes.

---

[60] *logos, harmonia, rhythmos, Rep.* 398d1–2.
[61] A point admirably shown by Budd (1985).

The 'luxurious' city is gradually being purged of many of its accoutre-ments. A discussion of rhythm and metre follows (399e8–400c6), in which the same basic principle applies. Different rhythms are appropri-ate to, or are 'imitations' (*mimēmata*) of, different ways of living—though Socrates leaves us to consult his contemporary Damon on the details.

The final passage of Plato's discussion of *mousikē* broadens into a positive account of the value of all the arts, briefly achieving an elo-quence comparable with the Diotima-speech in the *Symposium*: and indeed, Plato rounds off by saying that a discussion of *mousikē* ought to end in the love of the beautiful. Here it seems appropriate to translate *mousikē* as 'the arts', and the present passage thus differs from the Diotima-speech in the prominent role it gives to the arts in making the soul akin to, and a lover of, the beautiful.[62] The truly educated person must be able to recognize self-control and courage occurring in persons and actions, and see this as of a piece with[63] recognizing *likenesses* (*eikones*) of self-control and courage—that is, the likenesses of these human qualities as they occur in dramatic characters, styles of speech, musical modes, and an orderly manner of production in all the arts. It is thus that being a devotee of *mousikē* in its widest sense embraces an acquaintance with the human virtues.[64]

Why is 'nurture in the arts' (*en mousikēi trophē*) so important for Plato?— 'because their rhythm and harmony permeate the inner part of the soul, bring gracefulness to it, and make the strongest impression' (401d5–8). 'Gracefulness' is *euschēmosunē*, an unusual word meaning literally 'well-formedness', which Plato here uses to denote a virtue that can be shared by the soul and art-products alike. An early educa-tion in the arts forms the soul, then, in such a way that it spontaneously welcomes what is fine and good. Before attaining full use of reason, the young can be prepared by contact with beautiful sights and sounds—but only if their nourishment is carefully controlled. Not only the poets,

---

[62] It is another question whether it encompasses Plato's full-blown doctrine of Forms, as we said the *Symposium* does. Plato says that no one can become truly educated in the arts, or truly *mousikos*, until they learn to recognize the forms (*eidē*) of self-control, courage, and other virtues, and to perceive them in things they occur in, both the things themselves and likenesses of them (*kai auta kai eikonas autōn*). Although *eidē* is Plato's word for separate Forms when he is discussing them, the cautious reader should not import that doctrine into this passage. Cf. Adam, i. 168; Guthrie (1975), 459–60; Grube (1981), 82 n. 29; Annas (1981), 100.

[63] 'Part of the same craft and training' (402c7–8).

[64] There is no doctrine here of art's being able to 'imitate' Forms directly, despite the views of Grey, 299; Tate (1928), 21–3.

but all other producers—painters and the like, weavers, embroiderers, builders—must be 'forbidden to put the bad character that is unrestrained, unfree and graceless into their likenesses of living things or their buildings or any other of their works' (401b4–7). There is a relation between the character (*ēthos*) of the soul and the speech, rhythm, harmony, and form which occur in the arts. Plato calls this relation variously one of likeness, kinship, following or consequence, or *mimēsis*. Good form or gracefulness issues spontaneously from a well-formed soul. But stylistic good form in poetry and the visual arts, which is a likeness of the soul's good character, can also impress itself on a soul by habituation. By exercising gracefulness in the arts, and consuming well-formed products, one's soul becomes assimilated to them, and since they are a *mimēma* of the good character, one's soul becomes more like a good soul.

So Plato has a role for artists which is both positive and profound:

> We must seek out such craftsmen [*dēmiourgoi*] as have the talent to pursue the beautiful and the graceful in their work, in order that our young men shall be benefited from all sides like those who live in a healthy place, whence something from these beautiful works will strike their eyes and ears like a breeze that brings health from salubrious places, and lead them unawares from childhood to love of, resemblance to, and harmony with, the beauty of reason. (401c4–d3.)

The pursuit of beauty through the arts is thus seen as necessary in the education of the truly excellent human being, though it is not sufficient, but merely a preparatory stage prior to the full acquisition of reason.[65] I wonder if we do not believe something approximating to this? We give the arts a fairly prominent place in the education of the young. It has at least been part of our tradition to teach them, long before they reach intellectual and ethical maturity, to dance, to sing in tune, to follow a rhythm accurately, to paint, to notice form, to build; we select their fiction and drama, their musical instruments even, believing that omitting such steps risks impoverishing their overall development. Plato can be seen as giving elevated expression to a similar way of thinking.

As far as Books 2–3 of the *Republic* are concerned, therefore, Plato's critique of the arts is a thorough overhaul, not an outright rejection. But is that the end of the story? Plato retains the arts and charges them with the precious task of benefiting the souls of his young guardians, but it is easy to feel that the arts have really been undermined and replaced,

---

[65] As is spelt out by 401e1–402a4. See also Irwin (1977*a*), 202–3.

because Plato's aims are so antithetical to those that we normally recognize as 'artistic'. Thinking of Plato, E. M. Forster wrote that from the State's point of view the artist never quite 'fits in':

> The State believes in education. But does art educate? 'Sometimes, but not always' is the answer; an unsatisfactory one. The State believes in recreation. But does art amuse? 'Sometimes, but not always' is the answer again. The State does *not* believe in experiments, in the development of human sensitiveness in directions away from the average citizen. The artist *does*, and consequently he and the State ... must disagree.[66]

Plato opposes what we would call 'Art' as a motivating force in the life of an individual or a community. For he opposes the pursuit of diversity or novelty for their own sake, the seeking out of pleasurable experiences, the imaginative exploration of the morally reprehensible and ambiguous sides of human existence, the cultivation of the viewpoints of women and slaves which challenge the secure habits of the aristocratic *kalos kagathos*. The arts may be a preferred means of fulfilling Plato's educational and political ends, but we are bound to feel that he subordinates them rather violently to those ends, at the expense of their other potential values.[67]

To complain that Plato has omitted such characteristically 'artistic' values is not to revert to the view which I earlier called aestheticism. We can agree with Plato that form and content in the arts influence people's characters in ways that are morally and politically important, that the arts can be criticized for the inaccuracy of their portrayal of human life, and that if pursued for the sake of novelty and pleasure without being answerable to any values outside themselves they may be corrupting. We may even share his demand that some moral and political benefit from the arts is a condition of acknowledging their worth. But all this is compatible with valuing as beneficial precisely the 'experiments' and 'development of human sensitiveness' that Forster speaks of. This suggests that it is not so much what Plato says about the nature of the arts themselves that is objectionable, but rather his rigid authoritarianism and the narrowing vision expressed in his Principle of Specialization.

---

[66] Forster, 97.

[67] This is no doubt a particularly modern thought. In Aristophanes' *Frogs* Aeschylus and Euripides contend in a comic debate for the title of best poet, but despite great differences in style and social attitude they agree that what they *ought* to be doing is 'making people better in the cities' (*Frogs* 1009–10).

5

Mimēsis

BOOK 10 of the *Republic* contains Plato's most sustained and decisive critique of the arts. First he develops a general conception of *mimēsis*. Then he argues that poetry which is mimetic and aimed at pleasure should be banished from the model city (and from the well-governed soul) until it can demonstrate that it is not merely pleasant, but beneficial to cities and to human life (607b1–608b2). In Chapter 6 I shall consider the arguments that lead up to this banishment. But in this chapter I ask: What does the concept of *mimēsis* developed in Book 10 embrace? We cannot hope for a single clear definition of *mimēsis* covering all uses that Plato ever makes of the term.[1] At the most general level it tends to mean something which is like something else in some way. Often, though not always, this will be a copy or likeness which is less real than an original of which it is the likeness. In Book 10 Plato uses this notion to put forward an intelligible, if rudimentary, theory of artistic representation.

In the first sentences of Book 10 Socrates expresses satisfaction over the completed 'city of words' and cites as particularly pleasing 'the fact that we did not admit such poetry as is mimetic' (595a5). Much has been made of the disparity between this and the discussion of *mimēsis* in Book 3.[2] There, as we saw in the previous chapter, some poetry that uses *mimēsis* (dramatic characterization) was admitted as positively beneficial—behaving like the good and noble man in a dramatic context would make one grow more like such a person in one's own character and impart graceful form to the soul. We seem to face a choice: either Book 10's claim that the city excludes mimetic poetry

---

[1] Among numerous discussions of *mimēsis*, two which bring out its wide-ranging character in Plato are McKeon, and Halliwell (1986, 116–21). The attempt by Verdenius (1949, 16–18) to find Plato giving 'art' a worthy place in a 'hierarchical structure of reality' relies on uses of *mimēsis* in which one thing strives to emulate something higher (e.g. truth or divine harmony), or in which something is a sensible instance of a Form. Neither relates directly to Plato's conception of *mimēsis* in the arts.

[2] The disparity issue is raised e.g. by Greene, 50 ff.; Tate (1928), 16; Cross and Woozley, 277–9; Collingwood (1938), 47–8; Nehamas (1982), 48–54.

contradicts Book 3, or Plato is now using 'mimetic' in a radically different sense.

However, if we concentrate on the kinds of artistic practice rejected in Book 3, we find that Plato does not go back on what he said there. The key question (394e) was whether the guardians should be mimetic—whether *mimēsis* should be an end in itself for them. By giving a negative answer to that question, Plato in a certain sense did reject 'such poetry as is mimetic' (*mimētikē*): he rejected poetry whose dominant motivation was the production of pleasurable dramatic impersonation at the expense of any discrimination among role-models. Book 10 does not alter this situation. The fact that some sort of dramatic impersonation was retained as beneficial when it subserved educational and moral ends is less important.[3] Secondly, the focus of the critique of poetry remains, as we shall see, on tragedy and Homeric poetry. I shall argue that the two discussions use different senses of *mimēsis*, but that the *reference* of the term has a certain stability: instances of poetic *mimēsis* in the Book 3 sense are also the central topic of Book 10.[4]

What, then, is *mimēsis* in Book 10? Socrates asks: 'Could you tell me what *mimēsis* as a whole is?'[5] By 598b8 the answer has been given: 'Mimetic art [*hē mimētikē*] is far removed from the truth, and that is why . . . it can make everything, because it touches only a small part of each thing, and that an image [*eidōlon*].' As a means of reaching this answer, Plato discusses a painting of an object, such as a bed. So '*mimēsis* as a whole' embraces painting as well as some forms of

---

[3] Nehamas (1988, 215) and Ferrari (1989, 125) argue for continuity between Books 3 and 10 on similar grounds. Nehamas: 'Plato forbids not imitation, which he considers essential to education, but imitativeness, the desire and ability to imitate anything independently of its moral quality and without the proper attitude of praise or blame toward it. . . . When Socrates says in Book x that "all mimetic poetry" (*poiēseōs hosē mimētikē*) has been excluded from the city, he does not refer to imitation but only . . . to poetry which involves and encourages imitativeness: the conflict disappears.' Belfiore, in a detailed study (1984), makes a similar point: Plato opposes in both Books 3 and 10 what she calls 'versatile imitation' (*mimētikē*).

[4] Cf. Halliwell (1988, 5), who speaks of a 'shift in the use of the mimesis word-group from denoting dramatic enactment through direct speech (3. 392d5 ff.) to meaning artistic representation or depiction in a much broader sense'. It is fairly traditional to see a shift in the sense of *mimēsis*—though harder to find agreement on what the different senses are. (See Havelock, 20–6; Grube (1935), 185, 188; Cornford (1941), 324 n. 1; Cross and Woozley, 271–2; Annas (1981), 336; Else (1986), 44.) Belfiore's attempt to see the sense of *mimēsis* as constant between Books 3 and 10 lacks plausibility: the Book 3 definition is surely not 'making something similar to something else in sound or shape' (1984, 124–6) but is restricted to dramatic enactment or composition.

[5] *Mimēsin holōs echois an moi eipein hoti pot' estin*? (595c7).

poetry. It seems a fair approximation to say that in modern terms Plato is talking about *representation* in the arts, or at least one kind of representation, in which an artist represents something by making an appearance of it. *Mimēsis*, in Book 10, is making an appearance which by intention resembles things of some kind, but is not really one of them.

Plato's account of the human soul will enable him to argue that in poetry this sort of activity is potentially dangerous (595a5–b7). But the initial explanation of '*mimēsis* as a whole' is given in metaphysical and epistemological terms: Plato tries to establish what entities are made by *mimēsis*, and what knowledge its practitioner requires. In all this he relies on doctrines developed earlier in the *Republic*, so a brief sketch of some of these will help us here. Plato's model city, which we left with its specialized class of military guardians, soon acquires another specialized class selected from among their ranks: a class of rulers. Socrates' account of justice has it that if the city consists of three classes, rulers (to which he now transfers the name 'guardians'), military (now called auxiliaries), and the economic class of producers and traders, it will be a just city provided that each of these classes performs its own function properly without usurping the function of the others. Plato's attention shifts to the role of governing the whole city, and a new phase of the *Republic* begins when he suggests (in Book 5) that 'philosophers [should] rule as kings in the cities, or those whom we now call kings and rulers [should] genuinely and adequately study philosophy' (473c11–d2).

Philosophers are defined by their relation to the Forms, Fine and Ugly, Just and Unjust, Good and Bad, each of which is itself one, but which appear in multiple instantiations.[6] Contrasted with the philosophers, who look towards the single Form in each case, are people whom Plato calls *philotheamones* and *philēkooi*, lovers of sights and lovers of sounds. These people 'run around to all the Dionysian festivals omitting none . . . as if their ears were under contract to listen to every chorus' (475d5–8). But they are unable to 'look' towards Fineness itself or to enjoy it. They believe only in 'fine things', not in Fineness itself, and, thinking that the only fineness there is lies in a multiplicity of colours, shapes, and sounds (476b4–c7), they mistake a mere likeness for the real thing. In a long and difficult argument, Plato puts forward the view that it is the philosophers who have knowledge, while the lovers of sights and sounds have only belief. Knowledge,

---

[6] See *Rep.* 475e9–476a7, and 476b10–11 for *auto to kalon*.

then, is tied to Forms: someone who denies the existence of Forms, or is incapable of apprehending them, can have no knowledge.[7]

Since the sight-lovers' lack of knowledge is linked to their attitude towards enjoying the arts, we ought to consider where the deficiency of these unphilosophical aesthetes is supposed to lie. They believe, as surely everybody does, in many things or actions that are fine or beautiful. They seek out such things, to gain from them the pleasures of sight and hearing. What Plato particularly criticizes them for, however, is their failing to believe in what is distinct from the many things or actions: Fineness or Beauty itself. He complains that because they view reality as not containing Beauty itself, 'the many conventional opinions of the many, about beautiful and the others [*kalou te peri kai tōn allōn*], are rolling around, as it were, between what is not and what purely is'.[8] This strange wording seems to indicate that the sight-lovers go wrong primarily in the negative view they hold about beauty. Their opinions are many because they hold that beauty is no one thing at all. They judge on each occasion 'this is beautiful', 'that is beautiful', but when asked what makes all of these things beautiful (when asked, if you like, for their opinion about what 'beautiful' itself is), they do not believe that there is a single answer. Thus they are in the position of Hippias,[9] when he said that beauty was 'being made of gold' and on other occasions 'being made of ivory': they will have as many different opinions as there are different properties which make particular things beautiful. This is in line with a recent interpretation, according to which Plato's 'many beautifuls' here are the many sensible properties[10] which someone might believe beauty to consist in. The things which have one of these properties are and are not beautiful—meaning that some gold things are beautiful, some are not, some brightly coloured things are beautiful, some are not, and so on. We cannot say that any of the many 'beautifuls' 'is any more than it is not what anyone might call it'

[7] The traditional reading is that knowledge can be only of Forms, beliefs only of their many sensible instances. This has recently been questioned by Fine (1978 and 1990).

[8] 479d3–5, translation adapted from Reeve.

[9] *HiMa.* 289e2–290d6, discussed above (Ch. 3). Another relevant comparison is *Phdo.* 100c10–d8, where Socrates rejects the 'blooming colour' or 'shape' of a thing as the reason for its being beautiful, preferring instead the explanation of its participating in beautiful itself.

[10] See Gosling (1960); Irwin (1977*b*), 7–9; Fine (1990), 91. Hippias answers that fineness is a beautiful girl, and that it is 'being made of gold'. If he is a prototype of the sight-lovers, it is probably a mistake to think that they care to distinguish between the many beautiful *things* and the many *properties* that can make things beautiful. Cf. Gosling (1960), 116 n. 1.

(479b9–10). On this interpretation, to say that opinions about beauty 'roll about between being and not being' means that, among the things exhibiting those sensible properties which are wrongly held to constitute beauty, some are beautiful and some are not—which in turn means that the conventional opinions about beauty are and are not true.

In Books 6 and 7 Plato portrays the philosophers' knowledge and their more advanced education. At the pinnacle of their achievement is to be knowledge of the Forms, crowned by knowledge of the Form of the Good, which, like the sun in the sensible realm, illuminates and sustains the existence of everything in the realm of Forms. A method of reasoning, which Plato calls dialectic, will take them to knowledge of the highest of principles, from which they will be able to deduce further knowledge. Throughout this part of the book Plato operates in pictures or likenesses, which are a second-best to genuine knowledge and possibly deceitful, as Socrates himself warns.[11] Plato's set of similes relies on permutations of the relation between a thing and its mere likeness. X and Y are related as likeness and original when X resembles Y, but is not as real a thing as Y. Shadows and reflections are contrasted with the solid things of which they are mere likenesses; yet these things relate to the higher realm of Forms just as their own likenesses relate to them.[12] Forms, in particular the Form of the Good, are the only elements of reality which cannot be viewed as a likeness of something else. This is another way of marking them out as 'most real' and as the proper objects of knowledge.[13]

In his approach to artistic image-making in Book 10 Plato exploits this background, and sets out to locate the products of *mimēsis* within a hierarchy of likenesses and originals which still has Forms at its head. But rather than reproducing the metaphysics of Books 6 and 7 exactly, he adapts it to a new argumentative task.[14] Two features are worth noting: firstly, in the whole of Book 10 he does not use the usual term

[11] In the Sun simile Socrates disclaims knowledge of the Good, and says only 'what appears as the offspring of the Good and is most like it' (*Rep.* 506e3–4); he adds: 'be on your guard, lest I unwittingly deceive you and give you a counterfeit account' (507a4–5). The account of the Cave is also just a 'likeness' (*eikōn*: 515a4, 517a8).

[12] See the simile of the Divided Line (*Rep.* 509e1–510b5 and 510d5–511a8). The ascent in the Cave simile (514a2–516b7) uses repeated likeness : original contrasts to illustrate the transition from ignorance to full knowledge.

[13] At *Rep.* 476c2–7 those who recognize beautiful things but not the Form are said to 'think that a likeness is not a likeness but the thing itself which it resembles'.

[14] A point made by Halliwell (1988), 118.

eikōn for an image or likeness, preferring instead terminology to do with appearance (*phainomenon*, *phantasma*) with shades of apparition and magic attached to it, and the word *eidōlon* which tends to mean a false image, or a counterfeit.[15] (Recall the claim in the *Gorgias* that rhetoric is the mere *eidōlon* of true justice.) And secondly, Plato here has some curious ideas about Forms which he does not entertain anywhere else.

In some respects, then, we have to regard Socrates' opening invitation as disingenuous:

Do you want us to start looking in our usual way? We are accustomed to assuming one Form in each case for the many particulars to which we give the same name ... Let us then take any set of particulars you like. For example, there are many beds and tables ... But there are only two Forms for these two articles, one of the bed and one of the table ... We also usually say that the makers of these articles look to the Form when they make, one the beds, the other the tables, which we use. And so with other things. The Form itself is not the work of any craftsman, for how could it be? (596a5–b10.)

Plato thinks of the relation between the ordinary bed which we use and the Form of 'what a bed really is' as a relation between likeness and original. The Form is 'what is', hence the maker of the bed makes 'not what is, but something which is like what is, but is not that' (597a4–5). It is into this context of likenesses and originals that he introduces the painter who paints a picture of a bed. What does this painter make? The answer is now a natural one: the painter makes something which is not a bed, but which is a likeness of it. The practitioner of *mimēsis* is thus the maker 'whose product is at two removes from nature', or from what truly is. While the bed is not 'what is' (the Form) but merely something like it, the painting is in turn not a bed but merely something like it.[16]

As has often been said, the present passage is dubious when

---

[15] See Halliwell (1988), 118–19, on Plato's avoidance of *eikōn*, and the connotations of *phantasma* and *eidōlon*.

[16] Nehamas writes that Plato never 'accuses art of being an imitation of an imitation ... not once in *Republic* 10 is *mimesis* used to refer to the relationship between sensible objects and Forms ... nothing in the text implies that the relationship between a work of art and its subject is the same as that between a physical object and its Form or Forms' (1982, 60). The two relationships are of course not *the same*: the bed is not *a picture of* the Form, and the painting is not *an instance of* the bed. Yet Plato does say that the object : Form relationship is one of *being like*—the carpenter makes *ti toiouton hoion to on* (597a4–5). (Cf. Belfiore (1984), 125.)

considered for the contribution it makes to the Theory of Forms.[17] Socrates' hesitant speculation about the Form, 'we would say, as I think, [it] is the work of a god' (597b6–7), has him toying with an idea that Plato never entertains elsewhere: usually, since there never was a time when Forms were not, Plato does not need to consider who or what brought them into existence. Secondly, we may doubt whether it is proceeding in the 'usual way' to assume that *any* set of many particulars which we call by the same name has an associated Form. Thirdly, should we not be surprised that a humble craftsman is now granted a glimpse of the Form as the guiding principle in the production of beds, when earlier in the *Republic* much was made of the fact that only philosophers have access to Forms? We may even doubt whether Plato's view of Forms elsewhere would really allow him to think there are Forms of artefacts. (What do these have in common with the Fine itself or the Good?) On these issues Book 10 seems to some extent adrift from the main body of the *Republic*.

However, these anomalies do not detract from the clarity of Plato's explanation of *mimēsis*. His dominating concern is with the question what 'kind of maker' the practitioner of *mimēsis* is (596b12). This, together with the desire to place the product of the mimetic artist within the hierarchy of likenesses and originals, leads him to seek also a hierarchy of makers or producers. Once started along this path, he is forced to use an artefact as his example of an object depicted by the painter, simply because the painter has to be contrasted with a maker of a 'more real' product.[18] (Plato does not believe the absurd proposition that painters paint pictures only of artefacts.) His talk of a god making the Form can be explained as the completion of a hierarchy of three producers to match that of the picture, the bed, and the Form. Finally, an analogy has to be drawn between the intentions of the painter and the intentions of the carpenter. The painter intends to make something which is a likeness of a bed without being one, in the same way as the craftsman intends to make something which is a likeness of 'what a bed truly is' but without being that. This analogy could not work unless the carpenter's activity was allowed to be guided by some kind of cognitive access to the Form itself. Plato needs to specify the kind of artefact made by the practitioner of *mimēsis*; he sets himself the

---

[17] See e.g. Nehamas (1982), 54–5; Cherniss; Annas (1981), 227–32; Cross and Woozley, 284–6; Griswold (1981), 135–6.

[18] 'Had he selected e.g. mountains, it would be difficult to specify the middle term' (Adam, ii. 387).

additional imaginative task of contrasting three kinds of artificer. This goes some way towards explaining the oddities we have mentioned.[19]

What, then, does the practitioner of *mimēsis* make? A telling exchange occurs at 596e10–11: 'in a way the painter too makes a bed, does he not?—Yes, he does, but only the appearance of a bed [or "only an appearing one", *phainomenēn ge*].' The painter does not make nothing, but what he or she does make is only an appearing something. It is a case of 'making in a way, but in a way not', as Plato also puts it (596d3–4). The second peculiarity is that *mimēsis* can make an appearing thing of any kind. There is an easy way in which everyone could do this:

Carry a mirror with you everywhere; you will then quickly make the sun and things in the heavens, the earth as quickly, yourself and the other living creatures, manufactured articles, plants, and all that was mentioned just now.[20]

Yes, he said, I could make them appear, but I could not make them as they truly are. [Or: 'I could make appearing ones (*phainomena*), but not ones that really are in truth.'] (596d9–e4.)

This extraordinary comprehensiveness is meant to carry over from the 'mirror' example to that of the painter who provides the instance of *mimēsis*. In apparent denial of this, Plato says that the painter, rather than making a likeness of the Form, 'tries to *mimeisthai* . . . the works of the craftsmen' (598a1–4). But this is simply a comment on the particular example Plato chooses; it is not an expression of the view (which is anyway an absurdity) that painters paint pictures only of artefacts, as the conclusion of this passage shows: 'Mimetic art, then, is far removed from the truth, and that is why it can make everything, because it touches only a small part of each thing, and that an image' (598b6–8). The wide range of animals and plants, gods and humans, heaven and earth, nature as well as artefact—everything—is the true subject-matter of *mimēsis*.

At the end of the concluding sentence quoted immediately above, the

---

[19] I agree with Halliwell: 'We should read the present passage . . . as an *ad hoc* adaptation of Plato's theory of Forms. It is enough for his polemical purposes if the argument communicates the idea that there are criteria of truth which transcend the material world . . . and if mimetic art is convicted of being limited . . . to this lower world' (1988, 110). For Halliwell also 'the reference to god cannot be taken entirely seriously . . . Plato is obviously striving for a symmetrical shape to his argument' (114)— similar to the views of Cherniss, and Havelock (32).

[20] 'Just now' refers to 596c4–9. Excluded from the new list are 'the gods', and 'all things in Hades below the earth'—easy to paint, hard to hold a mirror to! (Cf. Halliwell (1988), 112.)

account of '*mimēsis* as a whole' is complete.[21] Already it was decided
that the appropriate name for the painter of a bed is *mimētēs*, the *mimētēs*
being the maker of a product at two removes from nature, that is, from
Forms: 'we are agreed on the *mimētēs*', says Socrates (597e10). The
final points are that this 'maker' attempts to make a *mimēsis* of an
ordinary thing, not of a Form, and that he attempts to make a *mimēsis*
of a thing not as it *is*, but only as it *appears*. Though both points may
need a little clarification, the latter is certainly not too difficult. A
painting of a bed must present to the spectator one way in which a bed
might *appear*. A bed stays the same, as regards what it *is*, from wherever it is viewed, but it appears in different ways. Painting must present
some way that a bed appears (or might appear) rather than presenting
the way it always is, and hence painting can be called 'a *mimēsis* of an
appearance [*phantasma*] rather than of the truth' (598b1–5). This is an
intelligible claim. Even if we are tempted to reply that a painting can
'capture the way something really is', we should ask ourselves whether
a painting can ever do this without presenting to us the way something
appears. The answer seems to be that it cannot. For example, if (in any
sense) a portrait may convey to us 'just how a particular person is', or
if a painter can show us the very 'chairness' of a chair,[22] they must
nevertheless do so by showing us one way in which the person or chair
appears, or might appear.[23]

The other claim Plato makes is that the painter does not attempt to
mimeisthai the Forms, but only things such as a particular bed. He thus
debars the arts, in so far as they are mimetic, from representing eternal
realities. This claim has generated a long history of regrets and denials
since Plato's time,[24] but in fact he has no choice in the matter. The only
proper sense in which a painting, or anything, could be an 'imitation'

---

[21] i.e. at 598b8. In Chapter 6 I argue that the following sentence begins a distinct phase
of argument, concerning the mimetic *poet* in particular.

[22] Ferrari (1989, 128), thinking of van Gogh.

[23] In Xenophon's *Memorabilia* (3. 10. 1–8) this issue arises in a conversation between
Socrates and the painter Parrhasius, who initially thinks it impossible to represent 'the
disposition of the soul' in painting (e.g. friendliness, hostility, nobility). He is convinced
by Socrates that it is possible—but note that the painter represents such moods and
character-traits by representing a friendly, hostile, or noble *look*. Related points occur in
Plato's *Cratylus*: music and graphic art make a *mimēsis* of the sound, shape, or colour of
things, not of their essence. Indeed, the kind of *mimēsis* which makes an image (*eikōn*)
of something *must* reproduce only limited features of its original. An attempted *mimēsis* of
Cratylus the man which went beyond his colour and shape, and became a complete replica,
would not be an *image* of him, but another Cratylus (*Crat.* 423d4–424a3, 432b2–c5).

[24] Two parts of the story often cited are: Plotinus, *Enneads*, V. viii. 1, and Schopenhauer,
i, Third Book.

of one of the Forms is by being large, or good, or fine, and thus standing in a certain relation to the Form Largeness, or Goodness, or Fineness. Here it is all one whether one says the thing is like the Form, strives to be like it, is a likeness of it, participates in it, or 'imitates' it.[25] It is the ordinary bed that would—in this 'metaphysical' sense—be a *mimēsis* of the Form of Bed. A painting that 'imitated' the Form of Bed *in this sense* would *ipso facto* be a bed as well![26] Now clearly paintings are a case of *mimēsis* in the different sense that Plato is labouring to establish: they make an appearance of a thing of a certain kind, not something that is of that kind. The question then remains why a painting could not, without of course being one of the Forms, nevertheless make the appearance of Forms. Why must it be restricted to making the appearances of beds and the like? But to this question there is a simple answer: Forms do not have an appearance. They belong to the realm of the intellect, not the sensible realm; they can never be perceived with any of the organs of sense.[27] The only 'restriction' placed on painting is that it must make a *mimēsis* of things that have, or possibly could have, an appearance. But this already rules out as impossible any painting of a Form.

A persistent strain of Platonism in the philosophy of art has tended to assert that the artist's ability is that of intuiting and making manifest some higher, eternal reality. Both the 'intuiting' and the 'making manifest' here are questionable. I have been asking what a painting of Goodness or Justice would be, and have answered: At most a picture of an ideally just or good *something or other*—that is to say, of the appearance of something or other—such as the painting of the ideal human being Plato imagines at 472d. But this may be thought to miss the point. For such a picture might yet make manifest to us, by way of the portrayed perceptible thing, what Goodness or Humanity itself is. However, now the distinct question of the painter's cognition of Forms must be raised. The painting of the appearance of a good human being

---

[25] See Halliwell (1986), 117 ff., on this kind of *mimēsis*. For Plato's various terms, see *Rep.* 597a4–5, 476c6, 510d7, 510e2–3, *Parm.* 132d1–4, *Phdo.* 74d9–e7, 100c4–6, 101c2–7, *Symp.* 211b2, *Phdr.* 250b1–5, *Tim.* 29b2, 39d7–e2, 48e6–7, 50c4–6. Plato indicates his uncertainty about what to call the relation between Forms and instances at *Phdo.* 100d5–8.

[26] For Plato a bed could not be a painting, and its maker could not be a painter (see Nehamas (1982), 60). In a brilliant move, Danto (1981, 12–13) points to two painters, Rauschenberg and Oldenburg, who have made works of art which *are* beds.

[27] See especially *Phdo.* 65d4–e4, *Rep.* 507b2–10, 508c1–2. Even that 'most evident' of Forms, beauty, is not *itself* seen; we see only its image (*eidōlon*) in a beautiful person at *Phdr.* 250d3–e3.

could reliably make manifest what Goodness itself is only if the painter by some means knows what Goodness is. But why should a painter as such know that? One of Plato's best points is that you do not need knowledge of what Goodness really is in order to make a fine, convincing appearance of some good person or thing.

There have been commentators who have refused to believe that art cannot imitate Forms, and who have evaluated Plato's contribution to the philosophy of art accordingly. If one believes that there *can* be artistic *mimēsis* of Forms, then either Plato is to be criticized for overlooking it, or—perhaps—he deserves credit for thinking that 'true art' can accomplish it after all.[28] A defender of the latter view is J. Tate, whose view is that Plato means us to distinguish 'good' and 'bad' *mimēsis*:

The distinction between the good and bad senses of imitation is, broadly speaking, a distinction between two kinds of artist, the ignorant on the one hand and the enlightened on the other. Here we have the key to understanding Plato's attitude towards poetry and art in general.[29]

It is vital to know whether this view is right or wrong. Let us therefore understand Tate's argument. The ground for the good/bad distinction was laid in Book 3, he claims, where *mimēsis* (dramatic impersonation) was to be judged good or bad only according to the nature of the model imitated, and where the enacting of good characters behaving well was 'good *mimēsis*'. Now in Book 10, Tate claims, Plato

leaves it to be understood that the poet who is imitative in the sense in which the guardians are permitted to be imitative will produce a direct copy of reality; he will be like the painter who uses the 'divine paradigm' . . . not like the painter who is content to hold the mirror up to nature.[30]

That a painting can be a copy of Forms is, it may be felt, too large a point for us to be 'left to understand' by Book 10. Tate, however, draws additional evidence from a passage in Book 6 where Socrates imagines an outline of the ideal city sketched by 'painters who would use the divine model' (500e3–4). These painters would 'keep looking back and forth, to Justice, Beauty, Moderation, and all such things as

---

[28] Criticism of Plato for overlooking artistic *mimēsis* of Forms comes from Grube (1935), 202, 206; Adam, ii. 393; Daiches, 20. Credit to Plato for believing in artistic *mimēsis* of Forms is given by e.g. Tate (1928); Verdenius (1949), 18; Golden, 123–4, 130. The discussion and bibliography of Nehamas (1982), 58–60 and 75–7, is invaluable here.

[29] Tate (1928), 21.   [30] Ibid. 19–20.

by nature exist, and they would compose human life with reference to these' (501b1–4). It is true that these imagined painters could be guided by knowledge of Forms. But how are we to imagine their picture of 'human life'? Any such picture must (to reiterate the point) present to us an appearance of some aspect of human life—how could it be 'a direct copy of reality', if that means a direct copy of Forms? Another problem is that Socrates' painters here are purely imaginary: we cannot take this as evidence for Plato's believing in any real artistic activity guided by knowledge of the Forms. The passage is an elaborate metaphor and is not really about painting at all. It is about philosophers.[31] To make more vivid the role he is assigning to philosophers, Plato asks us temporarily to think of them as if they were designers of some visible product, who have the philosopher's privilege of knowing the Forms. A careful look at the passage reveals that the 'fine picture' these 'painters' make is 'human life' itself. Philosophers, knowing Forms, make human life into a likeness of Justice, Beauty, and Moderation, that is, make life so that it is just, beautiful, and moderate. When the metaphor is explained we see that painting is not the issue. A similar passage is 484c8–d1, where Plato says that the guardians must 'as painters can, look to that which is most true, always refer to it, contemplate it as exactly as possible'. It has been said that 'not too much must be made of this passage'[32]—wisely, since again we are dealing with a simile, which gains its point because painters can make exact copies of the ordinary things (not Forms) which they observe carefully with their eyes. (It would anyway be very lame to say that the guardians must carefully attend to the Forms, like painters carefully attending to the Forms!)[33]

---

[31] As *Rep.* 500c9, e1 make clear. See Nehamas (1982), 59; Keuls, 41, 50.

[32] Grube (1935), 188. Also see Keuls, 50–1, for a sensible discussion.

[33] Other passages may appear to support Tate's idea that there can be artistic *mimēsis* of Forms. One is where Plato says that no one can become truly educated in the arts until they learn to recognize the forms of self-control, courage and other virtues, and to perceive them in things and in likenesses of things (402b9–c8). But, as we said in Ch. 4, it is not very likely that the 'forms' mentioned here are the Forms to be put forward later in the central part of the *Republic*. Plato is talking about recognizing instances of the virtues in people and things and in artistic images of people and things. Another passage is at 472d4–7, where Plato uses the simile of the painter who paints the model of the perfect human being. This shows that Plato could regard a painting as something admirable, if it depicted something admirable, and that he could imagine a painting which was not merely a slavish copy of what already exists. But what is painted here is not a Form, but 'an appearing man', an image of the way an ideal man might look. Tate's remaining point, that there is 'good' and 'bad' *mimēsis* in Book 3, does not help his position either. From the fact that modelling one's dramatic behaviour on one type of person is 'good'

So what philosophical position, if any, can we attribute to Plato in Book 10? His view is quite simple: to paint is to make only an appearance, not something real—a painting of an X is an intentionally made image, something which is a likeness of an X's appearance without being an X. In taking as his example a painting of an object, he is singling out the kind of thing we would call a representation and the activity we would call representing. But pictorial representation is not an easy phenomenon to analyse, and our use of expressions such as 'image', 'appearance', 'likeness', 'painting of ...' has left many issues unclarified. To begin with, Plato assumes that representation is a matter of resemblance. Recent philosophical writing has put such an assumption under strong attack.[34] If we are tempted to say that the painter makes something 'like' a bed, we are most likely to mean that *what is represented in the painting* is like a bed: that the bed we see in the picture is like real beds.[35] However, once we make this distinction between a painting's resembling a bed and the-bed-in-the-painting's resembling a bed, we bring into focus a striking feature of Plato's account: he never says that the painter's product is a painting, a marked surface, or a 'real' thing of any kind at all. What resembles a bed for him is the 'bed' that the painter 'makes'. The painter makes only an appearance, 'an object whose identity is constituted by the thing that it seems to be, not by any properties that it might have in its own right'.[36] It is in this sense that the traditional translation of *mimēsis* as 'imitation' is appropriate. The painter makes a bed, a person, or a bowl of flowers, which is not a real one. What the painter makes is not a real anything: it is always an imitation something. As Arthur Danto has put it, a feature of the imitation theory is 'the logical invisibility of the medium'.[37] We might naïvely consider the painting to be an intentionally produced set of physical marks in a physical medium on a physical

there is no inference to the claim that painting can represent Forms. In Book 10's sense the *mimēsis* of any type of person would be the 'making' of an 'appearing person'—and neither an appearing good person nor an appearing bad person would differ ontologically from an appearing bed.

[34] See e.g. Goodman, ch. 1, and Schier (1986), 2–9, and for further discussion, Budd (1991).

[35] See Wollheim, 18.

[36] Nehamas (1982), 63. Nehamas (ibid. 62) rightly notes a 'vacillation' in Plato's description of artists, between '*imitator* of an appearance' and '*maker* of an appearance' (cf. 598b3–5, 596e10–11 on the painter) or between '*imitator* of images' and '*maker* of an image' (600e5, 599d3 on the poet). What is represented is the appearance of things in the world, but what is *made* is also only an appearance.

[37] Danto (1981), 151.

surface[38]—but Plato does not consider that this is anything important, interesting, or pleasing in its own right. So he cannot think of evaluating the painter's choice of substances to paint with, or the painting's success in handling colour or line. The product of the painter's activity, for him, is just something secondary to other objects, a non-real bed or a non-real person.

It is relevant here to remark on a fact about the phrase 'a painting of . . .': it can be, but does not have to be, completed by an expression referring to some particular subject. When it is, we have, for example, a painting of Socrates, or of the particular bed on which Socrates died. It is plausible to say that the painting manages to be *of* these subjects by standing to them (or standing for them) in some relation parallel with linguistic reference. On the other hand, there can be a painting which is 'of a bed' not by being related in any way to any particular bed, but only in the sense that a bed figures as the 'representational content' internal to the picture, to understand which is to understand the picture at the most basic level. Plato is aware of the second kind of representation,[39] but he makes no theoretical distinction between these two ways of understanding 'painting of . . .' And this could be seen as a difficulty, in view of his comparison between painting and holding up a mirror to things. For something to be 'a mirror image of . . .' always does require some particular original of which it is the image. Plato concentrates on the fact that in both cases what is made is an appearing thing, not a real thing, overlooking the difference between the two cases: that the mirror image is essentially dependent on its more real original, both for its existence and for what it appears to be, whereas a painting of a bed, if that phrase is understood in the 'non-referential' way, does not have to have such a dependence on any other particular object.[40]

While Plato makes nothing of this difference, it is nevertheless unjustified to claim that Plato equates *mimēsis* with 'photographic realism', or even that this is a manner of representation that particularly concerns him. Commentators sometimes assume that Plato thinks of the painter as 'a mere mechanical copyist' indulging in 'uncritical copying

---

[38] I note in passing that this too has been disputed. For an initial discussion, see Wollheim, 11 ff. and 177–84.

[39] Two examples in the *Republic*: (A) The painting of the ideally beautiful human being (472d4–7) is not any kind of copy of a particular person. It is a 'non-relational' painting. (B) The painter 'of a cobbler, of a carpenter, of other craftsmen' (598b8–c1) *need* not copy some actual person. And the painting of the bed is the same.

[40] The same point is made by Danto (1981), 69.

of an object', 'exact copying of the way things in the world look', a
'mindless' or 'slavish reproduction of reality', and that he 'degrades
[painting] to the level of photography'.[41] This relies on taking the analogy with the mirror-carrier as a very tight one indeed. In a mirror, the
appearance of some existing particular thing really is reproduced both
exactly and mindlessly. But Plato does not say painting is holding a
mirror to the world (for that matter, he does not even say that the
mirror-carrier performs *mimēsis*, only that two are the 'same kind of
maker'). Nothing in the discussion requires there to be some particular
bed which is 'copied' by a painting which succeeds in being 'of a bed'.
And even a depiction of some actual bed does not have to be 'photographic' or 'exact' in its style in order to make 'an appearing bed'. It
merely has to bring a bed to mind in some natural way.[42] It is thereby
rendered derivative from a *kind* of real things—no one could recognize
images of beds if they did not recognize beds—but does not have to be
a 'slavish copy' of any particular thing.

What about the idea that Plato positively believes *mimēsis* to be the
production of an illusion? In the clearest and crudest sense, producing
an illusion is bringing about a false belief in the existence of a thing,
where that belief is engendered by the apprehension of what is only an
appearance, image, or imitation.[43] If this were Plato's view, it would be
open to two broad objections: (1) even in the case of painting, with
which Plato chooses to exemplify '*mimēsis* in general', it is an implausible view of the nature of representation (of a painting's managing to
be 'of a bed'), and (2) it gives a poor account of poetry, which will be
Plato's main concern in the remainder of the discussion. To take the
first objection first, paintings plainly do not very often work, or succeed
in being 'of' something, by engendering an illusion. There is a weaker
view which says that, when we see a painting which we understand to
represent (say) grapes, we are under an illusion of seeing grapes at least
some of the time (perhaps momentarily). But that view is no better. We
should bear in mind those many ordinary viewers who are never under
any illusion while looking at a particular painting of grapes, and who
are aware throughout that they see a flat, painted surface. The price

---

[41] Adam, ii. 393; Grube (1935), 203; Annas (1981), 336; Osborne, 65. Ferrari (1989,
127) parallels my criticism of these views.

[42] Two notions that have had much currency recently are 'seeing-as' and 'seeing-in'.
See Wollheim, esp. 205–26; and Scruton (1974), ch. 13.

[43] The well-known theory of Gombrich (1960) does not take illusion to involve false
belief (see Gombrich (1973) for elucidation). But I shall discuss the attribution to Plato
only of the cruder 'illusion' view.

they pay is not that they cannot access the content of what is represented. So representation does not entail illusion. If Plato held blankly that in all paintings *mimēsis* is a matter of inculcating illusions, then he held a crude and implausible theory.

A second illusionistic interpretation would have it that Plato deliberately limits the discussion to that sub-category of painting manifested in the tale of the painters, Zeuxis and Parrhasius—one of whom painted grapes so realistic that the birds pecked at them, only to be trumped by his rival, who fooled him by painting a curtain seemingly in front of one of his pictures, but actually part of the picture. Some have maintained that Plato is criticizing a change towards illusionistic styles occurring during his lifetime, in contrast with more conservative modes of painting of which he approves.[44] But there is no good evidence for this view.[45] The only relevant technique that Plato shows any interest in is that of *skiagraphia*, literally 'shadow-painting', which used small areas of contrasting colour, distinctly visible when viewed from close-up but not when viewed at a distance. Impressionism or Pointillism seem to be the nearest modern approximations, and by analogy with these the point of interest for Plato must be that what were 'really' diverse blobs or strokes could come to 'appear as' a homogeneous surface or a depicted object if viewed from far enough away.[46] He is, accordingly, suspicious of *skiagraphia* and prone to use it as a vivid example—sometimes purely in metaphor—of something which puts up an appearance that closer consideration reveals to be false.[47] It is fair to say that Plato treats *skiagraphia* as a genuinely illusionistic or *trompe*

---

[44] A view put forward by Schuhl, and Steven.

[45] See Demand, esp. 17 ff.; and Keuls. There is no clear indication of what style Plato would be contrasting 'illusionism' with. Some of the identifiable 'illusionist' techniques may have been well established by his day, rather than being innovations that could be contrasted with 'more conservative' art. And Plato generally seems more interested in illusionistic painting as an example of illusion rather than as a style of painting. Zeuxis is one of the few painters Plato refers to by name—but these references (*Gorg.* 453c–d, *Prot.* 318b–c, the latter calling him Zeuxippos (see Keuls, 90)) merely treat him as the standard example of a well-known painter, and criticize neither him nor any style of painting.

[46] Two references to *skiagraphia* outside the *Republic* indicate this: *Parm.* 165c–d, and *Tht.* 208e: 'I'm for all the world like a man looking at a shadow-painting; when I'm close up to it I can't take it in in the least, though when I stood well back from it, it appeared to me to have some meaning.' Later in Book 10 *skiagraphia* is said to exercise a kind of 'wizardry' that exploits the mind's propensity to succumb to optical illusions (602d1–3).

[47] Cf. *Rep.* 523a10–b6 (*skiagraphia* comes to Glaucon's mind as an example where 'perception does not achieve a sensible result'); and 365c4, 583b5, 586b8, where *skiagraphia* is a metaphor for something deceptive. *Laws* 663c2 is another example.

l'oeil style of painting. But does he limit *mimēsis* to this narrow genre? If so, then the second broad objection to Book 10 comes into play: as Julia Annas puts it, 'Plato . . . has done nothing to show that [the poet] imitates in the way that a *trompe-l'oeil* painter does',[48] rendering his case 'forced and unconvincing', because it is vastly implausible that a Homer or Aeschylus does something analogous to inducing a false belief in the existence of concave surfaces or real grapes.

There is no firm evidence for either of these illusionistic interpretations in the discussion of '*mimēsis* as a whole'.[49] Plato does not use the term *skiagraphia* here, only the more general word for a painter, *zōgraphos*. When he writes 'carry a mirror with you everywhere; you will then quickly make the sun and things in the heavens, [etc.]' (596d9–e3), the reference to 'making' is ironic: the 'sun' in the mirror is not the sun, it merely has the appearance of the sun. But something which has the appearance of the sun does not have to be an illusion of the sun. The emphasis is not on whether anyone has believed that something is there which is not, but rather on the question: What kind of thing would you have 'made', if you held up a mirror to reality? The same point, I argue, can be extended to the painter. The carpenter makes a bed and 'in a way the painter too makes a bed, does he not?—Yes, he does, but only an appearing one' (596e10–11). There is simply no reason to find a preoccupation with illusion here. Plato might have said: 'the painter produces not a bed, but something resembling a bed in appearance', or '. . . not a bed, but a bed-seen-in-a-picture', and his point would have been unchanged. If something is a mere appearance and not a reality, it does not follow that it is an appearance taken for a reality. The possibility of being deceived will be something to guard against; but, I suggest, deceit is not built into the examples which explain '*mimēsis* as a whole'.

As we saw, Plato sums up with these words: 'So mimetic art is far removed from the truth, and that is why, it seems, it can make everything, because it touches only a small part of each thing, and that an image' (598b6–8). He emphasized earlier, when discussing the mirror, that *mimēsis* is a capacity for making everything, in appearance at any rate. This is an important point, which provides another argument against

---

[48] Annas (1981), 338, 340.

[49] i.e., on my reading, up to 598b8. Belfiore seems right in saying 'There is no question of deception in *Republic* 10 until 598c, where the painter, "if he is a good painter", is said to be able to deceive "children and fools" by showing his works "from a distance"' (1984, 128 n. 23).

the illusionistic reading of these passages. Has anyone ever remarked on the extreme oddity of thinking that the artist can make an illusion of everything? Grapes and curtains hanging in front of the picture are part of a reasonably small repertoire of *trompe-l'oeil* subjects. No one seriously thinks there can be successful illusionistic renderings in painting of the entire range of animals, or of 'the earth and the heavens and the gods, all things in heaven and all things in Hades below the earth' which Plato says the mirror-carrier 'makes', adding that the painter belongs in the same class of makers (596e5–6). You can paint pictures of all these things, but not in an illusionistic manner. The all-embracing nature of *mimēsis* is of vital importance to Plato, as we see from his critique of poetry. There are some people who claim that Homer and the tragedians 'know all the crafts, all human affairs concerned with virtue and vice, and all about the gods as well'.[50] Plato wants to show that these people are wrong. *Mimēsis* can masquerade as comprehensive knowledge and can lead us to erroneous judgements about what is good. In that way, in the case of poetry, it can give rise to false beliefs—and indeed, for illustrative purposes, Plato will liken such false beliefs to visual illusions.[51] He uses the loaded terminology of phantasms and false images because he wants us to see the potential for illusion and error lurking in *mimēsis*. But that is a far cry from saying that a painting's being a *mimēsis* of a bed must consist in its perpetrating an illusion to which the spectator falls prey.

Plato has yet to convince us that any kind of poetry fits into the account given of *mimēsis* and has yet to show that, if it does, it will thus be revealed as dangerous. It has been suggested that Plato is inconsistent: the inclusion of poetry in *mimēsis* would support the view that poetry is a trivial and unimportant thing, yet Plato takes it very seriously as something harmful.[52] But even if it is Plato's intention to show that poetry is 'trivial', there is no real inconsistency here. If people devote large portions of their lives to the pursuit of something trivial, in ignorance of its triviality, that they do so is surely an important and potentially dangerous fact.

Is any poetry mimetic in the sense established? From the single

---

[50] 598d8–e2. Halliwell suggests (1988, 111) that Socrates' irony about *mimēsis* as a making of everything is 'in part directed against claims for the general wisdom and knowledge of poets'. 'In part' strikes me as an understatement. We readily think of Ion's claim that reading Homer makes him an expert on every subject (see Flashar, 42 n. 1). Plato never writes of such claims in relation to painting.

[51] See *Rep.* 598c1–4, 600e4–601b4, 602c7–605c5, and Ch. 6 below.

[52] Annas (1982), 11–12, and (1981), 342.

mention of any poet in the discussion of '*mimēsis* as a whole' (595c7–598b8) it can look as though Plato merely assumes without argument that tragedy is mimetic in the right sense. Here it is:

You would call the maker of a product at two removes from nature a *mimētēs*?
— Absolutely.
— The maker of tragedies will be this too, then, given that he is a *mimētēs*, someone naturally third from the king and the truth, and so will all the other *mimētai*.
— Probably.
— We are agreed on the *mimētēs*. (597e3–10, my translation.)

However, this may be read in two ways. The clause 'given that he is a *mimētēs* [*eiper mimētēs esti*]' may mean either '*since* the tragic poet is a practitioner of *mimēsis*' or '*if* indeed the tragic poet is a practitioner of *mimēsis*'. On the first reading Plato assumes without further argument that the tragic poet fits into the same mould as the painter of a bed. This would be unfortunate, for nothing has been said to establish that he practises *mimēsis* in the Book 10 sense.[53] However, the other reading—with 'if'[54]—leaves it to be established separately whether the tragic poet does practise *mimēsis*. This reading not only clears Plato of an illegitimate move, it also makes much better sense of Socrates' saying later 'Next we have to examine tragedy and its leader, Homer' (598d7–8), as if up to this point in the discussion the status of tragedy was an open question.[55] So I think we should not read Plato as assuming without argument that tragic poetry is an instance of *mimēsis* in the sense he is seeking to establish in Book 10.

The next question is whether, as some have claimed,[56] Plato now

[53] The tragic poet is obviously a mimetic poet in the Book 3 sense of using dramatic characterization, but that is not a matter for argument in Book 10. Plato at times finds it natural, as at the beginning of *Republic* Book 2 (373b5 ff.), to apply the classificatory term *mimētēs* to poets along with other performers and painters—cf. Halliwell (1988), 116. But again this does not address the issue of *mimēsis* in the Book 10 sense.

[54] Liddell and Scott give the first meaning of *eiper* as 'if really, if indeed', the second as 'if as is the fact' or 'since'. For 'if indeed' see Reeve, in his revision of Grube's translation. Shorey and Jowett also have 'if'. Other translators go for versions of the 'since' reading (e.g. Lee (1955), Grube (1981), Cornford (1941)). Halliwell (1988, 116) has 'given that', but in the commentary assumes the 'since' reading, remarking: 'This direct inference from painting to poetry is . . . a weak link in the argument.' On my reading there is no inference here, only the assertion of a conditional.

[55] Also—for what it is worth—the 'if' reading gives force to Socrates' saying that the maker of tragedies *will* be third from the truth (rather than 'is'), and to the non-committal answer 'probably' (*kinduneuei*). (But perhaps Socrates and Glaucon are just being hesitant about the 'third from the King' metaphor.)

[56] See Annas (1981), 336; Cross and Woozley, 277–8; Havelock, 24–6; Collingwood (1925), 166 (but repudiated by him in (1938), 46 ff.).

treats all poetry as a form of *mimēsis*. Since the opening remarks of Book 10 mention 'such poetry as is mimetic', our answer here should help us decide whether Plato is going to attack all poetry. If all poetry is mimetic, all poetry will be objectionable. Before examining that question, however, let us note that Plato's overwhelming emphasis in Book 10 is on one specific kind of poetry: that which is dramatic, and hence mimetic in the restricted sense established in Book 3. Later I shall split the Book 10 discussion into four main arguments against mimetic poetry, all of which have as their explicit targets Homer, who is called 'the teacher and leader of all those fine tragedians' (595c1–2), and the tragedians themselves.[57] Thus in the first argument Plato states that the maker of tragedies will be removed from truth, and calls for an examination not of 'all poets', but simply of 'tragedy and its leader, Homer' (597e6, 598d7–8).[58] In the second he concludes that 'the tragic poets, whether they write in iambics or in epic verse [the metres of tragic dialogue and Homer respectively] are mimetic to the greatest possible extent' (602b8–10); then a third argument is launched with the statement that mimetic poetry 'imitates people acting voluntarily or under compulsion . . .' (603c4–5), which suggests that mimetic poetry is essentially dramatic. And the final 'chief accusation' (605c6 ff.) concerns what happens when we 'hear Homer or some other tragedian imitating one of the heroes sorrowing . . .'. Each of the four main arguments, then, is aimed fairly sharply at Homer and tragedy.[59]

Calling these kinds of poetry *mimēsis* can be seen to have its point. Drama and the kind of character-writing found in Homer clearly have something in common with painting a picture, in that the dramatist and the epic story-teller make things we see and hear 'in a way'—namely persons and actions which are only 'appearing persons' and 'appearing actions', not real ones. The characters of epic and tragedy exist only in the medium of words, but their image (voice and shape) literally appears before us in the person of an actor or rhapsode. So epic and tragedy, which qualified as poetic *mimēsis* in Book 3, are also instances of the wider artistic *mimēsis* of Book 10. They are in the intersection between 'making oneself like another in voice or form' (Book 3 *mimēsis*) and artistic 'appearance-making' (Book 10 *mimēsis*) (see Figure 1). In

[57] Socrates' comment about his being denounced 'to the tragic poets and all the other mimetic ones' (595b3–5) is vague: there is no licence to read it as referring to all poets.

[58] The only other poets named in this argument are Hesiod, who provides a subsidiary illustration to the points made about Homer's achievements, and Homer's obscure companion Creophylus, who does him no credit as a teacher (600d6, 600b6).

[59] Cf. Grube (1935), 188, 190.

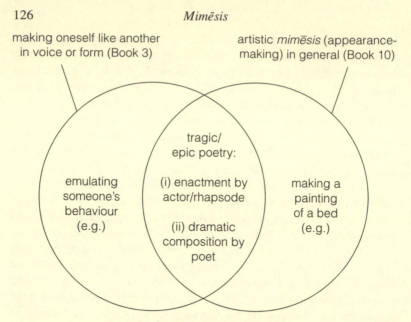

making oneself like another
in voice or form (Book 3)

artistic *mimēsis* (appearance-
making) in general (Book 10)

emulating
someone's
behaviour
(e.g.)

tragic/
epic poetry:

(i) enactment by
actor/rhapsode

(ii) dramatic
composition by
poet

making a
painting
of a bed
(e.g.)

FIG. 1. *Sense and reference of* 'mimēsis'

Book 3 Plato's topic was how our actions can be modelled on the behaviour of different types of person. The guardians' emulation of the good type of person in real life was one example, dramatic enactment of a character was another. But we realize in Book 10 that some enactment is also representation, and so can be classified in a different way, along with painting a picture. The sense of the term *mimēsis* changes between Book 3 and Book 10 without losing its reference to the same kinds of poetry, and it is still these which Plato is most concerned to criticize, though now predominantly from the point of view of the audience who apprehend the representation rather than that of the person who performs the enactment.

However, Plato now also speaks as if *all* poetry can be included in Book 10's circle of artistic *mimēsis*. He concludes prominently that 'all of the poets, beginning with Homer, are imitators of images of excellence [*mimētas eidōlōn aretēs*] and of everything else they write about' (600e4–6), and he describes 'Homer or any other poet' as merely a *mimētēs* of doctors' words (599b9–c2). Other passages which seem to treat all poetry as mimetic are 601a4–6, where 'the poet' does not understand anything but how to perform *mimēsis* and 603b4–7, where 'poetry' is the name given to the mimetic art (*mimētikē*) which is concerned with hearing rather than sight.[60] Does Plato really mean that all poets are mimetic? Given the chief target of his arguments, one could suggest that 'all poets' is merely elliptical for 'all tragic and epic poets' (mimetic poets in the Book 3 sense), and so on with the other passages mentioned. However, this is not a very convincing suggestion, given that the final few pages of Book 10's discussion of poetry are decidedly more comprehensive in scope. The 'ancient quarrel' (607b5) is between philosophy and *poetry*—not just something narrower called mimetic poetry. Plato says now that *poetry* is to be banished (607b1–3); and he explicitly objects to 'the Muse of sweet pleasure whether in lyrics or epic' (607a5–6). So it is hard to discount the view that in the earlier passages, even though focusing on Homer and tragedy, he means to label as mimetic 'all poets' and 'poetry' without exception.

This leaves us with a problem: in virtue of what does all poetry now qualify as *mimēsis*? Is there something common to all poetry which makes it analogous to the painting of a bed? Plato is not explicit about this: his references to any poetry beyond Homer and tragedy are vague, he does not debate the possibility of some poetry's falling outside the Book 10 heading of *mimēsis*,[61] nor does he tackle questions about the differences between pictorial and poetic representation. But if the discussion is to have any cohesion, he must have an implicit reason for regarding all poetry as a kind of *mimēsis*: he must believe that poetry, like painting, can 'make' everything—not really, but in image—and that its images lay hold only of the way things appear.

Think back to Book 3 and Plato's illustration of the difference between straight narration and narration using dramatic characters: the same story can be told either as a description of what Chryses did or as a scene in which we imagine Chryses himself speaking (393c11 ff.). Plato's own descriptive re-casting of the tale from the *Iliad* is unpoetic (393d8), but we can conceive of it told again using Homer's poetic resources, though still in purely descriptive narration. Is there not a sense in which the poet in either case will have 'made' something? Chryses is still there in both versions, he is the same man, he has the same daughter, he goes on the same mission with the same outcome. Characters, things, and events are (as it were) conjured up by the poet,

---

[60] Also 603c1, *hē tēs poiēseōs mimētikē*—if it means 'that kind of *mimēsis* which is poetry' rather than 'the kind of poetry which is mimetic'.

[61] I have previously suggested that Plato could recognize and approve poetry that was not *mimēsis* in the Book 10 sense (see Janaway (1991), 4). Anthony Price has convinced me that this claim cannot be supported.

and the difference between the two forms of narration brought to prominence in Book 3 is now irrelevant. So presumably what Plato thinks the generic poet 'makes'—and here the irony that *poiētēs* means 'maker' cannot but surface—is an imaginary scene containing characters, actions, and so forth. Poetry makes its own world, presenting before the receptive imagination Chryses, Agamemnon, the city of Troy, the Greek ships, the gods, battles, conversations, moral conflicts—thus the poet may 'make' any kind of thing without limit, but only in the way in which a painter makes a bed.

Does the similarity rest there? Plato concludes that 'all of the poets . . . are imitators of images of excellence and of everything else they write about' (600e4–6). The argument for this conclusion will be discussed in Chapter 6 below, but what does the conclusion mean? To be an 'imitator of . . .' embraces being a *maker* of something and being a *portrayer* of something.[62] So the phrase 'imitator of images' may, for Plato, mean someone whose product is an image, but it also implies that the models which the imitator attempts to portray are themselves only images. Earlier the painter not only made a 'non-real bed', but took as model the appearance of a bed from a particular angle. If the poet is analogously to be an 'imitator of images of excellence', then his or her product must be modelled, not on excellence itself (the Form), but on excellence as it can appear in the behaviour or the traits of some particular person or kind of person. Plato mentions that, for instance, a poet may be 'an imitator only of doctors' words' (599c2). The poet cannot be a doctor or do what doctors do, but can make a character who speaks and acts in the manner of some possible doctor. Such 'convincing portrayal of character' consists, for Plato, in the poet's approximating the world within the poem to one of the many ways in which things might *appear* to the audience.

So with ethical qualities the poet will know how to assimilate the content of the poem to possible episodes of observable behaviour which will seem to the audience those of a courageous or pious or wise person in particular circumstances. But that, for Plato, is not knowing such virtues *themselves*. Like the rhetorical manipulator of the *Gorgias*, the poet will not know what excellence is, but will contrive to present before the many a gratifying appearance of human behaviour, from which they may falsely take themselves to be learning of excellence (or

---

[62] See above, n. 36; also Adam, ii. 402.

the lack of it).[63] 'He will . . . make his imitation, without knowledge of where good and bad lies in each case. Instead, so it seems, it's what *appears* to be good [*kalon*] to the ignorant masses that he will imitate.'[64] The audience's perspective on *aretē* may well agree with that of Meno, who tells Socrates:

If it is manly virtue [*aretē*] you are after, it is easy to see that the virtue of a man consists in managing the city's affairs capably. . . . Or if you want a woman's virtue, that is easily described. She must be a good housewife, careful with her stores and obedient to her husband. Then there is another virtue for a child, male or female, and another for an old man, free or slave as you like; and a great many more kinds of virtue, so that no one need be at a loss to say what it is. For every act and every time of life, with reference to each separate function, there is a virtue for each one of us, and similarly, I should say, a vice. (*Meno* 71e2–72a5.)

Plato has in mind an audience who, like the 'lovers of sights and sounds', will not acknowledge even that there is a single Form of *aretē*—in their view, repeated acquaintance with particular episodes which manifest this or that courage or lack of it, this or that wisdom or lack of it, will suffice for 'knowing excellence'. There will be many excellences and deficiencies (virtues and vices) for this audience, and the poet will succeed if he or she gives pleasure by making recognizable images of some of them.

It is in this way, I think, that we must construe Plato's implicit reason for claiming that all poetry is a form of *mimēsis*. Poetry will lead us to apprehend imaginary versions of every kind of thing including people and their actions—images whose production is merely the successful attempt to 'convince' by simulating the myriad appearances of human life as the mass audience understands it. Knowing excellence, by contrast, is a philosophical enterprise which neither turns the gratifying image into an end in itself, nor looks for insight from the way virtues variously appear in different human circumstances. *Aretē* itself is an eternal and unvarying object of intellection, which poetry and poetry's audience neither comprehend nor even try to comprehend. Again Plato suffers less from a radical misconception about poetry than from his severe and outlandish conception of what qualifies as knowledge. One powerful reply to Plato—outlined in Chapter 8 below—begins with the

---

[63] Compare *Gorg.* 464d5–e2, 459d1–e1 and *Rep.* 598b8–c4 , 600e4–601b1.
[64] 602b, Halliwell's translation.

thought that there is a knowledge that is best acquired from imaginative engagement with images of human beings in the particularity of their actions and feelings.[65]

Another difficulty in the Book 10 discussion is that despite the apparently comprehensive critique of poetry, Plato nevertheless keeps some poetry in the city: 'Homer is most poetic and . . . stands first among the tragedians, but you must know for sure that hymns to the gods and eulogies of good men are the only poetry which we can admit' (607a2–5). For Plato to be consistent, the hymns and eulogies in his ideal city must escape his criticisms. Are they mimetic? Are they poetry? If they count as poetry and as mimetic, and if all mimetic poetry is to be banished, Plato's retention of them leaves the whole discussion in a hopelessly ragged state. The suggestion has been made that the hymns and eulogies do not count as poetry for Plato.[66] That is one way to make him consistent. However, the idea that what remains in the model city could not seriously be termed poetry betrays a highly questionable assumption that Plato approves only of what is dull. The sacred works of Palestrina probably contain nothing to which Plato would object, and the motet *Nuper rosarum flores* by Guillaume Dufay—which marked the consecration of Florence cathedral by the Pope, setting to music of great beauty and perfect proportions a text that refers to the act of consecration and its eminent executor—would not be out of place on a similar occasion in the model city. There is no correlation between our regarding something as high art and Plato's not liking it. Nor should we disregard the simple point that he calls his hymns and eulogies the only sort *of poetry* that he will accept in the city (607a4–5). As Collingwood remarks, when Socrates says this, 'no character is made to protest: "But was not *all* poetry to be excluded?"'[67]—which makes it look as if banishment for all poetry never was proposed. If this is an anomaly, it would be tedious to make too much of it: the essential point is to exclude any poetry subservient to 'the Muse of sweet pleasure' (607a5).

---

[65] I am echoing Nussbaum's comments: 'Certain truths about human experience can best be learned by living them in their particularity. . . . But we cannot all live . . . through all that we ought to know in order to live well. Here literature, with its stories and images, enters in as an extension of our experience, encouraging us to develop and understand our cognitive/emotional responses' (1986, 186).

[66] Annas remarks 'Plato is enough of a creative artist himself to know that such productions are not real poetry' (1981, 344)—though it is surely unclear what 'real poetry' is, especially to Plato.

[67] Collingwood (1938), 48.

The hymns and eulogies will not necessarily be judged 'most poetic' by standards that have prevailed hitherto, because they aim to benefit the citizens, not simply to please them. But they will still be poetry.

However, difficulties remain. If all *mimetic* poetry is banished, the hymns and eulogies cannot be mimetic. Yet if they are not mimetic, how can *all* poetry be mimetic? Again, I doubt whether we should press these questions too hard. The truth is that Plato wanders in his descriptions of the poetry he criticizes. Sometimes it is 'all poetry', sometimes Homer and the tragedians, sometimes something called 'mimetic poetry', sometimes the kind of poetry whose aim is pleasure. Late in the discussion he rejects '*mimēsis*' and 'poetry that aims at pleasure' all in one breath: *hē pros hēdonēn poiētikē kai hē mimēsis*,[68] a phrase which may be read as the single idea 'poetic *mimēsis* designed for pleasure' or as 'all poetry which aims at pleasure, including mimetic poetry'. The latter reading is possible because poetry's aiming at pleasure (rather than the good) would be sufficient objection regardless of whether or not it was a kind of *mimēsis*. But the single idea of 'poetic *mimēsis* designed for pleasure' takes us closer to the heart of Plato's worries.

For once again his greatest concern is with the governing aims of different kinds of poetry. We saw that the beneficial style of poetry in Book 3 could use *mimēsis*, but was not allowed to be 'mimetic' in its motivation. Now again there is one sense in which Plato's favoured hymns and eulogies will not be 'mimetic': they will not privilege the aim of appearance-making, of conjuring up a world of persons and things for the imagination. If appearance-making in itself is one's aim, one may endlessly delight the human soul. But this, as ever, cuts across the Platonic project of improving the soul and attuning it more closely to the truth. Plato might easily think (though he does not say) that even his hymns and eulogies, being poetry, would *use* imaginative appearance-making. What better way to honour a great, departed citizen in words and song than to make his bearing, his speech, and his actions as vividly present as possible? But what matters most is that the poetry of the city shall never regard imaginative appearance-making and its pleasures as autonomous ends.

Finally, before we turn to Plato's arguments against mimetic poetry, let us note that he does not seek to banish painting from the model

---

[68] 607c4–5. Halliwell (1988, 69, 155) treats the Greek phrase as a hendiadys: 'poetic mimesis designed for pleasure'. I agree with Halliwell that the *mimēsis* meant here is not *mimēsis* in general: 'Plato's earlier interest in visual mimesis has now been put aside.'

city.[69] He has been disparaging about painting, but his aim in discussing it is to reach an understanding of '*mimēsis* as a whole', as part of the attempt to show the true nature of mimetic poetry. While he announces clearly at the beginning that mimetic poetry is his target, and ends by banishing poets—except for the beneficial eulogizers—he says neither that painting is dangerous nor that he will exclude it from the model city. And the reason is plain: in Plato's experience of it, painting neither masquerades falsely as knowledge, nor corrupts our moral judgements by the appeal it makes to the emotions.[70] Poetry does both—or so the arguments of the sequel will attempt to show.

[69] This view is supported by e.g. Nehamas (1982), 47–8; Keuls, ch. 2; Urmson (1982), 136; Belfiore (1983), 49. Even so, Plato's hostility to painting may be variously assessed. We need not treat *everything* said of the painter as merely illustrative of points about poetry, as implied by e.g. Havelock, 32. Demand finds an 'attack against the painter in full swing' (8). And, obviously, if there is a critique of 'representational (mimetic) art as a whole' (Halliwell (1988), 6), it will be a critique of painting too.

[70] Ferrari seems in line with Plato's view: 'A poetic performance . . . engages its participants . . . in the whole "feel" of the human action it portrays . . . a canvas on a wall tends to invite sustained and relatively detached meditation rather than sympathetic participation in the portrayed scene' (1989, 109).

6

Against Mimetic Poetry

HEARERS of mimetic poetry will suffer damage to their intellects, Socrates claims, unless armed with the drug that will counteract it. The drug is knowledge of the nature of mimetic poetry (595b5–7), and the point is even clearer, he says, 'now that the parts of the soul have each been separately described' (595a7–b1), as they were earlier in the *Republic*. In fact the arguments against mimetic poetry come in two pairs: two arguments dealing with the parts of the soul appealed to and fostered by mimetic poetry come after a pair of epistemological arguments, concerning the poet's lack of knowledge.

The first of these epistemological arguments (598b8–601b8) purports to establish the conclusion that poetry is *mimēsis* and raises the con-comitant objection that poets lack knowledge. I shall call it the 'painter of craftsmen' argument, after the unusual analogy which frames it:

As, for example, a painter, we say, will paint us a cobbler, a carpenter, and other craftsmen, though he himself has no understanding of any of their crafts; but nevertheless he might deceive children and foolish people, if he were a good painter, by painting a carpenter and exhibiting him at a distance, so that they thought it was truly a carpenter.[1]

Here, I claim, Plato leaves his discussion of '*mimēsis* as a whole' and moves on to new business. What work does this passage do? It presents us with an example of what went before—an image of a thing of a certain kind, an 'appearing thing' and not a real thing, and hence a case of *mimēsis*. But it is, apparently, the oddest example to choose. Firstly, such a succession of craftsmen hardly provides painting with its most characteristic subject-matter. Since in the previous sentence 'everything' is what *mimēsis* can render, why pick on paintings of carpenters and cobblers? And secondly, of what interest can it be that children and fools might be taken in by certain images? Why build such atypical reactions into the 'example'? Thirdly, why include the detail that the painter does not understand the crafts belonging to those he makes

---

[1] *Rep.* 598b8–c4. My translation, partly based on that of Shorey.

images of? The earlier 'painter of a bed' did not (or need not) understand the craft of carpentry, because he was making an image of a bed
and not a real bed. That is fully intelligible. But the 'painter of craftsmen' is making an image of a craftsman—why then is his lack of
ability to make beds, or shoes, at all to the point?

I believe there is a satisfactory answer to these questions. Plato is not
now explaining the nature of *mimēsis* in general. We do not have to
regard all the features of this 'example' as intended to be typical of
painterly activity, or as defining features of *mimēsis*. At this point Plato
enters the second stage of his argument, in which *poetry* specifically is
to be scrutinized. That may seem to stretch incredulity even further,
since Plato does not mention poetry or poets at all in the passage
quoted. But the same example returns later, with a reference back to its
first occurrence, and this time Plato leaves us in no doubt as to its point:

Shall we then lay it down that all of the poets, beginning with Homer, are
mimētai of images of excellence and of the other things about which they make
poetry, and that they do not lay hold on truth, but as we were just now saying,
the painter will make what *looks* like a cobbler, even though he understands
nothing of the cobbler's craft and nor does his audience, whose perception
depends only on the shapes and colours? . . . In this way, I think, we will say
that the poet, understanding nothing but how to *mimeisthai*, lays on with words
and phrases the colours of the several crafts so that other such people whose
perception depends on his words think—whether someone speaks in rhythm,
metre, or harmony about cobbling or generalship or anything whatever—that
he speaks extremely well.[2]

Plato introduces the 'painter of craftsmen' stealthily, without explaining his function; but he then immediately embarks on an elaborate
argument concerning poets, whose culmination is the passage just quoted.
The 'painter of craftsmen' thus provides an analogy for the poet, and
in particular for the tragic or Homeric poet.[3]

Mimetic poetry portrays characters in action: 'human beings acting
voluntarily or under compulsion, and believing that as a result of these
actions they have fared well or ill, also suffering and rejoicing in
all this' (603c4–7). Sometimes these characters are generals, rulers,

---

[2] 600e4–601b1. This translation is also partly based on Shorey, but owes a lot to
Halliwell (1988).

[3] Halliwell's view (1988, 120) seems just right: 'Plato is using the extreme case of
visual illusion as a blatantly rhetorical means of preparing the ground for his main
argument—that poetry is falsely credited with a standing (that of ethical wisdom etc.)
which it has no claim to.'

prophets, charioteers, doctors—exponents of a *technē*. So when Plato
talks of the poet 'laying on with words and phrases the colours of the
several *technai*' this is part of what he means: using language, the poet
can create a character which the audience accepts as possessing any of
the many brands of human expertise. But, as Plato suggests, in addition
the poet's characters may have, acquire, or be seeking understanding of
the goods and evils of human life and of the ways of the gods: they are
locatable somewhere on the spectrum of ethical knowledge. Enmeshed
with the analogy between the poet and the 'painter of craftsmen', a
more familiar analogy is also at work: having ethical knowledge is
analogous with possessing a *technē*, and so making poetic characters
who appear to possess ethical knowledge is analogous with making
characters who appear to be exponents of a *technē*. The painted images
of cobbler, carpenter 'and the other craftsmen' are included, I suggest,
wholly for the sake of analogy and correspond in this way to the characters who appear in poetry, displaying to us what we take for virtues
(or the lack of them).

What then of the other questions we posed about the 'painter of
craftsmen' analogy? What is the interest of the mistakes of fools and
children? And of what import is the painter's ignorance of the crafts of
those he portrays? The point is that poets who write of generals and
rulers and charioteers do so in ignorance of any of these areas of human
expertise; and in like manner (as Plato sees it) poets who write of
human goods and evils do so while lacking ethical knowledge. To
make a successful poetic character, Plato is saying, it no more takes
knowledge of the truths about value in human life, than it takes expertise in shoemaking to make a convincing visual image of a cobbler.
This is his fundamental point. The fools and children are analogous to
those people who do not realize this—those who believe, falsely, that
poets themselves have knowledge of every conceivable kind.[4] The
analogy is thus slightly off-centre. Fools and children mistake a painted
image at a distance for a real thing. Those who ascribe knowledge to
poets do not mistake Homer's characters for real persons; what they do
is mistake the poet for a really knowledgeable person. Plato's rhetorical
point is that this mistake puts those who perpetrate it on a par with the
children and fools of the analogy.

Read this way, the analogy embodies a mismatch between (in the
case of the 'painter of craftsmen') mistaking *an image of a person* for

---

[4] Again I am in agreement with Halliwell here (see 1988, 121).

a real person with expertise, and (in the case of poetry) mistaking *the maker of an image of a person* for *a person with expertise*. But is that an objection? We must make sense of the mistake perpetrated about the products of the 'painter of craftsmen': there must be some analogous mistake with regard to the poet's product. The suggestion might be that people are deceived into thinking they are seeing real kings speaking and real deaths occurring, when they are experiencing poetic representations. But two points weigh strongly against that. It would have been laughable to suggest to the Athenians, with their vast collective experience of dramatic art, that an audience is commonly duped in this manner. And secondly Plato never elsewhere says anything to this effect: he never maintains that an audience are under any childish illusion of seeing real characters. (That the Athenians believed most of the protagonists of their poetry to be historical figures should not distract us. Some they *knew* to be real people, such as Xerxes, who appears in Aeschylus' *Persians*: my point is that even then the Athenians who saw this play did not think they were seeing Xerxes—and that Plato did not think they did.) What Plato does say in the passage we are about to examine is that people make foolish claims concerning the abilities of the poet. For his comparison with the 'painter of craftsmen' to be effective, Plato must reveal some mistake which it is clearly foolish or childish to make. He seems to have one vivid idea in mind throughout: that of people falsely believing in the existence of some real, knowledgeable person. On my reading there is an illusion of such a person both in the specially concocted example of the 'painter of craftsmen' and in the real case of the poet, so that the analogy is not hopelessly flawed.[5]

Now to the argument with which Plato supports his analogy of the poet with the 'painter of craftsmen'. I offer a schematic summary:

1. If someone *S* claims to have met a person who has knowledge of all the crafts (*dēmiourgiai*), and who knows everything each other

---

[5] An alternative reading of the analogy has been offered by Elizabeth Belfiore (1983). Belfiore agrees that the mistake Plato alleges about poetic *mimēsis* is not that of falling under the illusion of taking mere images for real things. But she also argues that in the illustrative half of the analogy, the 'painter of craftsmen' image, the mistake of the fools and children 'is not about ontology, but about a craft, carpentry' (44–5), and that the mistake made is, in both halves, 'veridical'—wrongly taking the content of painting (carpentry) and poetry (*aretē*) for true. This reading makes the analogy structurally more perfect than the one I propose. However, for some critical comments see Janaway (1991), 6–7.

person knows, only more accurately, then it is likely that *S* is simple-minded, and has been deceived by a magician and *mimētēs*, because of an inability to distinguish knowledge, ignorance, and *mimēsis* (598c7–d5).

Plato continues with the remark, 'Next we must examine tragedy and its leader, Homer'.[6] The point is that there are people who stand in just this relation to these poets:

2. We hear from some people that Homer and the tragedians know all the *technai*, and all things, human and divine, pertaining to excellence and evil (598d8–e2).

Plato would expect us to infer:

3. It is likely that the people making the claim of knowledge for these poets are simple-minded, and have been deceived by a magician and *mimētēs*, because of their own inability to distinguish knowledge, ignorance, and *mimēsis*.

The final conclusion Plato is aiming for is that Homer and the tragedians are nothing but *mimētai*, that they make only an image of the appearance of certain things, and hence are 'removed from truth'. But first he has to deal with the argument used by the friends of the poets, which is as follows:

4. (i) Homer and the tragedians are good poets (make poetry finely).
   (ii) A necessary condition for the ability to make (good) poetry about a subject-matter X is knowledge of X.
   (iii) Therefore, for any subject which Homer and the tragedians make poetry about, they must have knowledge of that subject (598e3–5).

Sometimes the views expressed in this little argument 4 (i)–(iii) are attributed to Plato himself,[7] despite the fact that he attacked an almost identical position in the *Ion*, and despite the fact that the overall argument works only if this is the reasoning of Plato's opponents. (He asks

---

[6] 598d7–8: This is the first explicit proposal, since the topic of '*mimēsis* as a whole' was broached (595c7), to examine poetry specifically; and note that not all poetry is included at this point.

[7] e.g. Nussbaum (1982), 84; Collingwood (1938), 49. Adam (ii. 396–7) is clear, on the other hand, that this is a view Plato is attacking, as are Halliwell (1988), 45, 121, and Osborne, 59–60. For Grube (1935, 190 n. 3), Plato agrees with 'the ordinary Greek view' that good poets have full knowledge, but 'does not agree that the so-called "good poets" like Homer have any such knowledge'. But Plato does not regard Homer as merely a 'so-called' good poet, nor does he share the 'ordinary' view he goes on to argue against!

shortly 'whether there is something in what they say, and in truth good poets do have knowledge'—only to deny that there is anything in what they say.) Furthermore, if 4 (i)–(iii) constituted Plato's own view, he would have to say that Homer is not a good poet. But he nowhere disputes Homer's claim to be a good poet, recognizes him as 'most poetic' (*poiētikōtatos*, 607a2), and expresses reluctance to criticize him (595b9–c3). (This also parallels a feature of the 'painter of craftsmen' analogy: it is if the painter 'is a *good* painter' that some people may be misled on seeing his work.)

So far, then, we have two views about the status of the poets, and Plato now offers to decide between them. He states the issue with complete precision. It is: whether the friends of the poets

have met with *mimētai* and been deceived, and on seeing their works do not perceive them to be twice removed from what is and easy to make for someone who does not know the truth—for it is appearances not real things that they make—or whether there is something in what they say, and in truth good poets do have knowledge of the things about which they seem to speak well to the many. (598e5–599a4.)

Plato does not deny 4 (i). Instead, he attacks 4 (ii) and (iii) with two counter-arguments. The first is as follows:

5.   (i) If anyone was able to produce both some real product X and images of X, then they would prefer to produce X.

    (ii) If Homer and the tragedians had knowledge enabling them to produce what they make images about, then they would not have chosen to make images about it.

    (iii) But Homer and the tragedians chose to make images or appearances, not real things.

    (iv) Therefore, Homer and the tragedians have no knowledge of the kind of real things they make poetry about (599a6–b8).

5 (iii) is Plato's own premiss.[8] It can safely be taken for granted that, *qua* poet, Homer makes appearances or images of things. The question is: what kind of ability does making them require? The argument 5 (i)–(iv) is valid. But, if 5 (iii) is uncontentious, 5 (i)—also Plato's own premiss—is not. Plato has no right to the assumption that poetry is an activity of such obviously low value. The upshot of his whole argument might be that poetry is worthless, but he should not assume that *en*

---

[8] Cf. the parenthetical remark 'for it is appearances not real things that they make' at 599a2–3.

route. So the first counter-argument against the friends of the poets is not convincing.

The second counter-argument to show that good poets do not require knowledge is a brief survey of the empirical evidence concerning the achievements of poets, mainly those of Homer.

6. (i) There is no evidence of Homer (or any poet) exercising abilities in medicine, generalship, government or education.

   (ii) Anyone who had such abilities to offer would not have been allowed by their communities to 'go about rhapsodizing' like Homer and Hesiod. (In other words, there would have been evidence of their exercising these abilities, if they had had them.)

   (iii) Therefore, the poets all lack knowledge and are mere *mimētai* (599b9–600e3).

This argument is no stronger. The supposed survey of evidence is based on (to put it mildly) too small a sample, and one could no doubt easily supply counter-instances where a poet has had some of the abilities mentioned. The second premiss is again dubious because it begs the question, attributing Plato's own low evaluation of poetry to the communities in which poets have lived.

However (especially for readers of the *Ion* and the *Gorgias*), it is not difficult to see that good poetry does not require knowledge, and all Plato needs, to show this, is one clear example where a good poet's work springs from no first-order knowledge of his subject-matter. If Homer is a good poet and lacked the knowledge in question, then such knowledge cannot be a necessary condition of successful poetic image-making. Plato appears at times to think he has shown that poets *cannot* have knowledge of what they make poetry about. What is more convincing is that they *do not need* such knowledge as a condition of making good poetry, that any knowledge a good poet were to have about *X* would be coincidental, and would not account for the goodness of his or her poetry about *X*—the reason being that good poetry is a form of good image-making, in Plato's sense, and nothing more. The poet's words conjure up an image of a sorrowing or jealous or cowardly person, of a person deciding what it is right to do or bowing before what honour dictates, and so on. Success in this enterprise can be no more—Plato alleges—than satisfying the audience, who lack knowledge of good and evil (vouchsafed, remember, only to philosophers who can grasp Forms), with a stretch of fictional behaviour they can accept as a credible portrayal. Success in the poet's enterprise does not, then, require the poet to have knowledge of good and evil either.

Plato brings home his conclusion in the way we discussed earlier: the good poet is analogous to the ignorant 'painter of craftsmen', who is nevertheless a good painter. Even if poets are not necessarily ignorant, the analogy holds. The convincing appearances of persons knowledgeable in various ways—the characters poets make—are liable to give rise to false beliefs about the poets' own capabilities. The beliefs that the poets' knowledge is compendious, and that knowledge of X is a necessary condition for making good poetry about X, can be shown to be false. Given the fact that these false beliefs are held, together with Plato's premiss 1 concerning the likely cause of such beliefs, there is a coherent case for concluding that Homer and the tragedians are *mimētai*. Their ability, in other words, is just an ability to make images of the way things of certain kinds appear, and is not essentially fed by knowledge. Homer and the tragedians (and all poets, Plato says) are in this sense 'removed from truth'.

Plato rubs salt in the wound by saying that because the poets know nothing except how to make appearances, but are thought to speak well about many topics, their activity must be one of 'enchantment' (*kēlēsis*, 601b1). It is the metre, rhythm, and harmony, or what Plato now refers to as poetry's 'musical colours' (601b2), which spellbind the audience, blinding them to the ignorance from which the poetry really stems. Strip these colours away from poems, and 'you know what they look like', says Socrates. (I think of Tolstoy's hilarious 'stripped-down' narration of Wagner's *Ring*: 'Three Norns plait a golden rope and talk about the future. They go away. Siegfried and Brünnhilda appear. Siegfried takes leave of her, gives her the ring, and goes away [etc.].')[9] What is left of poetry without its superficial means of 'enchantment' is bald and banal, like the plain faces of those who have lost their youth and with it their only attraction (601b6–7).

The second epistemological argument against mimetic poetry (601b9–602b11) is what we may call the 'user/maker' argument. This is distinct from what went before, and alleges that the *mimētēs* of any thing has neither knowledge nor true belief about it. Plato returns to a general point about *mimēsis*, illustrated by reference to another painter, who this time paints a horse's reins and bit. In contrast with the saddler and bronzesmith who would make the real reins and bit, the painter—of

---

[9] Tolstoy, 212.

course—does not understand how the reins and bit should be. But then Socrates suggests that 'not even the maker of them, the bronzesmith and saddler, understand that, but only the person who knows how to *use* these things, the rider.'[10] It is like this with everything, he continues: there are three *technai*, one which uses the thing, one which makes it, and one which imitates it. And only the user of something has knowledge of how it should be, that is, of the thing's 'excellence and fineness and rightness', also of its 'deficiency'.[11] The maker is compelled to consult the user, and thereby acquires a correct belief about the excellences and deficiencies of reins and bits, or flutes, or anything. The point is supposed to stretch to 'every artefact, creature, and activity': for everything, the criterion of its being fine, excellent, or right is what use it has (601d4–6), and only the thing's user will know what it takes to have an excellent thing of a particular kind. As a general principle this seems unlikely. Even allowing that everything has a 'use', many things do not have the kind of expert users who have superior understanding of excellences and deficiencies. The beds and tables from the earlier discussion are a case in point.[12] One even suspects that the majority of things we use have excellences and deficiencies which it takes a designer or producer to point out. I may understand why a thing is excellent *for my purposes* without knowing much about it at all. (Think of computers.) Another possible worry is that in the previous argument the *maker* of a bed could 'look to' the Form. *If* that entails knowing what makes some particular bed a good one (which is not clear), then it is odd that now the maker has only true belief.

However, the passage at least asserts a more refined charge against mimetic poetry. We might have swallowed the previous argument that Homer lacks knowledge of the various *technai* and of human excellence, but still think him and his colleagues useful for getting things right in a way which fell short of knowledge—mimetic poets may have and communicate true beliefs, for all that Plato has said. His real interest now is in the claim that mimetic artists have neither knowledge *nor true belief* about the excellences and deficiencies of what they represent.[13] Painting reveals that making the appearance of musical instruments, riding tackle, and so on, demands neither knowledge nor

---

[10] 601c11–13, translation by Halliwell (1988).

[11] *aretē, kallos, orthotēs* (601d4), *ponēria* (602a9).

[12] Halliwell's point (1988, 129). For other difficulties, see ibid. 129–31, and Annas (1981), 337.

[13] See 602a8–9 for exactly this claim.

true belief about the excellences and deficiencies of such objects. That is surely true. So will it not also be true that the mimetic poet, who makes only images of persons and actions, requires neither knowledge nor true belief about the genuine nature of excellence and deficiency? If so, Plato continues, the mimetic poet will be altogether lacking in wisdom (*sophia*, 602a11–13) concerning the things he writes about, but will not let that prevent him composing, for what he represents will be guided instead—reiterating a point from the previous argument—by 'what appears fine to the multitude who themselves know nothing' (602b1–4—cf. 601a4–9).

At the end of the 'user/maker' argument Plato's epistemological charges against mimetic poetry are complete:

We have a reasonable agreement that the mimetic practitioner knows nothing significant on the subjects of his imitation, but that *mimēsis* is a game and not a serious matter; and that those who put their hand to tragic poetry, whether in iambics or in hexameters, are all mimetic practitioners *par excellence*.[14]

The claim that Plato has made, then, is that the tragedians and Homer are practitioners of *mimēsis*, making only images of the way things appear, and that as such they lack both knowledge and true belief concerning anything they write about. They are good poets only because their use of metre, rhythm, and harmony succeeds in enchanting their audience. If their poetry has any value, it is only that of a pleasing game. Poetry itself does not have any serious ethical or educational weight. A prevailing theory that would counter this says that the ability to make good poetry must stem from knowledge of its chosen subject-matter. But this theory is false, and to accept it is to have been duped by a kind of 'magic'—the pleasure which fine poetry is capable of inducing. Plato's position is not substantially different here from what it was in the *Ion* and the *Gorgias*. The difference is that he can now claim to have developed, in the main body of the *Republic*, a positive account of what it is to achieve knowledge, and of the pursuits which do have ethical and educational weight.

The theme of 'enchantment' runs throughout the Book 10 discussion of poetry. Scholars have pointed out a number of allusions here to Gorgias' doctrine of the power of language.[15] For example, when Plato writes that the defenders of Homer have probably 'been deceived by

---

[14] 602b6–10 (Halliwell's translation).
[15] See Pohlenz, 463 ff.; Flashar, 68–72, 111; Belfiore (1983), 59 n. 32; Verdenius (1983), 30; Halliwell (1988), 128.

some magician and imitator they have met, into the opinion that he is all-wise',[16] the sentence is packed with Gorgianic words: *goētēs*, *exapatan*, *doxa*—magician, deceive, opinion. It may not be too fanciful to see a link with Gorgias in Socrates' opening announcement that he will provide an antidote to mimetic poetry. The antidote is a *pharmakon*, the word Gorgias uses when he compares the action of a speech to that of a drug.[17] Socrates' *pharmakon* is then a drug against a drug. Later he says in the same vein that we should repeat the truth about poetry to ourselves as a constant charm to ward off its spell (608a3–5). Plato apparently agrees with Gorgias that speech, when used by mimetic poetry, drugs and bewitches the soul. But whereas for Gorgias this was the only option—charming the soul and bending opinion was all that any speech could do—Plato contrasts this effect of speech with different practices (reasoning and discovering truth) that involve another *part* of the soul. Hence the other opening remark that the dangerous nature of mimetic poetry can be more clearly revealed 'now that the parts of the soul have each been separately described'.

There follow two psychological arguments against mimetic poetry, which I shall call the 'conflicting attitudes' argument (602c1–605c5) and the 'greatest charge' argument (605c6–606d7). They capitalize on earlier passages in the *Republic*, where Plato argued that each human soul has an internal structure and is not a unity. Conflicting attitudes such as desires can be explained, he claimed, as originating in distinct 'parts' or aspects of the self.[18] There is the reasoning part, with which we desire to think rationally and gain knowledge, there is the part which has appetites for things such as food and drink and sex, and there is the 'spirited' or emotional part 'with which we become angry', and which seeks honour and victory. The *Republic*'s most important single idea is that justice comes about, in the individual as much as in the city, when each of the parts which constitute the whole performs its own function, not seeking to usurp the functions of the others. In a healthy soul, the reasoning part rules, taking thought for the overall good of the individual and setting criteria for which of the appetitive desires is followed; the spirited, irascible part allies itself with the reasoning part.

---

[16] My translation of 598d2–3, *entuchōn goēti tini kai mimētēi exēpatēthē, hōste edoxen autōi passophos einai.*

[17] *Helen*, §14 (Diels–Kranz 82 B 11).

[18] The parts are introduced in Book 4 (434d–444e). Plato does not refer always to 'parts'—his terminology is vague and variable. Moline argues convincingly against equating the 'parts' with 'capacities' in modern psychology.

When the rule of the reasoning part is challenged or overthrown there occur various kinds of disorder or imbalance in the soul which lead to a more unjust and, Plato argues, an unhappier individual. Worst of all is to be governed by that part of us which has unruly and unnecessary desires—the kind which erupt in sleep, when one seeks gratification in gluttony, murder, and unchecked sexual intercourse, even with one's mother.[19]

It is notorious that Plato does not stick with these three parts of the soul in Book 10, but relies mainly on the thought that the soul has parts (or rather a part) other than the reasoning or learning part which is 'highest' and 'best' and fitted by nature to rule in us. However, there are points of continuity with the earlier discussions of the soul, which help us to understand the psychological critique of mimetic poetry. The first point is that in Plato's picture of the soul each of the 'parts' is regarded as a quasi-autonomous centre of attitudes.[20] Each 'part' is a centre of desires, beliefs, or belief-like ways of apprehending the world, and also has particular pleasures associated with it.[21] Plato can say that, when we are confronted with some state of affairs, each part of us will apprehend it and react to it independently. Part of us will desire and enjoy things which another part of us shuns and finds distressing. The second point of continuity is closely related: Plato relies on a principle enunciated in Book 4, according to which 'one thing cannot act in opposite ways or be in opposite states at the same time and in the same part of itself in relation to the same other thing'. 'If we find this happening', says Socrates, 'we shall know that we are not dealing with one thing but with several' (436b8–c1). I may, for example, desire something merely to satisfy an appetite, but also not desire it because I have learned it not to be good, or because I would be angry at the loss of

---

[19] 571b4–d4 (Book 9). The allusion to Oedipus seems to prepare the way for the critique of tragedy in Book 10. Gould makes much of this connection, and thinks that Plato's remark about 'not refraining from any kind of food' may allude to the tragic figure Thyestes, who eats his own children at a banquet (see p. xviii, 30).

[20] Moline, esp. 6–14, brings out this point. See also Annas (1981), 131, 142–6.

[21] Burnyeat's succinct remark is helpful: 'it is as mistaken to suppose the lower two parts of the soul incapable of thought or judgement as it is to deny desires and pleasures to the top part' (1976, 35 n. 22). See 580d3–581c6 (each part has its kind of pleasure and desire; each is predominantly a *lover* of something); 571c3–d4 (in sleep the 'animal' part of us autonomously exercises desires and experiences pleasure); 574d5–575a6 (ethical beliefs are overwhelmed in the individual by the beliefs of his lustful part); 442c10–d1 (an individual has *sōphrosunē* (self-control) when 'all the parts hold a common opinion that reason should rule'). See also Irwin (1977*a*), 191–2, 195; Lovibond, 36 ff.; Penner (1971), 100–3; Moline, 10–12.

esteem which having it would bring. If I seek out and take pleasure in something and at the same time wish to avoid it, then I am not, for explanatory purposes, merely one thing.[22]

So the question is: What in a human being does *mimēsis* relate to when it exercises its power? (602c4–5). *Mimēsis* is 'at third remove from the truth',[23] so it can hardly be the wisdom-loving *logistikon*, the part 'by which we learn', that *mimēsis* engages. To illustrate a split in the soul here, Plato reverts to painting, and explicitly discusses visual illusions:

The same magnitude does not appear to our sight to be the same size when we look at it from nearby or from a distance . . . And the same things seem crooked when we see them in water and straight when we see them out of it; the same things appear concave or convex because our eyes are confused by colours, and every confusion of this kind clearly exists in our soul. *Skiagraphia* relies upon this weakness in our nature and is nothing short of bewitchment [*goēteia*]; so does conjuring and other such trickery. (602c7–d4.)

That we succumb to optical illusions does not itself illustrate that the soul is split into parts. But now follows the crucial point: at the same time we are able to use measuring, counting, and weighing, which work against the tendency to believe that we see a genuinely bent stick, or a genuinely concave surface among the painted scenery, and so on. These activities are the function of the *logistikon*, the calculating or rational part of the soul (602d6–e2). The basic argument here is as follows:

1. It is impossible for the same thing to hold opposed beliefs about the same object at the same time.
2. We believe at the same time (e.g.) that we see a flat surface and that we see objects with depth.
3. Therefore, two distinct parts of us must hold these two beliefs.

Brushing aside the most obvious philosophical worry—whether this type of illusion involves false *belief*[24]—we can understand how Plato, arriving at the view that there is complexity within the soul, must

---

[22] Plato's example of Leontius being angry with himself for wanting to look at dead bodies (*Rep.* 439e7–440a6) raises an interesting question: are we considering conflicting attitudes directed towards a single object, or a conflict between, say, a desire and an aversion to that desire? (See Irwin (1977a), 191–2.) This distinction lurks under the surface of Book 10's discussion of attitudes to grief.

[23] The point reiterated at 602c1–2, just before the question of parts of the soul is addressed.

[24] Raised by Halliwell (1988), 134.

locate the propensity to error in 'one of the inferior elements in us' (603a7–8). Being duped could hardly be the function of a *better* part of us. The most obvious way to take the division in the soul here is as a split between the *logistikon* and part of the soul distinct from the *logistikon*.[25] Then the argument continues more or less as follows:

4. It is the function of the *logistikon* to correct our beliefs by applying the standards of measurement and calculation.

5. Therefore, it is the function of something other than the *logistikon* to believe that depth is perceived, even when the correct belief (that we see a flat surface) has been arrived at by measurement and calculation.

Having reached the idea that some 'inferior part of us' is in play, Socrates makes one of his rudest pronouncements about the arts, saying:

Painting, and mimetic art [*hē mimētikē*] as a whole, produces a work that is far from the truth; it consorts with a part of ourselves that is far from intelligence and is its companion and friend for no healthy or true purpose. . . . Mimetic art, being an inferior thing and having intercourse with something inferior, produces inferior offspring.[26]

The metaphor is deliberately insulting: mimetic art is nothing but a cheap prostitute with which a cheap part of the mind can have a good time. In substance these remarks are hard to reconcile with the 'non-illusionistic' interpretation I have given of *mimēsis*. The problem is this: How can Plato be in a position to conclude that all *mimēsis* appeals to an inferior part of the soul? He claims that illusionistic painting appeals to an inferior part of the soul on the grounds that it induces conflicting beliefs: optical illusions are explained in terms of two differently functioning parts of the soul, and *skiagraphia* exploits the mind's propensity to optical illusions. But this tells us nothing about *mimēsis* as a whole, unless *mimēsis* as a whole is conceived as illusionistic. Unless the earlier talk about 'an appearing bed' is taken after all to refer to an illusion, Plato's argument here cannot work. Either he has no

---

[25] The view of e.g. Adam, ii. 408, 466–7; Crombie, i. 146, and probably the majority view (although among those who hold it there is no consensus about whether it makes for coherence or not—for contrasting assessments, see Annas (1981), 338–9, and Belfiore (1983), 50–6). A minority view is that the *logistikon* itself has two contrary attitudes and is split into two parts (see Nehamas (1982), 64–6, and Murphy, 239–41, criticized by Halliwell (1988), 134).

[26] 603a10–b4. My translation, adapted from Grube's.

right to his conclusion that all *mimēsis* appeals to an inferior part of us, or his overall theory of *mimēsis* is the implausible illusion view.

It may be that Plato makes no distinction between 'appearance of X' and 'illusion of X'. This would not be surprising since his terminology for both is the same. (What we earlier translated as 'the appearance of a bed' was *phainomenē klinē*, literally 'an appearing bed'. When he talks of illusions it is *to phainomenon meizon ē elatton*, literally 'the appearing larger or smaller', or 'what appears larger and smaller'.) If *mimēsis* always makes only 'appearances', and if there is an inferior part of the soul which is prone to believe in 'appearances' that are at variance with measurement, it may look as if we need no further argument for the conclusion that *mimēsis* always appeals to the inferior part of the soul. But take images of people in mimetic drama or in an ordinary non-illusionistic painting: if we are able to gaze on these without the kind of conflict of beliefs that Plato explains by invoking the soul's different parts, then there is no direct argument yet for the conclusion that these works as such—mainstream examples of *mimēsis*—appeal to an inferior part of the soul.

We discover, however, that the attack on mimetic poetry is not really furthered by Socrates' general disparagement of *mimēsis*. For he says immediately that we must not trust the comparison with painting, but must give a separate account of mimetic poetry. The ensuing argument against mimetic poetry does not rely on the analogy with visual illusions:[27] it has nothing to do with illusions as such, and everything to do with conflicts of attitudes of a different kind. The vicissitudes of life give plenty of opportunity for 'internal dissension' within the soul (603d2–3). One's child dies—Plato's example. One feels intense grief and has the desire to lament endlessly, to abandon oneself to sorrow. But one also has the desire to act rationally, to do what is for the best. This can be used to show another split in the soul. Simple, unreflective expression of grief is one attitude towards a death. But one may take a different attitude to it, reflecting that the value of such events is never clear-cut, and that the importance of anything human is not very great (604b10–c1). Moreover, one may challenge one's own desire to indulge in grieving, and, while still having that desire, seek also, at least in public, to moderate one's grieving, subordinating it to other concerns rather than submitting to it. One has two conflicting attitudes, then,

---

[27] As emphasized by Adam, ii. 408–9, and Halliwell (1988), 136—the latter against Annas' claim (1981, 339) that the present analogy with painting is by itself supposed to 'prove' something about poetry.

towards one's own propensity for violent and prolonged expression of grief, pulled one way by rational desires for the good, another way by the grief itself.[28] By analogous reasoning to that used before, there must here be two parts of the soul. There is a part of us which calculates, deliberates,[29] and (metaphorically now) measures our behaviour.[30] Another part, which Plato calls 'irritable' and 'variegated',[31] behaves like a child crying and hugging its own wound (604c8–9) and gives in uncritically to emotion. The part which seeks to moderate grief and act always in a consistent manner, calmly seeking the best according to 'reason' and 'custom', is the familiar *logistikon*, the superior rational part which governs in a healthy soul. However we read the analogy with visual illusions, the two cases of conflict have a common feature: the desire to indulge the disorderly, childish part of us persists despite rational judgement to the contrary, just as we continue to fall prey to optical illusions however well-established our correcting beliefs may be.[32] It is this pertinent observation about two cases of conflicting attitudes which gives a solid core to the otherwise rather troubled analogy.

But now the most important question is: How can the conflict of attitudes towards grief and its manifestations be used against mimetic poetry? Plato first lights upon grief and other emotions within the represented story. The objects of poetic *mimēsis* are 'people acting voluntarily or under compulsion, and believing that as a result of these actions they have fared well or ill, also suffering and rejoicing in all this',[33] and

[28] Cf. *auto to pathos*, 604b1. *Pathos* 'covers . . . both the objective suffering and the corresponding emotion' (Halliwell (1988), 138); Gould, 32 n. 3, takes the *pathos* to be 'the pitiable event', in this following Adam, ii. 410.

[29] The best part of us engages in calculation (*logismos*, 604d5) about how to behave so as to secure the best long-term outcome. One should deliberate (*bouleuesthai*, 604c5) about how to arrange one's affairs as reason (*logos*) chooses.

[30] Plato's way of speaking of 'moderation' keeps the link with 'measuring' alive: *metriasei . . . pros lupēn*, 'he will be measured with regard to his sorrow' (603e8).

[31] *aganaktētikos, poikilos* (604e1–2, 605a5). The former epithet reminds us of the 'spirited' part of the soul from Book 4, the latter of the appetitive part (Nehamas (1982), 67). (See also Adam, ii. 406.)

[32] See Penner (1971), 100–2; Nehamas (1982), 65–6; White, 253.

[33] 603c4–7. There is probably another reference to Gorgias here—he said of poetry 'at the actions and physical sufferings of others in good fortunes and in evil fortunes, through the agency of words, the soul is wont to experience a suffering of its own' (*Helen*, §9). Plato later echoes this when he says: 'Only a few will reflect that the enjoyment will be transferred from the spectacle of another's sufferings to one's own'. 604e5–6, *allotriou . . . pathous hē mimēsis autois gignetai* also puns on the same passage of Gorgias. See Belfiore (1983), 59 n. 32.

this kind of subject-matter tends to be full of people indulging their emotions, governed by a part of themselves other than the *logistikon*. The calm, rational, good-seeking reaction to events does not lend itself to depiction and would not make for a drama pleasing to the mass audience (604e3–605a6). Guided by the aim of producing pleasure rather than that of making the spectators better, poets depict multifarious behaviour which lacks the measure and composure associated with the best part of the soul. This, Plato then suggests, strengthens and nourishes that inferior part of the soul in the spectator, setting up a civil war within us, whose end result is the destruction of the *logistikon* (605b4–5). So mimetic poetry encourages us to acquire attitudes towards our emotions, and propensities to behave in certain ways, all learned through the gratification of a pleasing image, rather than by applying thought to which way of feeling and acting is best.

Though its conclusions are broadly parallel to what we have seen elsewhere, this argument is ambitious and full of slippery assumptions. Plato assumes that dramatic portrayals of characters guided by emotion and/or appetite will be enjoyed only by a corresponding 'inferior' part of the spectator—presumably because he thinks that what we enjoy about these portrayals is feeling (or imagining that we feel) what the characters feel, and hence engaging the same part of the psyche as we see expressed by them. He also assumes that this enjoyment will change us by progressively strengthening the part that does the enjoying, and that someone who enjoys seeing a dramatic representation of some way of behaving will come to behave in that way in life outside the drama. Perhaps Plato's position is not altogether unfamiliar: many people today believe that the depiction of violence feeds an aggressive part of us that may vent itself in real actions or in a more tolerant attitude towards real violence which we witness. But Plato's assumptions may still be questioned. He regards drama as a wholly permeable medium, as if our response could not be to the dramatic representation as such and did not essentially discriminate between a real course of events and a fictional one.[34] This assumption seems naïve. However, the issue is addressed more subtly in the second psychological argument against mimetic poetry.

This second psychological argument presents Socrates' 'greatest

---

[34] See Nehamas (1988) on this (esp. 218–19), and on the modern parallel: 'the greatest part of contemporary criticisms of television depends on a moral disapproval which is identical to Plato's attack on epic and tragic poetry' (222).

charge' against it[35]—that it is powerful enough to 'corrupt' or 'impair' even good men, with very few exceptions, and so is dangerous. As basis for this charge, we must confront another psychological fact:

> When even the best of us hear Homer or some other tragedian making a *mimēsis* of one of the heroes sorrowing and stretching out a long speech of lamentation or a chorus beating their breasts you know that we enjoy it, surrender ourselves, share their feelings and earnestly praise as a good poet the one who affects us most in this way. (605c10–d5.)

However reflective we are, however governed by reason, however desirous of the good, we still cannot resist feeling a pleasure in tragic drama, which arises out of an identification with the characters' emotional situation. Danger lurks in the poet's uncanny ability to draw us into the feelings of the drama and provide a pleasure which will override whatever reflective capacities we may have. In these circumstances, regarding ourselves as safe because of the remoteness of the fictional sufferings, we are prone to indulge the very part of ourselves which, in the previous argument, we saw to be at variance with the *logistikon*:

> The part which is forcibly controlled in our private misfortunes and has been pining to weep and adequately lament, as it is by nature desirous of this, is the very part which receives satisfaction from the poets in the theatre and enjoys it. That part of ourselves which is the best by nature [the *logistikon*] . . . relaxes its watch over the wailing part because it is watching another's suffering and there is no shame involved for itself in praising and pitying another man who, in spite of his claim to goodness, grieves excessively. Moreover, there is, he thinks, a definite gain, namely pleasure, and he would not welcome being deprived of it by despising the whole drama. Only a few will reflect that the enjoyment will be transferred from the spectacle of another's sufferings to one's own, and that one who has nurtured and strengthened the part of him that feels pity at those spectacles will not find it easy to hold it in check at the time of his own misfortunes. (606a3–b8.)[36]

In feeling pity, we indulge the 'lower', 'wailing' part of ourselves because of the sheer fact that it brings pleasure to do so, and this

---

[35] Socrates says 'we have not yet made the greatest charge against it' (*ou . . . to ge megiston katēgorēkamen autēs*, 605c6). What is the 'it'?—poetry, *mimēsis*, or mimetic poetry? The pronoun *autēs* seems to refer back, but there is no clear noun (such as *poiēsis, mimēsis, mimētikē*) for it to refer to. However, 'the mimetic poet' (605b7) was the subject of the previous paragraph, and Homer and the tragic poets are the principal target of the 'greatest charge'.

[36] The translation 'the wailing part' (for *tou thrēnōdous toutou*) I owe to Belfiore (1983), 57.

indulgence spills over into our real-life attitudes. However, the most serious charge has several further sophistications. Firstly, we do not merely experience pleasure in 'sharing' the character's emotions, but we consciously assign a positive value to the having of this pleasure. And secondly, the circumstances in which we can gain this pleasure, sunk in concentration on a theatrical performance, rob us of the ability to consider whether what we are experiencing will smuggle itself into our attitudes towards our own lives, and remove our capacity to take a view about whether this is beneficial. The pleasure of mimetic poetry is so strong that it takes away the power to decide rationally whether submitting oneself to this pleasure is beneficial or not. But thirdly, Plato charges, what we grow accustomed to feeling and approving in a drama will shape our responses in ordinary life, whether we realize it or not. The same point covers comedy as well: we take a pleasure in seeing the ridiculous enacted, but run the risk, while off our guard, of becoming 'comedians in our own life', of taking indulgent pleasure in things which our better judgement would bid us take seriously as objects to be hated.[37] Along with the dispositions to pity, grief, and ridicule, mimetic poetry also 'nourishes and waters' many others which 'ought to wither' and should not gain the upper hand in the polity of the soul: many 'appetites, pleasures, and pains', including those concerned with sex and anger.[38]

Thus the greatest charge against mimetic poetry is that, willy-nilly, we receive from it a training in many real-life feelings and ethical attitudes, which works by by-passing rationality, giving pleasure to a 'lower', indulgent part of the soul, and thereby disabling the power to reflect on the question of its own influence and value.[39] The charge that Plato is naïve about *mimēsis* may be softened to some extent by this argument. He does not overlook enjoyment of the dramatic representation *per se*, nor the rational defences which can in principle prevent reactions to fiction from spilling over into real life. Instead he makes the positive claim that drama, with its apparent 'zone of pleasure divorced ... from ethical consequences',[40] encourages an emotional involvement that disarms those defences even when they are strong and confuses us as to whether we approve of the representation *per se* or

---

[37] See 606c2–9.

[38] See 606d1–7. The list includes both 'appetitive' and 'spirited' elements.

[39] Plato's psychology here has been found both 'crude' (Crombie, i. 150) and 'of considerable interest and importance' (Belfiore (1983), 61).

[40] Ferrari's phrase (1989, 138).

the type of person and action depicted. As Giovanni Ferrari puts it, 'so far from ignoring the phenomenon we know as aesthetic distance, Plato is in fact directing his attack upon it.'[41]

Aesthetic distance, then, feels like a safe distance, but it is not. Indeed, it is not even a true distance, because, while on the rational level we know the fiction for what it is and deliberately reckon on benefiting from harmless pleasure taken in it, on a less discriminating level we *feel* in an involved way emotions concerning the fictional situation. Because the psyche is split, we can be 'in' the drama, even while we claim to be appreciating it from 'outside'. The effect of this circumstance, Plato alleges, is that enjoyment is 'transferred from the spectacle of another's suffering to one's own'. It is not just that I become more prone to indulge my pitying and fearful part in real life—itself a bad effect, according to Plato. I also learn the habit of *enjoying* sufferings and later cannot resist aestheticizing my own life. So 'aesthetic distance' is doubly dangerous, for Plato. It not only lulls us into an unhealthy state of complicity with the worthless parts of our psyche, but also breaks out of its proper artistic sphere and eats into life itself. The calculating *logistikon* cannot resist because, by the time it realizes the danger, it no longer rules the soul.

The well-known 'banishment' follows. Against the claims of those who say that he educated Greece in human affairs and still can teach us how to organize our lives, and in the face of his being 'most poetic', Homer is not to be received into the model city. Why not?

Hymns to the gods and eulogies of good men are the only poetry which we can admit into our city. If you admit the Muse of sweet pleasure, whether in lyrics or epic, pleasure and pain will rule as monarchs in your city, instead of the law and that rational principle [*logos*] which is always and by all thought to be the best. (607a3–8.)

The power and comprehensiveness of his poetry make Homer seem to be an educator, but his real success is only in engendering pleasure of a certain kind. Plato is not exactly opposed to pleasure, but rather to pleasure and pain *ruling* in the place of rational truth-seeking. His reasons for excluding poetry are now complete, he says.[42]

Plato seeks in these final paragraphs to locate his attitude to poetry in a traditional 'ancient quarrel' between philosophy and poetry, and

---

[41] Ferrari (1989, 138).   [42] 'Poetry', without qualification: 607b1–3.

is at pains to spell out his motivation. It is not from 'harshness and boorishness' that he attacks poetry (though poetry has often descended to mere abuse of philosophy[43]), but, on the contrary, as a lover who has been convinced that his attachment must cease because it will bring him no good, and forces himself to stay away (607e4–608a5). He even wishes that poetry could put forward an argument for its own value, because it is hard to cast off something one has been brought up to cherish, and because if poetry really does have a positive value, we shall benefit greatly. We should listen to a defence of poetry, from any source, in a friendly spirit. But the task of any defender will be a stiff one: to show that poetry is 'not merely pleasure-giving, but beneficial to cities and to human life' (607d8–9).

Plato banishes mimetic and pleasure-giving poetry from the 'city of words', but envisages that in the real world it will continue to be there. 'We shall listen to it', he says[44]—but the important question is: With what attitude? Plato's answer is that we should sacrifice an almost irresistible pleasure for the sake of a higher principle: the truth about what is good or bad.

As long as it is not able to put up such a defence, we shall listen to it but repeat to ourselves like an incantation the argument we now put forward and be careful not to fall again into that childish and popular love. We shall go on repeating that such poetry must not be taken seriously as if it had any contact with truth and were a serious matter, but that the man who is anxious about the government of his soul must be careful when he hears it, and that what we have said about poetry must be believed. . . .

The struggle to become good or bad is important, my dear Glaucon, I said, much more important than people think, so that it is not worth being led on by honours, wealth or any office, nor indeed by poetry, to neglect justice and the rest of virtue.[45]

We must certainly consider how we might make the defence of poetry which Plato invites—a task of some difficulty which I reserve until my final chapter. But how good is the prosecution case in the first place?

---

[43] 607b6–c2 quote a few instances of such abuse, whose sources are, unfortunately, unknown.

[44] Gould (221) takes the view that this 'probably means, not "as we enjoy poetry", but "as we listen to poetry's defence of itself"'—but (whether or not the text supports Gould's idea) would not poetry's defence of itself also be poetry? Plato pointedly contrasts poetry's self-defence with a defence in prose by non-poets (607d6–9).

[45] 608a2–b8 (Grube's translation, slightly adapted).

Many writers[46] have been convinced that there is no case to answer—
on the grounds that Plato's arguments are bad, unclear, or insincere—
or else that Plato can be brought to drop the charges: we secure an
admission that in other places he explicitly or implicitly defends poetry
(or some restricted class of 'real' or 'good' poetry). Either way, *Republic* Book 10 can be made to emerge as something that a philosopher of
art does not have to worry too much about. Whether Plato's views
elsewhere mitigate the attack on poetry can be answered only when all
the evidence is in, and we still have to examine a number of works
written later than the *Republic*. But what of the idea that Book 10 itself
does not present a case worth worrying about?

One problem here is the temptation to detach the discussion of
mimetic poetry from the central themes of the *Republic*. Few would
wish to concede to Plato outright his views of knowledge and truth,
pleasure, desire, and the best constitution for the human soul, let alone
his doctrine about the manner in which philosophy can lead us to knowledge in the ethical sphere. But for all that, and for all its own doctrinal
quirks, Book 10 is the final chapter of a systematic ethics and epistemology, and if we treat it as a self-contained treatise on the arts, many
of its assumptions will seem gratuitous and baffling. We ought to be
asking whether the account given of the arts would be persuasive to
someone who accepted the *Republic*'s account of the soul and how it
acquires justice. If you believe that the *logistikon* should govern in a
healthy individual, and that nothing should be allowed to hamper it in
its quest for the eternal truth about what Good is, and that fostering
pleasures associated with the appetites and emotions will set up the rule
of something other than the *logistikon*—then when you find intelligent
people sitting in enjoyment of a representation of Medea planning the
murder of her children, should it be beyond contention that this is a
perfectly fine thing for them to do? Should it be *obvious* to Plato why
this kind of activity has a positive value? The first prerequisite for

---

[46] They protest too much: Plato is assailed with 'gross illogicality and unfairness',
'passionate, hopelessly bad arguments', 'trivial or sophistic arguments which he can not
himself have regarded as conclusive', and a position which is 'quite unacceptable' (how
dare he!)—but then again it is said that he is only 'enjoying himself by over-stating his
case', that a 'comparison with other dialogues makes it quite clear that [these sections of
the *Republic*] do not contain his considered opinion', and that we should 'construct a
nobler and more generous theory of Aesthetic Art' on his behalf. Perhaps there is a
hidden 'commendation of good art' even within Book 10 itself, or is Plato 'struggling
after a theory of aesthetics which does not find full expression before Hegel'? (Sources:
Warry, 55, 65; Annas (1981), 344; Greene, 54–5; Cross and Woozley, 281; Crombie, i.
147; Adam, ii. 393; Grube (1935), 192; Grey, 298.)

allowing the case against mimetic poetry to come to court is to realize that its issues are ones which Plato cannot avoid raising if his work is to have integrity.

The second prerequisite is to examine our own prejudices. In particular, that anachronistic and loaded concept, 'Art', should not be deployed until we have understood what Plato achieves without using it. We may be tempted to imagine teaching Plato this concept of ours, and patiently leading him out of error: 'You see, these things that you are attacking are Art. If something is Art it invariably has the following value ... and does not really need any further justification.' ('Thank you for clearing that up', he might reply—though this strategy would rebound on the champion of Art, if the concept is, as I argue later, an almost vacuous one for the purpose.) But we should first establish what, if anything, is wrong with his position as it stands. Otherwise there is little chance of a fair hearing, since 'attacking Art' appears to count as either blasphemy or blatant stupidity.

Plato's epistemological arguments, as I have interpreted them, fail to convince in points of detail: recall the implausibility of the user/maker dichotomy, the sweeping empirical claims about poets' lack of practical expertise, and the question-begging assumption that no one would want to make a *mimēsis* of something if they could make a real thing of the same kind. The psychological arguments, for their part, rely heavily on the principle that conflicting attitudes cannot stem from a unitary entity, and on a puritanical prescription[47] about which psychological reactions and modes of behaviour one should approve in oneself. Overall Plato proceeds on a naïve notion of artistic representation, as the production of 'appearing things' whose status is wholly derivative from the kind of thing they appear to be. He is sometimes under suspicion of making no distinction between appearance and illusion. He uses illustrative analogies—the painter of craftsmen and the 'bent-stick' visual illusion cases—which are over-stretched and potentially misleading, and he is, perhaps, vague as to whether his points apply to all poetry and which poetry really counts as mimetic.

Yet, despite these flaws, there is a coherent and interesting case to be heard. Firstly, what do mimetic poets characteristically do? They represent persons acting, suffering, and exhibiting varied psychological reactions to events in their lives. Their best subject-matter is provided

---

[47] 'Extreme emotional puritanism' (Halliwell (1988), 151). But if 'puritanism' means a blanket hostility to all pleasure, Plato is not guilty of it (Ferrari (1987), 99).

by characters in situations which call for a wide range of elaborately expressed emotions. If *mimēsis* is understood as the intentional production of an appearance of a thing of some kind, then clearly these poets perform *mimēsis*, and may be classed with the most usual kind of visual artist. However, in dramatic poetry, *mimēsis* has an especially potent effect on the human mind. It produces images of persons and their actions so successfully that the spectator is drawn to feel emotionally involved in the drama. Poetry uses a number of 'musical' means— rhythm, metre, and harmony—without which the narration would not be captivating to the same degree. To feel emotions along with characters who are portrayed by such poetic means affords an intense pleasure. When poetry enchants us so much that we identify with the characters and feel its powerful effect on us, we praise its producer as 'a good poet'.

It would surely be hard to deny any of this. The next part of the case asks: What value do these activities of producing and hearing mimetic poetry have? Essentially, two prevailing views are canvassed and rejected. The first says that the mimetic poet is an educator, whose ability to write finely stems from knowledge, or at least from true beliefs about human affairs in all their many aspects—the value of mimetic poetry is that we learn from it, often about weighty matters. Plato dismisses this view, and in so doing makes a good point: the theory of poetry which explains its success in terms of a compendious knowledge on the part of the poet is a foolish mistake. We must realize the difference between the ability to make a fine, pleasurable, enchanting, and (as we say) convincing artistic representation, and the ability to know or even be right about the highest truths of human existence. It is implausible to say that the two could not even coincide. But where Plato is surely right is in saying that they are distinct and may float free of each other, and that those who think otherwise are sunk in a deep error which not only renders their philosophy of poetry childish but makes any proper ethical thinking impossible.

The second view which Plato opposes locates the value of mimetic poetry in the pleasure it gives. We count this pleasure itself as a benefit. But pleasure ought not to be self-guaranteeing: we must ask why, if at all, the pleasure characteristic of mimetic poetry is good for us to have, and in order to do so we must analyse its nature. Plato suggests, with great plausibility, that we are not beings in full rational control of our reactions, and that mimetic poetry appeals to the psyche by engaging a more primitive 'wailing' part of us. While our rational defences are relaxed, because we are aware that the situation is remote, poetry, with its ability to create a convincing world in appearance and its splendid, involving 'musical colours', makes us feel emotions which in other circumstances we might choose to check as unworthy or dangerous. Once one has surrendered oneself, the emotions are hard to resist and the pleasure in feeling them is intense. To keep oneself away from such experiences is akin to separating from someone with whom one is in love. Who would maintain, after this analysis, that Plato lacks insight into the nature of mimetic poetry or understanding of why people think it is a good thing? He understands these matters well, but thinks we must tear ourselves away from pleasures if by rational argument we can recognize them as undesirable.

In broad terms what Plato has said about the nature of mimetic poetry—what it is and does—is persuasive. That, together with its roots in his ethics and epistemology, makes his prosecution worth hearing. There are some obvious points for the defence to fasten upon. Something is still missing from Plato's account of what it is to take pleasure in a representation, and we are likely to wonder whether our reactions to tragedy really spill over into our lives in such a wholesale and pernicious way. We may claim that even repeated exposure to drama does not change the whole balance of the soul, or that it does, but in a beneficial way. Or we might suppose its effect harmless enough that the value of mimetic poetry is found, after all, in a perfectly innocent pleasure. But Plato's monolithic standards for what constitutes a healthy individual and what it is to understand good and evil also stand out as targets. Plato may have some misconceptions about the arts, but let us not forget that he also pits them against a vision of attaining excellence and truth to which nothing human could ever be equal.

7

Myth, Madness, Pleasure, and Play

AFTER writing the *Republic*, Plato entered a period of development, self-criticism, and innovation.[1] What change, if any, did his views about the arts undergo? The later works have been enlisted in various ways as positive visions of the arts. For example, Iris Murdoch has said of the *Timaeus*: 'This splendidly complex mythical image of the creative process suggests and indeed demands interesting analogies with art of the mortal variety',[2] a view W. J. Verdenius appears to endorse: 'The world is called a divine work of art'.[3] But this is not really true. In the *Timaeus* the cosmos is created by the activity of a divine being; it is something fine—indeed, the finest (*kallistos*, 29a5, 92c8) of all things that have come into being. It exhibits an orderliness that can be regarded as aesthetic. But there is little justification for comparing the cosmos with art.[4] Plato's god is a *Dēmiourgos*, a craftsman or maker, not an 'artist'. He is said to make an image or visible likeness of the Forms, but, as we have seen, such terms are prevalent in Plato's metaphysics for any relation between an original and its less real derivatives. Plato has a beautiful idea about music's place in the world-order:

All audible musical sound is given us for the sake of harmony, which has motions akin to the orbits of our soul, and which, as anyone who makes intelligent use of the arts knows, is not to be used, as is commonly thought, to give irrational pleasure, but as a heaven-sent ally in reducing to order and harmony any disharmony in the revolutions within us. Rhythm, again, was given us from the same heavenly source to help us in the same way; for most of us lack measure and grace. (*Tim.* 47c7–e2.)

Why deny that the interest here is partly 'aesthetic'? But the chief ideas—that orderliness must win out over pleasure, that grace should be

---

[1] These traits are apparent in *Theaetetus* and *Parmenides*, though I do not discuss these dialogues here. The only assumption about chronology required by this chapter is that *Phaedrus, Timaeus, Sophist, Politicus, Philebus*, and *Laws* are all later than the *Republic*. In practice I treat the *Laws* as Plato's last work.

[2] Murdoch, 56.

[3] Verdenius (1949), 13. Else (1986, 60–1) has essentially the same thought.

[4] Cf. Bosanquet, 29, for the idea that beauty and not art is at stake here.

impressed on the soul—come straight out of the *Republic*; there is no evidence that Plato's position has changed.

Some may find a softening towards the 'artistic' in the fact that the *Timaeus* presents itself as a *mythical* image—a 'likely story (*muthos*)' (29d2). But again, it is unclear how much can be made of this. Firstly, it is nothing new: the *Gorgias*, the *Phaedo*, and the *Republic* all end with myths composed by Plato. Secondly, how much of Plato's motivation in using a myth is what we would call 'artistic' and how much, for example, does he regard it as a probable 'scientific' hypothesis?[5] The general question of the status of Plato's myths has been much debated. What we should ask here is whether his writing them conflicts with the treatments of poetry and the other arts we have examined so far. The strongest possible affirmative is that the myths constitute Plato's own 'defence of poetry',[6] or at least are of value to Plato and his reader in just the way that poetry would be.[7] However, even if there are consciously poetic elements in the myths, Plato has not necessarily, in writing them, undermined or modified his own critique of poetry. That would be true only if he had previously condemned all poetic writing absolutely. But we should remember that he positively wanted poets to produce myths for his young guardians, the complaint being simply that existing poets told unsuitable myths which were a bad likeness of the truth.[8] The myths he himself invents might be regarded as the kind of composition that would be allowed in the model city.

In the *Phaedo* Socrates expresses a decided attitude to his myth about the soul in the afterlife: it would be a mistake to insist on its truth, but 'that either this or something like it is true ... *is* fitting and worth risking, for one who believes that it is so—for a noble risk it is—so one should repeat such things to oneself as a spell'.[9] Socrates has just produced a series of muscular arguments for immortality, and searches for a noble enough myth to match his belief. Notice that the myth's role is presented in the same terms as that of the argument (*logos*) against mimetic poetry in the *Republic*—a charm which preserves us against corruption or error.[10] Myth may serve as 'a prolongation

[5] 'A *mythos* is a tale. Not all tales are fictions' (Vlastos (1939), 382).

[6] The claim made by Elias, 36: 'The myths are Plato's poetry, designed ... in the manner of their telling to supply the defence he has called for.'

[7] 'The essential charm of these Myths is that of Poetry generally' (Stewart, 46). (This charm is said to lie in 'its power of inducing, satisfying, and regulating what may be called Transcendental Feeling'.)

[8] See Belfiore (1985).   [9] *Phdo*. 114d2–7, translation by Gallop.

[10] Here the dangers are of lacking confidence in the soul and neglecting it in favour of the pleasures of the body (*Phdo*. 114d8–e3).

into the unknown of the lines established by philosophical argument',[11] but it is also a tool interchangeable with argument in that it shares the same goal: to attach us more securely to what we ought to believe in.

Why myth as well as argument? One answer lies in the *Republic*'s division of the soul.[12] Because each of us is a plurality, to address the *logistikon* alone would fail to persuade us. If each element within us has its own pleasures, desires, and modes of understanding, more than one treatment (charm, spell, *pharmakon*) will be required to draw the soul towards justice or make it embrace a doctrine such as that of immortality. Myth can present an attractive and worthy picture which satisfies us in ways that argument cannot. If we think of it as working on the soul in parallel with the poetry, music, story-telling, and encomium-singing which Plato wanted to retain in his ideal city, we see that Platonic myth is not at odds with his critical views about poetry. It may use poetic means, but does so in order to counteract or replace mimetic, emotion-stirring art-forms. It does not proceed in total ignorance or disregard of truth, but seeks an image complementary to the truth which has been, or might be established by argument. It does not masquerade as all-embracing expertise, or feed the childish part of us at the expense of order in the soul, or disable our moral thinking, or luxuriate in spurious paradigms of behaviour. It does not challenge philosophy, but is a part of philosophy, which will assist in guiding the whole person towards a love of truth and goodness.

Nevertheless it could be maintained that Plato is a poet, and that his doctrinal opposition to poetry is undermined by his own practice as a writer. Apart from his use of poetic images and diction, there is the fact that he constructs his works using dramatic *mimēsis*. Socrates is a character, painted in words. Plato 'hides himself' much more thoroughly than Homer,[13] and even plays self-consciously with the character who is usually his mouthpiece, making him hide among parodies, rhetorical exercises, and layers of fictional narrators. While the words of Plato's texts may proclaim that mimetic art is to be kept at bay, his methods, it might be argued, show him doing just what he attacks. This way of thinking can be challenged, however, in two principal ways. Firstly, although Plato is a poetic writer, and although he enjoys himself in a thoroughly 'literary' fashion, this need not undermine his serious

---

[11] Dodds (1959), 376.   [12] Here I follow the insight of Moline (esp. 16–19).
[13] This fact, at once obvious and neglected, is brought into relief by Kosman, esp. 73–8.

statements of philosophical doctrine. Secondly, it is a mistake to think that what he practises is the same as what he preaches against. His whole manner of writing is, possibly, calculated to woo away the 'friends of the arts' to philosophy.[14] But his ends are the discovery of truth and an insight into how to live a good life. He does not object to pursuing these goals using *mimēsis* and poetic diction, but rather to those who either neglect these goals in favour of 'artistic' aims, or mistakenly think that to produce fine poetry is already to have reached them.[15]

One dialogue which is peculiarly alive to poetry's possibilities and engages most self-consciously with issues surrounding myth, argument, and rhetoric, is the *Phaedrus*. Socrates (inspired, as he suggests, by whatever deities inhabit the banks of the Ilissus, and by the cicadas who sing overhead) composes a 'mythic hymn' to love, beauty, and the philosophical life, juxtaposing it with a more careful philosophical argument about the nature of rhetoric. The dialogue, artistic throughout in its portrayal of scene and characters, and offering great potential for self-reflexive comment on its own methods of discourse, seems to be telling us that if rhetoric needs philosophical dialectic, the reverse is also true.[16] How differently this all strikes us from the stern voice of *Republic* Book 10—no wonder that writers are prone to announce the *Phaedrus* in particular as Plato's recantation, his true defence of what he had previously attacked.[17] Yet nothing here is simple.

Let us begin with the much-quoted passage where Socrates praises the 'greatest of goods' (244a6–7) that stem from different forms of 'madness', among which a

---

[14] The idea that Plato is consciously trying to supplant an old art-form with a new is present in Nietzsche: see *The Birth of Tragedy*, sect. 14 (90). And see Nussbaum (1986), 122–35, for the idea of Plato's works as 'a theater constructed to supplant tragedy as the paradigm of ethical teaching' (129).

[15] Ferrari (1989, 145) is sensible on the *differences* between Platonic dialogue and conventional drama. See also Gould, 12.

[16] See Ferrari (1987), esp. 34, 38.

[17] Martha Nussbaum writes as follows (with my interpolated lettering): '[a] 'poetry inspired by "madness" is defended as a gift of the gods, and an invaluable educational resource. [b] Socrates presents his deepest philosophical insights in poetic language, in the form of a "likeness" ... [c] philosophy itself is said to be a form of *mania*—of "possessed", not purely rational activity ... [d] the *Phaedrus* is ... more hospitable to poetry and the poet than the *Republic*, and less certain about the distinction between poetry and philosophy' (1982, 80–1). I agree with [b] and partially with [d], but argue against [a], which is clearly a separate point. I have not space to discuss properly [c]'s claim that philosophy is held to be 'not purely rational', or the wider implications of the *Phaedrus*' moral psychology. But I find Price's comment apt: 'Plato, the arch-rationalist, is at last doing justice to unreason; but we shall not find him changing sides' (67).

kind of possession and madness [*mania*] comes from the Muses: taking a tender, virgin soul, and arousing it to a Bacchic frenzy of expression in lyric and other forms of poetry it educates succeeding generations by glorifying myriad deeds of those of the past; while the man who arrives at the doors of poetry without madness from the Muses, persuaded that expertise [*technē*] alone will make him a good poet, both he and his poetry, the poetry of the sane, are eclipsed by that of the mad, imperfect and unfulfilled.[18]

What conflicts with the *Republic*? Not the familiar idea that *technē* is insufficient for good poetry and that good poets require divine intervention: although the *Republic* does not mention inspiration, this idea is consonant with that dialogue's chief complaint that poetry is far removed from knowledge. Certainly nothing in the *Republic* requires Plato to believe that those traditionally recognized as good poets are *not* inspired. So we may assume that the belief in poetic inspiration found in the earlier dialogues has persisted, and surfaces again in the *Phaedrus*. However, two ideas do appear to clash with the *Republic*: the idea that good poetry is straightforwardly a fine thing for humanity, and the idea that it educates us through its glorification of ancient times. In the *Republic* Homer's being 'most poetic' was no indication of his true worth—virtually the opposite was the case (*Rep.* 607a1–5; cf. 387b1–6). And the elaborate set of arguments in *Republic* Book 10 is precisely aimed to repudiate those who say that Homer educated Greece. The conflict cannot be explained away by saying that Plato here means to confine admiration to the less pleasure-giving portion of poetry which is admitted in the *Republic*.[19] For how could the reader be expected to guess that poetry 'inspired by the Muses' was now meant to exclude not only Homer (about whose divine inspiration so much is made in the *Ion*) but all the pleasure-giving works traditionally considered 'most poetic' and rejected in the *Republic*?[20]

In the *Phaedrus* it is now said that good, inspired poetry is a fine thing and that Homer (no mere technician) really educates us. But is it credible that Plato should thus assert, in a rather showy rhetorical manner, the negation of a conclusion for which he had laboured through so many pages of the *Republic*? As it is the character Socrates who is made to utter both that argument and this simple statement, do we not need some hint of a reason why he has changed his mind? Perhaps we

---

[18] *Phdr.* 245a1–8. Rowe's translation, with my addition of 'alone' (the Greek is *ek technēs hikanos poiētēs esomenos*).

[19] The suggestion of Hackforth (1952), 62, with reference to *Rep.* 607a.

[20] See Tigerstedt (1969), 55.

may begin to reconcile the two passages by reflecting on their different contexts of utterance. A serious argument was called for to complete the picture of the model city. By contrast, Socrates has here arrived at a crux in a game with the speech-loving Phaedrus: having tried to beat the speech-maker Lysias in praising the cynical non-lover, he is ashamed of his dishonesty, and wishes now to praise love, but still in mythical, poetic manner. His speech praising love precisely as a form of madness can be made more palatable by a rhetorical preamble cataloguing different forms of beneficial madness. It is in place to say something celebratory, and indeed quite conventional, invoking the Muses and the 'myriad deeds' of the ancient past.[21] If its rhetorical function can be understood in this way, the passage by itself will not require Plato to have recanted anything from the argument of the *Republic*.[22] He is not necessarily using this passage to enunciate any serious doctrine of his own, or of Socrates', about the nature or value of poetry.

Elsewhere in the *Phaedrus* poetry is not especially praised. In the main body of the mythical speech on love, when Socrates places his reincarnated souls in order of importance, he assigns the soul of a poet sixth place out of nine, below gymnasts and seers, and above only craftsmen, farmers, sophists, demagogues, and tyrants. Those inclined to think that 'Plato's true voice' must be showing through in the opening praise of poetry find this low ranking rather a shock. But is it not just as likely, given what we heard in the *Republic*, the *Ion*, the *Gorgias*, even the *Symposium*, that we are nearer to the true voice here in the list of souls? What Socrates actually says is 'for the sixth place, the fitting life will be that of a poet or some other life from among those concerned with *mimēsis*' (248e1–2). Hackforth writes with supreme assurance that 'Plato must be thinking of that sort of poetical *mimēsis* which is condemned in the *Republic*; it need not, and indeed cannot, imply that every sort of *poiētikos bios* [poetic life] is so low in the scale of values', and that 'Plato cannot have in mind the inspired poetry of 245a'.[23] But why not? The *mimēsis* attacked in the *Republic* includes that of the greatest poets, and they are precisely the ones whose success

---

[21] Plato includes the opposition between *mania* and *technē* which is his own doctrine elsewhere; but it is possible to use, for rhetorical ends, expressions of what one genuinely believes. Ferrari (1987, 113–19) treats the opening praise of poetic inspiration as aimed non-ironically at the historical past, but in pointed contrast to contemporary poets.

[22] The wholly 'ironic' reading is supported by Woodruff (1982*b*), 150 n. 17: 'Plato never has Socrates speak sincerely of poetic inspiration'. See also Tigerstedt (1969), 50–3.

[23] Hackforth (1952), 84. (Hackforth accepts Tate's account of good versus bad *mimēsis* (Tate (1928)), which I criticized in Ch. 5 above.)

Plato elsewhere puts down to inspiration. Besides, if Plato had wanted to assign his sixth-ranking life to a 'bad' or 'uninspired' poet (or any other specific kind), he could easily have added a few words to accomplish that.[24]

We have to accept that this passage ranks the poetic life without qualification, and implicitly that of other artists, comparatively low in the scale of things. If we can regard the praise of poetry in the introduction to the speech as something of a preparatory rhetorical flourish, not a statement of doctrine, there is no serious inconsistency. If, on the other hand, Plato means us to take both passages in earnest, there is a jar in tone,[25] and possibly a direct contradiction—it would at least be odd to maintain that five other kinds of life surpass a life devoted to one of the 'greatest goods' (244a6–7). However, we have seen Plato elsewhere recognize the fineness of a poet's output while refusing any great value to the poet's own capacities.[26] In the *Ion* Homer's fine works are among the blessings of madness, but presumably Homer's life, being low on the scale of knowledge, was less of a life than some others. If we seek 'Plato's voice' (a perilous exercise in this dialogue especially), it is easiest to hear it in the low ranking of the poet, and in the distancing of fine poetry from *technē*.[27] We have much less reason to ascribe to him a serious belief that inspired poetry is truly educational.

The highest form of life put forward in Socrates' myth provides another opportunity for those who hope that Plato is embarked on a rehabilitation of the arts. The highest life belongs to 'a man who will become a lover of wisdom or of beauty, or devoted to the Muses [*mousikos*] and to love' (248d2–4). What to make of the contrast between this life and that of the sixth-ranking poet or mimetic practitioner? Some abandon caution at this point: 'No other meaning than

---

[24] Nussbaum (1982, 89) points out that the sixth-ranking poet 'is not said to be Muse-inspired'. True, but nor is he said to be the 'ordinary' poet who trusts in *technē* alone. See Verdenius (1962), 133; Ferrari (1987), 118 and 257 n. 11; Tigerstedt (1969), 55; Price, 65 n. 9; Burnyeat (unpublished).

[25] Ferrari (1987, 119) sees this as a calculated effect.

[26] Burnyeat (unpublished): 'He thinks, as he always thought, that the marvellous and useful pronouncements they make are no credit to them, but to the god who speaks through them.' (Cf. Rowe, 169.)

[27] Collingwood seems right that even in the *Phaedrus* 'poetry is enthusiasm or inspiration . . . but . . . *on this account* the poet comes low in the scale of souls' (1925, 167, my emphasis).

creative artist' can be given to these words.[28] But there is no good reason for this anachronistic suggestion, and Nehamas' deflating comments seem especially apt:

Taking 'musical' to refer to some sort of artist, commentators have seen Plato here distinguishing between a true artist and a mere imitator. But the *Phaedrus* has been discussing the soul and the proper relations between its parts. The best lives are lived by the most harmonious souls. . . . The 'musical', in this as well as in other contexts, is not the artist but the gentleman who patronizes the artists and knows what to take from them.[29]

In other words, the so-called 'creative artist' is, for Socrates, if anywhere, in the sixth-ranking position, and distinguished from the cultured philosopher/lover at the top. Poetry and mimetic art are distanced from the best life of the philosopher. The distancing is carried out in a very different mood from the banishment in the *Republic*, using a different image, but there is no fundamental reversal in Plato's position.

This may seem an insensitive way of reading the *Phaedrus*. Firstly, it may be thought, the power of Socrates' mythic hymn on the value of love is so great that Plato must have meant to embrace poetic madness implicitly in the same account. This is not a very convincing thought on its own. But there are signs scattered around that Socrates regards himself, in speaking the myth, as rising to poetic heights in a state of inspiration. Assuming that Plato is firmly behind what the myth says about the lover and his soul, how could he not regard with reverence the very poetic inspiration which he says produces the myth? Here, I believe, the *Phaedrus* is far from offering any simple answer. The purpose of Socrates' bouts of 'inspiration' in the dialogue has been much debated. In rather over-larded fashion he professes that his first speech is inspired by something 'divine' outside of himself (235c5–d1, 237a7–10, 238c5–d3, 241e1–5). But this is the very speech where he speaks falsely and is shamefully dishonest. If we take seriously the idea that Socrates is inspired, Plato is reinforcing the old message that inspiration is no guide to truth. On the other hand, there are reasons to regard the talk of inspiration as on the playful side—a way for Socrates

---

[28] Oates, 59. Similarly incautious claims about the *Phaedrus* are found in Beardsley, 44: 'the artist may have his own insight into the nature of ideal beauty'; and Partee (1971), 87, for whom the poet is 'only slightly inferior to the philosopher in his access to absolute knowledge'. It is hard to see how these claims could be supported.

[29] Nehamas (1982), 60. (Tate (1929, 22) is once again the opponent cited.)

to excuse the poetic diction[30] which Phaedrus is compelling him to use, and to excuse Socrates' words as not really his own. The second speech, the one which presents the wonderful myth of the philosophical lover's soul, is also expressed in 'somewhat poetic language', ostensibly again to please Phaedrus (257a3–6). But Socrates at one point describes it as the best palinode which lies within his power, suggesting that he is either not inspired, or inspired in some way 'from within'. It is unsafe simply to put Socrates on a par with a poet inspired to madness by the Muses.[31]

Looking back on his mythic speech in a more sombre mood, Socrates cites its poetic qualities as grounds for its being only an 'amusement' or 'play'. But these remarks are especially hard for the interpreter to treat straightforwardly. What degree of evasion should we read into this description of the mythic speech: 'by expressing the experience of love through some kind of simile, which allowed us perhaps to grasp some truth, though maybe also it took us in a wrong direction, and mixing together a not wholly implausible speech, we sang a playful hymn in the form of a story' (265b6–c1)? ('And it gave me great pleasure to hear it' responds Phaedrus, as if that were all that mattered.) What do we make of Socrates' view that, although some rather dry principles of philosophical method came to light,[32] 'to me it seems that the rest really was playfully done, by way of amusement (*paidiai pepaisthai*)' (265c8–9)? Is the mythic speech being dismissed as not serious at all?[33] The only trouble is that we do not know how playful Socrates is being when he says that the earlier speech was merely playful. The philosophical headway made in the myth suggests that its playful invention cannot be dismissed with total seriousness.[34] So is the myth itself 'seriously meant', and, if it is, can the idea of its being composed in mad, spontaneous inspiration be anything other than a 'playful' touch? Such questions are left hanging because the very

---

[30] 'Almost dithyrambic' and even epic diction (238d2–3, 241e1–2.).

[31] My reading here is strongly influenced by Burnyeat (unpublished) and Woodruff (1982*b*), 150 n. 17. However, Price (66–7) argues that 257a3–4, 'the best palinode of which I am capable', is compatible with Socrates' being inspired, and points out that Socrates appears to invoke external inspiration later in a more general way (262d3–6, 263d5–6).

[32] 265c9 ff. The reference is to the method of collection and division, which we shall shortly see exemplified in *Soph.*, *Pol.*, and *Phil.*

[33] Implied by Woodruff (1982*b*), 150 n. 17.

[34] For other passages where Socrates calls his own discourse playful, see 262d2, 278b7.

distinction between 'serious' and 'playful' is one which the dialogue keeps undermining.[35]

In the last part of the *Phaedrus* Plato reasserts the primacy of philosophical knowledge over both rhetoric and any form of writing that can be called poetic. Rhetoric could be scientific—it could be the genuine *technē* which it was not in the *Gorgias*[36]—if only it were preceded by dialectic, the philosophical method which establishes the truth about the just and the good, and about the nature of the human soul on which persuasion is exercised.[37] The truly knowledgeable rhetorician, who did not just tack together any old methods picked up empirically, would be a philosopher. (On the other hand, of course, dialectic would be incomplete without rhetoric: the mythic speech gave the only account of the soul which was humanly possible, in terms of a simile (246a4–6).) Plato's complaint that anything set down in writing is mute and powerless has had great influence on recent deconstructionist writings.[38] But we must remember that he uses the point to discriminate the philosopher from the mere writer, or the poet. His point is that unless one already has knowledge prior to encountering the written marks, they will remain a mere amusement, a play of signs. A person who writes without knowledge will be rightly called a poet or author of speeches, and is comparable to a rhapsode (278d8–e2, 277e5–9). These people are nothing but writers: in a wonderfully telling phrase, Plato speaks of someone who 'does not possess things of more value than the things he composed or wrote' (278d8–9). In stark contrast stands the philosopher, who

has composed these things knowing how the truth is, able to help his composition when he is challenged on its subjects, and with the capacity, when speaking in his own person, to show that what he has written is of little worth. (278c4–7.)

If Homer's words had been like that, a temporary aid or reminder which he could reject or revise as it suited him, if he had knowledge of the nature of justice and goodness and had mastered the craft of dialectic—then he would be a philosopher (278c2–d6). Philosophy is thinking, probing, questioning, with a firm scientific method, and for it

---

[35] As many authors attest: Tigerstedt (1969), 57–9; Hackforth (1952), 14; Price, 72 n. 24; Ferrari (1987), 269 n. 48; Burnyeat (unpublished).

[36] That dialogue's contrast between a *technē* and a mere knack (*tribē, empeiria*) is repeated in the same terms (*Phdr.* 260e4–5, 270b5–6).

[37] See 260e5–261a5, 262c1–3, 270e2–5, 272d4–7, 276e1–277a4.

[38] In the wake of Derrida's essay.

fine words are never enough. A poet or writer of speeches is someone who is stuck at the level of words, and will not let them go, because beyond them there is no knowledge and no method that will ever attain it. Such is the reappraisal of the relationship between philosophy and poetic writing on which Plato draws the *Phaedrus* to a close. Hardly a reprieve for Homer.

The *Phaedrus* may be said to enlarge the *Republic*'s conception of philosophy. Philosophy now is compatible with rhetorical persuasion and poetic diction. It can reach up to the border-line between playful and serious, between self-possessed and inspired. It must persuade with myths as well as analyse, it must be alive to visible beauty and the madness of love. But two words of restraint are required. The philosopher's activity must always be governed ultimately by a search for truth and excellence; the philosopher's soul must still be ruled by its best, that is to say its rational part, and this is not undone by the idea that love and inspiration are a fundamental part of the philosophical life.[39] Secondly, there is merely less of a difference between poetry and philosophy than was alleged in the *Republic*. Though philosophy legitimately embraces poetic methods, it can never abandon itself to them. Nor is there any advocacy here of a life devoted to poetry or uncritically taken up with endeavours that are primarily mimetic or pleasure-giving. A philosopher can and must use poetic means, but out-and-out poets of the kind dismissed from the *Republic* should not think themselves recalled from exile.[40]

In many of the later dialogues we find Plato still concerned with his conception of *technē*. The most likely inference from *Phaedrus* 245a is that he thinks there is a poetic *technē*. Why else would he trouble to note the opinion of some poets that *technē* is sufficient for writing well?[41] Later there is not only a *technē* of rhetoric, but a *technē* possessed by the tragedian and the musician (268c5–269a3), who would scorn those who try to write in an amateurish, haphazard way. *Technē* is not sufficient, but it is necessary. When in other dialogues Plato

[39] Plato does not, in this sense, depart from his 'rationalism'. See Price, 67; Irwin (1988), 380; Dodds (1951), 64, 218–19.

[40] As recent commentators have put it, philosophers are allowed to use 'poetic images as structures that point away from themselves' (Moravcsik (1982, 44)) towards things of true value, and to make 'a poetic and philosophic call to the philosophic life' (Ferrari (1989, 148)).

[41] Woodruff (1982*b*, 149 n. 11) believes the remark about the insufficiency of *technē* 'consistent with the idea that poets have no skills'. But surely Plato is less likely to say that poets believe *technē* sufficient, if he thinks there is no such *technē*.

exercises his new method of division (or definition by progressive classification), mimetic art is classified as a form of *technē*, as are painting, sculpture, and music. Some earlier commentators were drawn to these systematic passages in the hope of finding Plato's 'definition of art'.[42] But as I said in Chapter 2, I think that this idea should be resisted. Firstly, these passages were written late in Plato's career, using a method which he did not possess in the early and middle dialogues, so it would be dangerous to assume that his way of systematizing here will provide any definite structure for passages up to and including the *Republic*. Secondly, we must keep alive a sense of the strident oppositions between poetry and genuine *technē* in the *Ion*, *Gorgias*, and *Republic* 10. Thirdly, as we shall see, no single systematic account emerges in any case: the late passages classify the arts by dividing *technē* in a number of different ways, and rather than constituting a single theory of art, they are continuations of a number of earlier ideas, particularly from the *Republic* and *Gorgias*.

None of the arts emerges with much greater credit than it enjoyed in those dialogues. This passage from the *Politicus* (or *Statesman*) is especially trenchant:

Might we agree to name a fifth class [of *technē*] including all things concerned in decoration and painting, and everything which produces representations whether using these or using music and poetry? They are produced simply to give us pleasures, and all may justly be included under one description . . . We use the expression 'diversion' [*paignion*] . . . this is the name we can apply to all of these things. For none of them has a serious purpose; all are performed for pure amusement [*paidia*].[43]

Plato could scarcely have grouped 'the arts' together more succinctly or dashed more decisively any hope that his earlier views would be recanted. 'Amusement' is here a pejorative term—even with the playful *Phaedrus* fresh in our minds, it is hard to find this classification ironic. The same notion of mimetic art as *paidia*, amusement or play, appears in the *Sophist*: 'Could you think of a more expert or delightful form of amusement than the mimetic [*to mimētikon*]?' (*Soph.* 234b1–2). In this passage the sophist is being nailed as a mere producer of images, and to this end Plato rehearses some key thoughts of *Republic* 10.— What would you think if you met someone who understood how to produce everything from a single *technē*? That would be a fine kind of

---

[42] See above, Ch. 2, n. 1.
[43] *Pol.* 288c1–10. Translation by Skemp, slightly adapted.

amusement. The sophist, if he does this, would be in the mimetic category, which means he would be a kind of wizard or wonder-worker. The art of painting, after all, if it displays its products at a distance, can deceive the foolish among children into thinking that the artist has wide-ranging capacities, and the sophist seems to pull off a comparable trick with words.[44]—Plato holds fixed his earlier view of *mimēsis* and repeats parts of it (sometimes word for word) to create a vivid comparison with his present quarry, the sophist.[45]

The *Sophist* does offer something new, however. The method of division leads Plato to seek greater precision about the class of 'image-making' crafts. Having divided off the productive from the acquisitive crafts, he makes a distinction between the making of images (*eidōlopoiikē*) and the making of originals or real things, and then sets to work making further divisions. The making of images is itself of two kinds: the making of likenesses (*eikastikē*) and the making of phantasms or semblances (*phantastikē*). A genuine likeness is one which conforms to the original in all three dimensions and whose every part has the same colour as the original (*Soph.* 235d7–e2). To make a likeness (*eikōn*) on this definition is to make a perfect replica. 'Is not that what all mimetic artists try to do?' asks Theaetetus naïvely (235e3–4). It is not. Very often artists depart from the true proportions of the object they are depicting. Colossal sculptures and paintings, which must be seen from a limited viewpoint, are not made in true proportion, since otherwise their upper parts would look too small and their lower parts too large. So artists 'leave the truth to take care of itself' and concentrate instead on what will *appear* fine. They do not really make *likenesses* then, but something that only seems like the original—a seeming or *phantasma*. This phantasm-making variety 'is a very extensive class, in painting and in imitative art (*mimētikē*) as a whole' (236b9–c1). Having made a distinction which allows *mimēsis* to be genuine likeness-making, and which would provide an opportunity to show greater leniency towards mimetic painting or poetry, Plato shows no inclination to place any of the arts he previously attacked into this new class.[46]

---

[44] See the passage 233d9–235b6. On the rehearsal of ideas from *Rep.* here, cf. Cornford (1935), 198.

[45] The mirror-carrying wonder-worker in the *Republic* was already referred to as 'an amazing sophist' (*Rep.* 596d1).

[46] The point is more telling if we look more closely. Ostensibly the wider class to be divided into two is called *eidēlopoiikē*—the making of images. But Plato uses *mimētikē* as a direct synonym for this (235c2, d1, 236b1; see also 235e2, *mimēma*, and 235e3, *mimoumenoi*). Thus, while all of *mimētikē* is still the making of images, as it was in

Later in the *Sophist* Plato makes further subordinate divisions within image-making. The results of the whole discussion are best conveyed in diagrammatic form—see Figure 2.[47] The final set of divisions which eventually pens the sophist in his correct box is notable for its complexity. The term *mimēsis* is now reserved especially (*malista*, 267a8) for the making of visual or auditory semblances with one's own body or voice, moving back closer to the sense of *mimēsis* developed in *Republic* Book 3. (A painter, using implements and materials, could not in this sense be practising *mimēsis*.) On the other hand the wider notion of *mimētikē* is treated as synonymous with image-making in general,[48] and retains more or less the sense established in *Republic* Book 10. The divisions lower down appear to offer some hope that Plato will be more discriminating in his view of the arts. The sophist falls into the category of *doxomimētikē*: he produces his semblances only on the basis of opinion (*doxa*) and has no knowledge. On the other hand, an artist might produce a semblance of someone which was born out of genuine knowledge of them. Plato hints that a successful *mimēsis* of Theaetetus must spring from knowledge of him (267b11–12). Just after this he switches to the obvious point that some people, without having knowledge of justice or excellence, can make themselves seem to embody it. We are left wondering whether a category of artists has not been glossed over. We know that Homer and his tribe make only images of excellence—even 'semblances' rather than fully faithful replicas. But,

---

Republic 10, not all of it is the making of mere phantasms, or something far from the truth (as at *Rep.* 598b3–8). Yet Plato does not note any consequences for the mimetic arts which he discussed before. Tate (1932, 163–4) adduces the discussions of image-making in *Soph.* as support for his reading of the *Rep.* as involving 'good' and 'bad' artistic *mimēsis*. But if the evidence for that distinction in *Rep.* is wanting (see Ch. 5 above), it is better to say that Plato has moved on to a new distinction. Tate also seems to make an error when he says that the *eikastikē/phantastikē* distinction is 'virtually the same' as the distinction lower down (see Fig. 2) between *mimēsis* with knowledge and *mimēsis* without (= *doxomimētikē*). This can scarcely have been Plato's view of the matter.

[47] A further complication, omitted from Figure 2, is Plato's division of both *autopoiētikē* and *eidōlopoiikē* into human and divine making, *Sophist* 265b–266d, which can be seen as another modification of the analysis in the *Republic*. Here the idea of divine production of a Form is replaced by divine production of ordinary things in nature such as ourselves, animals, and plants. This is divine original-making (*autopoiētikē*)—a doctrine which Plato remarks as somewhat controversial (see 265c5–e6). Since images also occur naturally in the form of dreams, shadows, and so on, the category of divine image-making (*eidōlopoiikē*) needs to be added. But these changes do not affect Plato's account of human making, where the division between e.g. an original house made by the craft of building (*autopoiētikē*) and a corresponding house-picture made by painting (*eidōlopoiikē*) —'like a human dream for those awake' (266c9)—is standard and familiar.

[48] See above, n. 46.

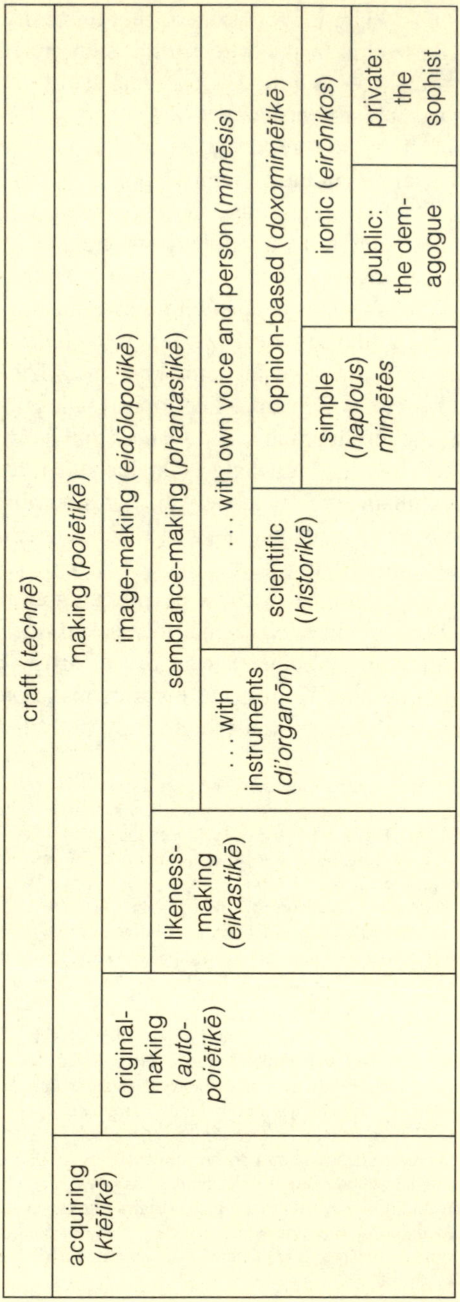

FIG. 2. *Division of* technē, Sophist *219a–c, 235b–236c, 264c–265b, 266d–268d*

according to the new conceptual scheme, a mimetic poet may make semblances of human beings and their virtues and vices, *knowing* all the while about such matters. For there is the category which Plato calls 'a sort of scientific (*historikē*) *mimēsis*' (267e2)—there is *mimēsis* with knowledge.

Now Plato does not step aside from his pursuit of the sophist to make any pronouncements about poetry. He does not even give us any example of this possible *mimēsis* with knowledge. Yet surely if he had had the *Sophist*'s divisions before him when he wrote the *Republic*, he would have found it difficult to move from classifying Homer as a mimetic artist to condemning him for lacking knowledge. The whole rhetoric of the poet's being only a maker of *eidōla*, only a *mimētēs*— would have been seen as corrupt if a practitioner of *mimēsis* can perfectly well have knowledge. Indeed, if we were to follow the hint that a *mimēsis* of Theaetetus requires knowledge of Theaetetus, Plato would lose even his firm point that fine semblances can sometimes proceed from ignorance. A similar reflection may attach to the last division which Plato makes within opinion-based *mimēsis*. Those who practise *mimēsis* without knowledge may, he says, be either sincere or insincere —'simple' or 'ironic'. While the sophist and his public counterpart, the demagogue, are manipulators fully aware of their ignorance, another kind of mimetic artist is conceivable, who in all good faith takes his mere opinions for knowledge. Such a 'simple *mimētēs*' would not be deceitful, merely in error. Even if Homer were not granted *knowledge* of human life, one might hold out at least for his sincerity.[49] Again, though, the text does not enlighten us as to who the sincere if mistaken *mimētēs* might be. If one is optimistic,[50] there is a basis here for a retraction of some of the criticisms of *mimēsis* in the *Republic*. There is also, of course, the basis for a more fine-grained *attack* on Homer and the tragic poets. But Plato favours us with neither.

A third division of the crafts in the late dialogues occurs towards the end of the *Philebus*, where they are classified according to their precision or imprecision. The ambitious topic under discussion is what should be the proper ingredients of the best human life. *Mousikē* is chief among the imprecise branches of knowledge, and Philebus, the champion of pleasure, wants to include it 'if our life is ever to be any life

---

[49] Tate (1932, 164) suggests plausibly that Plato would probably have placed Homer in the unconsciously ignorant section of *doxomimētikē*.

[50] Verdenius exemplifies the over-optimistic, when he uses *Soph.* 233e–236c as the basis for a Platonic claim about 'good art' and 'true artistic representation' (1949, 21).

at all' (*Phil.* 62c3–4). Socrates allows it in, but wrinkles his nose at the liberality of including all forms of knowledge, including even an inferior form such as music, which has been shown to be 'full of guess-work and *mimēsis*'.[51] We saw (in Chapter 2) how Plato distanced music and tragedy from the category of *technē* on the grounds that they were unprincipled and imprecise activities. In the *Philebus* a similar point is made by distinguishing superior from inferior kinds of *technē*:

Suppose . . . that one abstracted arithmetic, measurement, and weighing from all *technai*. The remnant in each case would be pretty meagre. . . . After that one would be left with guessing, by constant use and experience[52] training one's senses and then using one's capacities for estimating, which many people call *technai*—capacities that develop their power with laborious practice. . . . Music is full of this, in so far as it determines which notes are concordant on estimates born of practice rather than by measurement. Of music all flute-playing falls into this category and lyre-playing, for it involves searching by guess for the proper point on each string as it sounds.[53] Consequently there is a considerable admixture of imprecision, and little to rely on. (*Phil.* 55e1–56a7.)

Building and arithmetic are, by contrast, precise, and 'purified'; build-ing is 'more of a *technē*' than other branches of knowledge (cf. *tech-nikōteran*, 56b6). Plato treats music as the paradigm of the imprecise class (56c4–6). It is unclear how widely we are to take *mousikē* here, but his point extends to poetry, if there are (as we suggested earlier) no principles of poetic composition. So Plato is as prone as ever to demean the arts as not hospitable to *logismos*.[54] And if we add to this the *Philebus*' special treatment of 'pure' pleasures (discussed in Chapter 3), recalling that they expressly exclude the pleasures taken in tragedy, comedy, and representational painting, then this dialogue's view of the arts seems once more in line with that of the *Republic*.

Having examined the different forms of knowledge and the 'pure' and 'impure' pleasures, Socrates and Philebus are ready to assemble the components of the best of lives. Including all knowledge and *technai*, even the sloppy ones like music which are not of supreme importance,

---

[51] The reference to *mimēsis* here is unmotivated by the discussion in *Phil.* itself (cf. Gosling (1975), 133–4).

[52] *empeiriai kai tini tribēi*—the same terminology as at *Gorg.* 462c4–7, 463b4, 501a7.

[53] The translation departs from the Oxford Classical Text here, adding the reference to lyre-playing on the excellent grounds that 'few flutes have strings' (Gosling (1975), 126), and reading *phthengomenēs* for *pheromenēs* in 56a6.

[54] Already in the *Republic* Plato had stated that every true form of *technē* or know-ledge necessarily partakes of number and calculation (*logismos*) (*Rep.* 522c1–8). See also *Pol.* 283e3–284d8.

Socrates nevertheless sees no place at all for any pleasures except those that are pure. The rest, he argues, are not true pleasures, and are not even truly pleasures at all. The tiniest patch of pure white is more truly white than oceans of off-white. By analogy, the pure enjoyment got from a fleeting glimpse of a perfect geometrical figure would more truly be pleasure than the most intense delights of a protracted love-affair, or of years spent unravelling Sophocles' character-portrayals. Never mind which *feels* more pleasing—Plato does not flinch: 'any pleasure however slight and inconsiderable it may be, so long as it is purified of all distress, is pleasanter, truer and finer than any other whatever its size or quantity' (53b10–c2). The best of lives will not be devoted to pleasure, but nor will it be devoid of it. Pleasures there will be, but only those that are conducive to intelligent thought and the pursuit of the truth. In a speech put into the mouths of Intelligence and Thought, who welcome the true, purified pleasures along with those that accompany virtue, health and self-control (63d2–64a3), we hear a tone reminiscent of the *Republic*'s concern to protect the intellect from destruction. Intense and violent pleasures are rejected as a form of disruptive *mania* (63d6), wreaking havoc in the psyche. Even if we tried to 'square' the *Philebus* with the *Phaedrus*—probably we should not[55]—much of what passes for 'madness' is still, to Plato, dross to be left behind. His prime concern is that life should be ordered, controlled, not exceeding the due measure (66a6–7), and have its parts in a state of overall harmony: 'proportioned and beautiful . . . perfect and satisfying'.[56]

We can 'construct a limited aesthetic' out of the materials in the *Philebus*.[57] It is not sought among the wondrous high-art products of Plato's culture, but derived from still higher considerations concerning the orderliness and excellence of life as a whole. Existing art forms such as tragedy, comedy, and the representational visual arts would be excluded from the best life in the *Philebus*, as would the emotional kind of pleasure Plato thinks people generally take in music. The shapes, colours and sounds that are conducive to pure pleasure are austere in the extreme. 'The paintings of (for instance) Mondrian and Ben

---

[55] As Hackforth sensibly urges (1958, 99).

[56] 66b1–2, in Hackforth's translation (1958). His comment on the distinction between *metron* (measure) and *summetron* (proportion): 'in the formula of the first we are looking at each part or factor of the good life by itself . . . In the formula of the second we look at the good life as a whole, or (which is the same thing) we apprehend the relations of its parts' (138).

[57] Murdoch, 9.

Nicholson', writes Iris Murdoch 'might be thought of as meeting his requirements, [but] would I think be regarded by Plato as histrionic and dangerously sophisticated'.[58] There remains modest ornamentation of buildings and utensils, and the direct simplicity of folk art.

Plato is much concerned with pleasure also in the *Laws*. We have asked whether Plato shows any fundamentally changed attitude towards the arts in works after the *Republic*. So far the answer weighs towards the negative, but our clues have been picked up as Plato addresses the topics of love, rhetoric, sophistry, pleasure, and craft. In the *Laws* we hit on a substantial body of evidence: an extended re-examination of the arts and their role in a human community, in which Plato no longer aspires to delineate a model 'laid up in heaven', but turns to the formulation of a social structure which he thinks will actually work. Consequently, we hear far more detail than we did in the *Republic* about the cultural practices of which he approves.[59] The city of the *Laws* will make careful provision for recreation or play for all its citizens, of whatever age. There will be religious festivals at which poetic compositions are performed, choruses in which song and dance are enjoyed, competitions for solo rhapsodes, lyre-players, and *aulos*-players, training for all in lyre-playing and the reading of poetry and prose.[60]

Paidia, amusement or play, assumes an important social role. The whole of life should be spent 'at play—sacrificing, singing, dancing' (803e1–2). Play is defined as an activity giving harmless pleasure (667e5–8), but Plato is adamant that such pleasure cannot be left to develop of its own accord. Play must be regulated. Children must always play the same games, under the same rules, otherwise the city becomes unsettled. For if the young are allowed to innovate, they will become different from their parents and seek a different life (797a9–b4, 798b6–d1). In general, Plato asserts, 'change, except in something evil, is extremely dangerous' (797d9–10)—a statement which puts at its bluntest the deep cultural conservatism that repeats itself throughout this long work. Plato admires the Egyptians whose laws decree that the paintings of the present follow the same rules as the paintings of ten thousand years ago (656d1–657a2). If there are decidedly better and worse ways of painting, composing, and dancing, and these can be discovered, then it is legitimate, Plato believes, to ensure by persuasion,

---

[58] Murdoch, 16.

[59] This, I think, is the main reason why Plato appears to 'take poetry more seriously' in the *Laws*. Cf. Ferrari (1989), 107.

[60] See 653c7 ff., 764d5–e3, 809a6–813a3, 814d8–817e3, 828b7 ff.

compulsion, and the penalty of law, that the better are adhered to. Compulsion reigns everywhere in the interstices of the system: performers, critics, and teachers of the arts are under the eye of cultural directors who themselves are compelled by the state to implement fixed standards.[61] The gloom descends as we learn that the legislator must 'think up every possible device to ensure that as far as possible the entire community preserves in its songs and stories and doctrines an absolute and lifelong unanimity' (664a4–7). The arts must not be personal to any one: they are decidedly 'of the state'.

Plato insists that the right standards of evaluation for the arts are those of morality. This is partly because he sees the arts as more pervasive in life and learning than we do. No one will count as educated unless he or she is continually an active participant in a chorus, knowing how to sing and move with a sense of the order and disorder present in rhythm and *harmonia*. The educated person must be able to sing and dance well or finely (*kalōs*). But what does it mean to perform these activities well? (654b6–9). Instead of developing any aesthetic criterion, Plato sticks to the idea that 'all movements and tunes associated with spiritual or bodily excellence . . . are good (*kala*)' (655b3–5). So to sing well is to sing a song that is good (654b11–c1), and a good song is one which has the effect of making you good, or (which in the end will amount to the same thing) presents you with an accurate likeness of goodness.[62] Pleasurable recreation is thus required as a part of education which tunes the individual's sense of pleasure and displeasure (653b1–c4, 659d1–e2). It is not enough to know what good and evil are; the truly educated, those truly possessed of *aretē*, will also feel attachment or affection for the good, and distress towards its opposite.

The more specific prescriptions in the *Laws* implement these general principles about moral standards, correct models, and enforced uniformity. Thus poets must be constrained to portray brave and self-controlled men, dances must be a *mimēsis* of selected warlike and peaceful character-traits, hymns must honour gods, heroes, and departed citizens who have served the community, the rhythms and modes employed in song must match up with the words so that it is crystal-clear what they imitate, purely instrumental music should not exist, orderliness should be impressed on artistic products even at the expense

---

[61] A catalogue of compulsions and penalties is easily built up: e.g., 656c3–657b3, 660a3–8, 660e2–5, 661c5–8, 670c9–d1, 799b4–8, 800a4–b1, 801c8–d6, 804d3–6, 809e7 ff.

[62] See e.g. 655d5–656b7.

of pleasure, new styles which people happen to enjoy should be suppressed, showmanship, buffoonery, and malicious ridicule should be curtailed, each separate genre should stick to its own without any mixture, performances which arouse strong emotions should be frowned upon, tragedy should not be allowed to propose its view of life as an alternative to that enshrined in the state's practices, no poet should say that the just and good are anything but fortunate and blessed, and so on through many autumnal variations on themes first heard in the *Republic*.[63]

Plato argues that the standard for judging *mimēsis* in particular should not be pleasure.[64] When we attach value to anything, it can be because of three factors: attractiveness, correctness, or benefit.[65] If either benefit or correctness can legitimately be invoked, then pleasure cannot be the proper criterion of value. In the case of the arts of image-making, they have an attractiveness, because we take pleasure in representation; but the function of these arts is to produce likenesses, and here correctness comes into play (*Laws* 667c9–d7). 'What is equal is equal and what is proportional is proportional, and this does not depend on anyone's opinion that it is so, nor does it cease to be true if someone is displeased at the fact. Accuracy, and nothing else whatever, is the only permissible criterion' (668a1–4). To judge the fineness of visual images requires knowledge of what is being represented and how a thing of that kind ought to be (668d5–669a4). The same applies to *mousikē*, the whole of which he now declares to be mimetic and eikastic (668a6–7). His conclusion could fairly be said to apply across all the arts:

Anyone who is going to be a sensible judge of any likeness (*eikōn*)—in painting and music and every other field—should be able to assess three points: he must know first of *what* this or that likeness has been effected, second how *correctly*, and third how *well*.[66]

Hence *mimēsis* must carry with it a standard of correctness that tests value in a way that attractiveness cannot override. 'No *mimēsis* at all should be judged . . . by the criterion of the pleasure it gives' (667e10–668a1).

People usually think that 'the power of music to give pleasure to the soul is the standard by which it should be judged', but that doctrine is,

---

[63] See 660a3–8, 660e2–5, 669d5–670a3, 700a7–701b3, 797b4–c6, 800d1–6, 801e1–10, 802c4–6, 802e2–5, 812d4–e5, 814e6–815a1, 816e2–817d8.

[64] *Mimēsis* is again used in a pretty wide sense here. All of *mousikē* is image-making and representation (*eikastikē te . . . kai mimētikē*, 668a6–7), which includes the way in which rhythms and modes correspond to character-traits (see e.g. 655d5, 798d8–9).

[65] *charis, orthotēs, ōphelia* (667b5–7).

[66] 669a7–b2—strongly adapted from Saunders's translation.

we are told, intolerable and blasphemous (655c8–d3, cf. 657e1–3). It leads to an appalling relativism in which any idea of 'correctness' in music is lost and only what in fact pleases—and pleases the great mass of onlookers—can count as 'good'.[67] Against this 'theatrocracy' Plato plausibly holds that something can be liked by the majority of a community and still not be good. To maintain standards he wishes to abandon the practice of majority voting in artistic contests, and institute as judge a single person of strong character and insight who is qualified to pronounce on the value of the performances and ignore the whims of the masses. It is this judge who must like the performance: so in this sense 'pleasure is indeed a proper criterion in the arts, but not the pleasure experienced by anybody and everybody' (658e6–8). Plato is in favour of pleasure as long as it is regulated.

Plato's anti-relativism here stems from a concern with ethical standards. Although he condemns the view that one can be a sufficient judge of an art-form without specialist knowledge of it (670b8–c2) and wishes his cultural leaders, the chorus of elders, to have such expertise, he then says something curious about the author of the city's choral songs and dances: 'The author [*poiētēs*] is more or less obliged to have a knowledge of rhythm and harmony, but there is no necessity for him to be able to assess ... whether the imitation is a fine [*kalon*] one or not' (670e4–6). It is the elders, with their knowledge *of what is good*, who will guide the population towards artistic behaviour which is right from an ethical point of view. Hence the author is not looked to as the final arbiter of value: 'While we shall enlist poets and musical men, exploiting their capacity for poetry, we shan't—with rare exceptions—put our trust in their pleasures and desires.'[68] Plato wisely sees that the choice is not a straightforward one between pleasure and lack of pleasure. Someone brought up on disciplined art will not be able to take pleasure in a free-for-all, and vice versa, but it is no less *pleasure* that one feels in either case (802c6–d5). What must prevail is not the question whether pleasure is felt, but which practice makes better or worse people (802d5–6). That means taking the policy-making power away from artists themselves and putting it in the hands of a stolid censor of at least fifty years of age.[69] Pleasure will then be taken in something properly ordered,

---

[67] See 700e1–4. 'Theatrocracy' is in the same passage, 701a3.

[68] 802b6–c2, heavily adapted from Saunders's translation.

[69] 802b1–3. Plato stipulates a minimum age for the controllers or authors of artistic products also at 765a1–2, 829c7. The interlocutors of the *Laws* keep emphasizing that they are advanced in age, and that they are trying to construct the state from an old man's point of view.

which is not only aesthetically correct, but imitative of, and productive of, the good.

Plato imagines the poets of his state looking for guidance from its legislators. They can claim to be inspired, but are aware that this is not enough:

> There is an ancient story, legislator, which we poets never tire of telling and which all laymen confirm, to the effect that when a poet takes his seat on the tripod of the Muse, he cannot control his thoughts. He's like a fountain where the water is allowed to gush forth unchecked. His *technē* is that of *mimēsis*, and so he is obliged, when he represents people with contrasting characters, to contradict himself, and he doesn't know which of the opposing speeches contains the truth. But for the legislator, this is impossible: he must not let his laws say two different things on the same subject; his rule has to be 'one topic, one doctrine'. (719c1–d3.)

With this passage we come full circle. As in the *Ion*, inspiration is a condition in which one does not properly possess one's own faculties and has no hope of knowing the truth. For the first and last time Plato discusses inspiration and *mimēsis* in a single passage.[70] But he makes no new points. Because the poet's *technē* is only that of image-making (*tēs technēs ousēs mimēseōs . . .*, 719c5) he or she is necessarily distant from the truth of the matters depicted—this differs little in essence from the claim of the *Ion* or from the *Republic*'s idea that 'understanding nothing but how to imitate, the poet gives colour to certain crafts with words and phrases' (*Rep.* 601a4–6). Plato's fear of the ambiguity and diversity of viewpoint inherent in *mimēsis* is also as strong as it ever was.

There are traces of a more conventional, less hostile attitude to inspiration in the *Laws*. 'Poets as a class are divinely gifted and are inspired when they sing so that with the help of Graces and Muses they frequently hit on how things really happen' (*Laws* 682a2–5). Similarly, the old men of Plato's state may hope to have the help of a 'divine' voice in telling suitably improving stories (664d3–4). The tone is reminiscent of the claim made for poetic inspiration in the *Phaedrus*. But again Plato does not rehabilitate mimetic poetry on the grounds of its inspirational origins. The tragedians who plead to enter the city are described as 'divine men' (817a7–b1), but they are still not permitted to put on their performances, except in the unlikely event that what they

---

[70] As pointed out in Else (1986), 63.

say is the same as, or better than, the doctrines on which the city itself
is founded (817d4–8).

And here Plato's citizens make a startling announcement to their
artistic visitors:

> Most honoured guests, we are tragedians ourselves, and our tragedy is the finest
> and best we can create. At any rate, our entire state has been constructed so as
> to be a *mimēsis* of the finest and noblest life—the very thing we maintain is
> most genuinely a tragedy. So we are poets like yourselves, composing in the same
> *genre*, and your competitors as artists and actors in the finest drama, which true
> law alone has the natural power to 'produce' to perfection. (817b1–8.)

Plato steals the epithets 'tragedian' and 'poet' and the language of
dramatic production, but this should not lead us to think that *a kind of
poetry* or *a kind of art* is here given approval. What is proposed is a
displacement of tragedy. Plato truly 'sets up the philosophical life . . .
as an alternative to the life of the tragic hero, and . . . makes the writing
of philosophy an alternative to the writing of tragic drama'.[71] Since the
city of the *Laws* is, like its predecessor in the *Republic*, a city of words,
there is little difference between recommending the city's way of living
as an image of the best and finest life, and recommending in the same
terms the discourse which describes it, a fact on which Plato plays
when he recommends the *Laws*, the very text that he is writing, as the
best model to give to educators in the state. Plato's Athenian stranger
says that all the words he has uttered in the dialogue 'as it seems to me,
not without a certain inspiration from the gods' (811c8–9) are the best
possible model of what is suitable in the curriculum, and show a similarity with 'a sort of poetry' (811c9–10). This is Plato's provocative
way of saying that his own most sober thoughts must replace poetry as
an educational means. Philosophy is the greatest *mousikē*[72] only in the
sense that everything cultural or artistic must be shaped by, and subordinated to, the disciplined life of rational enquiry into truth and the
good.

[71] Halliwell (1984), 58.   [72] *Phdo.* 61a3–4.

Plato and the Philosophy of Art

WITH Plato's critique before us, it is time to consider what a 'defence of art' against it may amount to. How should we rise to the challenge of *Republic* 10, and show that poetry and all the arts are positively important, that a life without them would be not just less diverse, but genuinely diminished? In one sense to convince Plato of this is a redundant exercise. Education for him will already involve impressing graceful form and orderliness upon the soul, training us to feel pleasure through the apprehension of sights and sounds, including some fictional representations, but with a strong emphasis on good proportion, rhythm, and harmony. The community will consolidate its values in works of celebration and solemnity governed by the same considerations. So a complete life for Plato will contain music, dance, poetry, and the visual arts—perhaps more centrally than the lives of many people today—and will have its foundations in cultivating a love of things with fine form and appearance. Plato does not attack everything we call art, and would be able to find great value in many works which we prize for their formal beauty and spiritual profundity.

We cannot rest with this, however, if we recall the main lines of Plato's hostility to certain existing art forms. He is against turning dramatic enactment and fictional representation into ends pursued in their own right, and against the kind of life that is motivated by these ends. The first plank of his argument is that we acquire beliefs and other important habits of attitude-taking from *mimēsis*. Behaviour which we enact impresses itself on us: we become like the fictional characters we impersonate, acquiring tendencies not merely towards their kinds of action, but towards their gestures, inflections, moods—a whole insidious rhythm and harmony (or disharmony) that pervades our lives. Likewise, behaviour which is enacted for us in a drama influences our beliefs, desires, tolerances, and the attitudes we adopt towards our own ways of behaving. But dramatic representation activates our emotions at a level beneath our conscious control. We are sophisticated enough to make light of it, to rationalize the fiction as distant, unreal, and only for enjoyment; but in all of us there is also something unsophisticated, the childish, wailing part, the part for which images are enough, which loves to be carried along by the portrayed emotions and to indulge in them without discrimination. Plato's allegation is that devoting oneself to *mimēsis* in an unregulated way endangers two essential distinctions: between what is true and what is a plausible appearance; and between what is for the best and what is merely pleasing. The person who pursues *mimēsis* as an end in itself becomes like the 'lower' part of everyone's psyche, in not making these distinctions where it counts.

Plato holds that *mimēsis* can be allied to a concern for truth, and that it can be ethically and politically correct, that is, controlled by externally established standards to ensure that only appropriate paradigms are put forward. Then it is a powerful force for the good. But (contrary to what many of us believe) the pursuit of the good and the unregulated pursuit of *mimēsis* cannot be yoked together into a stable or satisfactory team. The pleasures of participating in *mimēsis* are so great and so deeply-rooted in the psyche that they will always be a potential danger. If *mimēsis* remains, only its subordination to the rational, ordered pursuit of truth and the good can make it acceptable. Plato's own portrayal of philosophical dialogue and his mythical word-paintings exemplify the right kind of subordination, and so do not fall foul of his critique.

Even where art is not mimetic in either of Plato's specialized senses (dramatic or representational) he argues that the same subordination is necessary. If not conscripted into the rational search for genuine moral excellence, the arts will tend to aim at pleasure. They provide shapes, sounds, colours (even 'musical colours') which gratify immensely in their own right, seemingly without engaging the issue of harm or benefit. Yet, for Plato, all such forms impress themselves deeply on the soul, contributing to its balance, or grace, or subtlety, and ultimately to the capacity to learn in ordered fashion about matters of the greatest import. Thus to leave pleasure unregulated and functioning as the single arbiter over the arts initiates a gnawing away at all the institutions by which we determine objective values. To be governed by pleasures, even the 'harmless' ones, is to lose the power to evaluate one's own preferences by any true measure, like the abhorrent 'democratic person' of the *Republic*, who deliberately allows an equal weight to any and every desire that occurs in the soul (see *Rep.* 559d–561e).

Thus, although Plato gives the arts a worthy place for reasons that are not entirely alien to us, his arguments bite hard into many traditions and assumptions of our own culture. Think of Shakespearean drama— an artistic paradigm—where we appear to have a whole world before us in image, and see deep into the heart of characters whose beliefs and attachments are irreconcilable. This is unlikely to survive Plato's test. The same will apply to a Thomas Hardy novel, a Puccini opera, or a narrative film such as *Citizen Kane* or *The Godfather*: mimetic, full of fine images and thoughts, meticulously beautiful, presenting characters, involving the emotions—but have those who enjoy these works subjected them to an inquiry about moral truth or the author's right to claim knowledge? Think also of non-mimetic, pleasure-giving displays: what is the *good* in a Rachmaninov concerto, why value a modern-day *aulos*-player such as Charlie Parker? Many of our artistic practices look vulnerable under Plato's interrogation. So, if we imagine ourselves in debate with him, something must be said.

Other elements in Plato's position may save us from having to provide a highly elaborate theory of art. We shall almost certainly wish to reject his Principle of Specialization and the wider abhorrence of diversity and experiment which it manifests. Nor are we likely to believe in the theory of Forms, the conception of ethics as a sphere of 'higher' knowledge of an eternal Good, the suppression of the emotions under the rule of the rational *logistikon*, the idea that understanding must satisfy the rigid requirements of a *technē*, or the proposition that pleasures (unless 'pure' or 'correct') are likely to distract us from what is rational and good. Take away these doctrines, and there remains an open door through which the arts may walk and take up their place in a worthwhile life. Enjoy sights and sounds for their own sake, experiment and diversify, weep over fictions, let pictures hold you captive— why not? We have no reason to think that this will prevent you from learning about moral values or make you a deluded or deficient human being. So perhaps the argument can end there: we accept that these art forms are long-standing (if frequently changing) conventions, and defend them simply as part of our way of life, as 'what we do'. As Aristophanes said:

> The graceful thing
> is not to sit
> by Socrates and talk
> and cast aside the Muse
> and all the great matter
> of the tragic art.[1]

---

[1] *Frogs* 1491–5. Translation by Levi, 179.

The arts are there, as independent cultural traditions; some may think the wisest option is simply to embrace them for what they are, and not impose an alien critique upon them. Philosophy of art can seem at best irrelevant, at worst destructive of something precious. Since in practice even aestheticians tend to keep quiet and enjoy the performance, the same stance may seem attractive as a lifelong policy. To open oneself to the power of even a few significant artworks—probably a different set in each person's case—may be more effective than any general theory of art a philosopher can devise.

It seems excessively evasive, however, to resort so soon to this retreat from philosophy—Plato shows us, if nothing else, that what we hold dear must not be exempt from all questioning. What we may usefully point out, none the less, is that Plato demands an evaluation of the arts from outside; instead of adopting the perspective of someone who lives and breathes in an artistic culture, he aspires to stand somewhere else and ask 'What is the point of that?' No doubt many aspects of human life can be made to appear strange if we pretend to abandon all participation in them. Almost anything we habitually do and which imbues our lives with significance can seem to have that significance removed if it is interrogated in a harsh enough light. This will especially be the case with something so subtly ingrained in the psyche and so definitive of culture as the arts appear to be. But we can refuse such an inquisition: the over-examined life does not reveal why it is worth living for a human being.

Is that sufficient, though? Surely there is a more positive account of the arts to be given? Some thinkable strategies are unattractive here because they are forms of capitulation to Plato. Firstly, there is the thought that art is a gratuitous but harmless enjoyment of leisure time, like breeding tropical fish: people like doing it and find it thoroughly absorbing and it gives them plenty to talk about. We can imagine someone urging that the value of art is of this kind. But to adopt this line would not be a 'reply to Plato', but an acquiescence, taking a single Platonic notion—the arts as *paidia*, a pleasing pastime, not to be taken seriously—and exaggerating it further. Secondly, in a similar category, there is art as sheer instrumentality. Art, we might say, has its place because it is socially useful, politically powerful, it trains us as good citizens or as correctly class-conscious opponents of the society we inhabit. Of course art has always had such uses, but if its very *value* is going to be of this order, then we flow once again into a Platonic stream. Nobody much likes Plato's political ends, but if we say that art's value is as a political or social means, we shall not be disagreeing with him fundamentally *about art.*

My third unattractive strategy is one which has often seemed the most promising: the view of art as the supreme route to a knowledge Plato thought reserved for philosophy—art as uncoverer of eternal Ideas, or some similar 'higher' reality. This view has a long history, starting with Plotinus and moving through Renaissance and Romantic guises, among others. At the beginning of this century a historian of literary criticism could write that 'some form of the Ideal Theory is indeed necessary to the critic: the beauty of literature is hardly accessible, except to one who is more or less a Platonist',[2] while a Plato scholar was firmly convinced that 'the famous lines of Wordsworth on King's College Chapel "They dreamt not of a perishable home,| Who thus could build," are more truly and characteristically Platonic than Plato's attack upon poetry and painting'.[3] Thinking in this way, commentators tried to save Plato from disgrace by discerning their own view of art in the Platonic writings themselves. I have argued repeatedly that such a reading is erroneous. I suspect that anyone who is not already 'more or less a Platonist' about literature will find no hints that Plato is one either. However, even if Plato did not think so, it is still at the back of our minds that the artist is concerned with uncovering truth and may have special cognitive access to something eternal and universal. So why is the Platonist reply not the most effective reply to Plato?

There are two reasons. Firstly, it requires us to believe that a realm of Forms or some 'higher reality' exists, and that the mind has some peculiar cognitive access to it. Accepting a metaphysics as extravagant as Plato's, and an epistemology as mysterious, is too high a price to pay for the benefit of correcting his view of art. Indeed, our account will be all the worse if it is required to postulate knowledge of eternal Forms solely in order to give a value to art, when so many other areas of human endeavour, from science to public administration, give us little or no call to believe in such entities. That is making art too special for its own good. Secondly, as a positive strategy it would be unappealing, since it would in effect collude in a Platonic subordination of the arts to philosophy, making them worthy only by borrowing the latter's quest for knowledge of the absolute.[4] The two reasons combine: since not even philosophy understands itself any longer as a quest for eternal

---

[2] Saintsbury, 18.   [3] Adam, ii. 393.

[4] Cf. Danto's view (1986, 16) that Hegel's *defence* of art has the effect of patronizing it as 'philosophy in one of its self-alienated forms'.

Forms, we should not force the same implausible task on the arts instead. This leaves it open that art is in some way concerned with truth, but there is no call to construe truth on the Platonic model.

Can we defend what Plato attacks by relying on the concept of art? The modern reader may look at Homer, tragedy, mimetic painting, florid dithyrambic performances, and the more adventurous musical modes, and think 'If only Plato had conceived of all these practices as *art*, he would not have objected to them!' Unfortunately, this line of thinking leads us in no clear direction. Plato lacks (as I put it) the concept of Art with a capital A, but he knows quite well what he is talking about; we, with the concept, do not. We do not know what art is, or at any rate what value we are attributing to something by calling it art. Consider first what a farrago the concept is. Even from the outset, when eighteenth-century Europeans began to place the diverse activities of poetry, painting, music, sculpture, and architecture firmly together under the common heading 'the fine arts', distinguishing them thereby both from crafts and sciences, the principle of unity was already in doubt: either they all 'imitated beautiful nature', or they aimed at pleasurable entertainment and could be dubbed the 'polite' or 'elegant arts'.[5] The latter idea was surely the more fruitful: it led to the modern elaboration of 'the aesthetic' as an identifiable area of value. Art could then be understood in terms of the aesthetic. But there have been numerous subsequent attempts to provide a definition of what makes such things art and other things not. To use the concept 'art' nowadays is to inherit salient chunks of this history, but not necessarily to possess a concept with a philosophical edge clear enough for a response to Plato.

For example, do we concentrate on the eighteenth-century ideas that art has pleasure as its object and requires a cultivated taste to appreciate? Or do we, in a more Romantic vein, locate the key element in the mental powers of the artist from which the work of art issues, dignified perhaps by the title 'genius'? Some have seen art as essentially a type of activity, in which a person crystallizes his or her emotions,[6] whereas others have seen it more as a privileged set of objects whose form moves the receptive perceiver to a certain kind of response.[7] Both of

---

[5] See Kristeller (1952). Kristeller (1951) is also required for the full narrative.

[6] I think here especially of Collingwood (1938).

[7] Merely two examples: 'There must be some one quality without which a work of art cannot exist ... Only one answer seems possible—*significant form*. ... I mean a combination of lines and colours ... that moves me aesthetically' (Bell, 87–9). 'Art is most simply and most usually defined as an attempt to create pleasing forms' (Read, 16).

these views set themselves in opposition to the 'imitation of nature' view (traditionally regarded as the oldest definition of art, and of course claiming Plato himself as ancestor), so that in the earlier part of this century it was customary to decry representation as inessential, in favour of expression or form.[8] Another familiar variable in theories of art is whether art is or should be morally significant. That pair of extremist contemporaries, Tolstoy and Oscar Wilde, tend to be invoked to point up this debate, saying on the one hand that true art must transmit sound moral feelings from person to person or be worthless, and on the other that art is 'immoral' and aims at 'emotion for the sake of emotion', having nothing to do with anything else in life.[9] Probably few agree with either extreme—but they illustrate the great diversity with which the essential point of art has been conceived. Revisionists, in the hope of making the concept begin to be clear, have been over-ruthless in ruling certain generally accepted forms as not art 'proper'. If art is 'significant form', many representational paintings need not count among the definienda. If art is 'expression of emotion', works which are calculated merely to arouse emotions such as amusement or patriotic feeling or religious awe, need not be art 'properly speaking'. If art is 'transmission of moral and religious feeling', the opposite applies. Fundamental antagonists seem curiously agreed about the general kinds of thing which fall within the range of the term 'art', which are more or less the *beaux arts* of the eighteenth century. But their stories are unhelpfully diverse.

Recognizing at last that the various things called art in modern times share no single obvious set of properties, philosophical aesthetics has moved into a new era. Writers in aesthetics fight shy of the question what gives art its value, because they no longer seriously believe that there is an elusive essence—the 'one common quality', the nature of 'art proper'—to dispute about. With such a view, no unanimous declaration about *the* value of art can be expected. A still stronger line, impressed by successive waves of the avant-garde in this century, says that the whole point about the concept of art is that it is thoroughly revisable, open-ended, allowing for radical change in practice. The activities of Duchamp and his successors down to today's conceptual, performance, and installation artists have widened the understanding of what can be art, and posed fundamental questions about how it comes

---

[8] See Collingwood (1938), 42–6; Bell, 91 ff.
[9] Tolstoy, esp. 49–54; Wilde, 380.

to be so. Some writers have resorted to institutional and historical definitions[10] where art is simply a classificatory term: that which bears a certain relation to the actual institutions of making, performing, consuming, and learning about paintings, plays, musical pieces, literature, is art; or art is simply that which intentionally bears some specifiable relation to what in the past was accepted as art. Such theories claim that the only fact about art as such is that it has been classified as art—and they do not pretend to tell us what is of value in having things so classified. Nothing prevents us asking what is important about the institutions we have, but again we may expect only a shifting answer, an answer responsive to historical change and unable to deal in essences. What institutional theories do not tell us is whether institutions which are called 'art' arise or persist *because* things of genuine value are produced or discovered within them.[11]

We can proceed, then, only if we resist our own Socratic inclination to demand a single, common characteristic in answer to the question 'What is . . .?' The concept 'art' will yield us no straightforward reply of the form 'Art is . . .' or 'The value of art is . . .'. It is a concept which can seem to stand for the perpetual possibility of change—the last thing to fit into the cities of the *Republic* or the *Laws*—or merely a permissive empty space travelling through history, to be filled variously according to circumstance: now ethical, now beautiful, now soothing, now harrowing, now truthful, now superficial, now deliberately ambivalent. Art is what Plato would call *pantodapos*: it is manifold, capable of being anything and everything. He would regard this as an admission of defeat, an acknowledgement of the very disunity he puts his finger on: people say that the arts are fine because they give pleasure, but they also say that Homer gives a profound and comprehensive education. (They also, remember, have the quite unfounded thought that to make fine poems which give pleasure qualifies you as an ethical teacher.) Now art itself proves to be fickle. Question it on its moral seriousness and it becomes full of superficial beauty; praise its charms and it pretends to be deep. Is its point to be a likeness of reality, or a study in balance and form, harmony, line, and colour? Should it please, challenge, or change us? Art begins to look worse than the person in *Republic* 3 who becomes 'double' through following two masters. Nevertheless, whatever defence we give must acknowledge the abundant

---

[10] Two much-discussed attempts are Dickie, and Levinson.
[11] Cf. Wollheim, 160 ff.

diversity of the arts, and so must reject any insistence on a monolithic answer.

Thus far our strategy is one of resistance: evasion of over-intense inquiry from outside our own way of life, and refusal of the assumption that a plurality of answers is a defeat. Resistance can be undertaken in a more radical spirit, however, resulting in what may be called an 'anti-philosophy' strategy. There is truth in the idea that Plato had to attack mimetic poetry in order to found his philosophy at all: he had to make room for the distinctions between truth and appearance, goodness and pleasure, or goodness and mere opinions of goodness. The dialectical method and what it valued could not be assimilated into a theatrocracy, so a radical break was required. Once philosophy has established an absolute dominance, it is easy for it to regard the arts as alien or puzzling. Plato is too early in the process to be other than hostile; later (the narrative is that of Danto[12]) philosophy becomes confident enough to welcome the arts as something of a domestic pet. A defender of the arts might seek to exploit this story and reverse the direction of dominance. Philosophy—at least in Plato's conception of it—may itself seem the questionable act of violence against which one must rebel in order to restore art to its proper value.

This is one aspect of the influential diagnosis given by Nietzsche in *The Birth of Tragedy*. Socrates, the archetypal philosopher, whose 'logical urge' was 'absolutely prevented from turning against itself',[13] looks at tragedy with his 'one great Cyclops eye', and of course finds 'Something rather unreasonable . . . so motley and manifold that it could not but be repugnant to a sober mind, and a dangerous tinder for sensitive and susceptible souls.'[14] The Platonic dialogue, Nietzsche writes, 'was, as it were, the barge on which the shipwrecked ancient poetry saved herself with all her children: crowded into a narrow space and timidly submitting to the single pilot, Socrates, they now sailed into a new world.'[15] If the archetypal philosopher, as he stands scrutinizing tragedy for its rational justification, is the very rock on which it is wrecked, we may conclude that the antagonism between tragedy and philosophy is genuine, and that attempts to neutralize the 'ancient quarrel' are misguided.[16]

---

[12] Danto (1986), 1–21.   [13] Nietzsche, *The Birth of Tragedy*, sect. 13 (88).
[14] Ibid., sect. 14 (89).   [15] Ibid. 90–1.
[16] Cf.: 'art, in which precisely the *lie* is sanctified and the *will to deception* has a good conscience, is much more fundamentally opposed to the ascetic ideal than is science: this was instinctively sensed by Plato, the greatest enemy of art Europe has yet produced. Plato versus Homer: that is the complete, the genuine antagonism' (*Genealogy of Morals*, iii, sect. 25 (589–90)).

In Nietzsche's story, the Socratic cultural force measures tragedy against the standard of intelligibility[17] and thereby kills it, because tragedy's excellence lies not in its appealing to the rational mind, but in a fusion of the Apollonian and the Dionysian, the radiant image and the terrifying enactment of the individual's destruction. The Apollonian image of the hero is a dream, an appearance, whose function is to amaze, and to transmute into something bearable the Dionysian glimpse into the abyss which the drama as a whole presents. Plato's suspicions are accurate, on this view: tragedy is wizardry, it trades in *Traum* and *Rausch*—dream and intoxication. The later Nietzsche builds on this opposition between philosophy and art. Art, for him, is a set of fabrications—'we possess *art* lest we *perish of the truth*'[18]—and Plato must be hostile to it because of his all-governing aspiration towards truth. Now Nietzsche urges us to resist that aspiration, which for him manifests the 'ascetic ideal', a longing 'to get away from all appearance, change, becoming, death';[19] if we become suspicious of that allegedly life-denying ideal, then we must be suspicious about our own 'will to truth': 'the value of truth must . . . be experimentally *called into question*'.[20]

It is salutary to reflect that the status and origin of the Platonic philosophical enterprise is not above suspicion. Plato's own use of *mimēsis*, myth, and poetic language suggests an awareness of the difficulty of self-justification:[21] the life devoted to rational enquiry into the truth is not defended simply by engaging in rational enquiry, but has to be pictured, acted out, and metaphorically conveyed. However, to adopt a radically anti-philosophical stance—trying to undermine Plato by posing the question 'Why is truth so important to you?'—generates at best an uneasy pluralism: we dare not regard either philosophy or the arts as a secure enough platform from which to assess the value of the other. Our questions about the arts themselves are, meanwhile, left hanging. So instead of merely refusing complicity with the Platonic mode of inquiry, we must attempt a more positive account of the arts. The emissaries charged with defending mimetic and pleasure-giving poetry arrive in the model city—what do they say? 'Philosophy as Plato conceives it is naturally antithetical to the arts, their nature and value is diverse and difficult to capture, and one should look at them only

---

[17] *Birth of Tragedy*, sect. 12 (82–4).   [18] *The Will to Power*, aphorism 822.
[19] *Genealogy*, iii, sect. 28 (598–9).   [20] Ibid., sect. 24 (589).
[21] Cf. Griswold (1988), who understands the 'ancient quarrel' as concerning the fundamental viability of philosophy itself, and finds that some of Plato's modern critics, including Nietzsche, lead us to an 'irreducible pluralism' (see esp. 152 ff.).

from within the cultural life in which they play a significant role.'—A preamble, but surely there is more? I shall propose two lines of thought, which I call the aesthetic defence and the cognitive/ethical defence.

First let us try to develop the aesthetic defence in outline. Plato's very complaints that the arts are concerned with pleasure, appearance, and play rather than fostering moral goodness or extending our knowledge, allow room for the thought that their point is, as we would say, aesthetic, and so not reducible to anything whose point is moral or cognitive. Although Plato talks of fine things which give pleasure without any other benefit, he does not envisage a proper defence of the arts emerging from this notion. To move to a convincing theory of the aesthetic, we must try to specify a kind of response, be it pleasure or satisfaction or liking, which is *sui generis*, irreducible to other forms of response, and possessing a unique value for the person who has it. Following Kant, we might suggest that this is a response to the experienced perceptual form of an object, and one which is not grounded on any desires we may have towards the object. The Kantian notion is *disinterested pleasure*, and although both 'disinterested' and 'pleasure' are terms liable to be disputed, we can take this as a model for the kind of response on which the aesthetic defence is to build. This aesthetic way of responding enables us to make a distinctive kind of judgement, which cannot be reduced to any other kind. Aesthetic judgements do not assert that an object is morally good, or that it fulfils a purpose, nor do they state a knowledge-claim about it. They are not based on the kind of expert-principle which Plato sought in the ideal *technē*. Nevertheless they have standards of correctness of their own. They do not merely assert a subjective like or dislike, but are judgements which claim validity for the whole community. The reasons I have for my judgement are also reasons for others. There can thus be standards of aesthetic value to which a whole community in principle assents.

This framework will allow us to reply to Plato on two specific points. He alleges that artists, if allowed their freedom, will attempt to instil pleasure in an audience in a wholly indiscriminate manner, pandering to whatever preferences they may have. And, secondly, he claims that the arts lack any proper autonomous measure of success or failure: they can be measured by external standards for truth or moral value, but to rely on the pleasure they give is to have no real standard of judgement—the poet must look for this to the lawgiver or philosopher. With some conception of a specifically aesthetic response we can reply to the first point by saying that the artist need not be out to cause pleasure in

an unqualified manner. Not all pleasures are aesthetic pleasures. Enjoying something which one finds aesthetically good can (in principle)
be distinguished from enjoying something for sentimental reasons, or
because it arouses acquisitiveness or sexual feeling or plays on one's
prejudices. Because of this differentiation of the aesthetic response, it
becomes possible to distinguish propagandistic, pornographic, or merely
entertaining works from those whose point is aesthetic. On the second
point we can say this: It is true that success and failure in the arts
cannot be measured by the kind of objective standard required by a
technē. An aesthetic judgement is based not on generalizable principles
of correctness, but on the particular response which an observer has.
But there are, nevertheless, genuine aesthetic standards. An aesthetic
judgement claims that the work *is* a good or bad one, going beyond a
mere report that some subjective response has occurred. The judgement
is shareable. A community can come to agree that a work is aesthetically fine or aesthetically poor, by agreeing in their aesthetic response to
it, and by discourse which fixes the reasons for that response. So although the aesthetic domain is in a sense unprincipled (*alogon pragma*),
it is not without standards. Art can have genuine standards which need
not be moral or cognitive.

There is no doubt that the aesthetic defence fills a lacuna in the
Platonic picture. Not to acknowledge that there are aesthetic responses
(however they are to be theoretically described), that some things are
valued because we can respond aesthetically to them, and that some
judgements about the arts are judgements of aesthetic value which purport
to be communal rather than merely subjective, is to miss a great deal.
To give but one example, the elaborate world of musical performance,
reception, criticism, and education would be unintelligible to someone
who did not believe in the existence of aesthetic responses, judgements,
and values.

Any renewed Platonic challenge must now be cast thus: if aesthetic
value is irreducible to moral or cognitive value, and if the point of the
arts is their providing aesthetic value—what is then so good about
having the arts in our lives? Or, to put it bluntly, what is the value of
having works with aesthetic value? This is a strange question. But it is
important to see why. For the proponent of the aesthetic defence may
be tempted by the following analysis: 'Plato, in demanding that the arts
always contribute towards making his citizens healthier and wiser and
his community more cohesive, was guilty of instrumentalism—of seeking a value for works of art only in some further end to which they

could serve as a means. Adopting the aesthetic defence against Plato means demarcating a unique and irreducible species of value. If we then go on to ask for the value of having works with aesthetic value, we lapse back into instrumentalism and fail to give an account in which aesthetic value is autonomous.'

However, the opposition between autonomous and instrumental value here is too simple. A distinction can be drawn between *evaluations* of works of art and *apologies* for them.[22] The former are answers to the question 'What makes this a good painting or tragedy?' and the latter to the question 'What makes art a good thing to have in one's life?' If we assume that answers to the first kind of question will be evaluations in aesthetic terms, then since presumably nobody wants an apology for bad art, the second question will indeed amount to the following: 'What makes art which is aesthetically good a good thing to have in one's life?' The question is strange not because it misconceives aesthetic value as a form of instrumental good, but because it strays again into scrutinizing aesthetic practices from an external, alienated standpoint. By contrast, fully to imagine the absence of the aesthetic from someone's life would give sufficient insight into that life's impoverishment, and render the question practically unaskable. A total non-aesthete, who never listens with pleasure to any music, never reads a poem or novel, never visits an art gallery, never produces anything 'artistic', and takes no interest whatever in the pleasing appearance, order, or structure of any part of the world he or she experiences, would arguably be deficient in one of the characteristic aspects of human life. It only remains to point out that the most frequent and fruitful exposure to the aesthetic is gained by participating in the many traditions of poetry, drama, music, and painting which already exist. They are one obvious way to remain in touch with one of the characteristic aspects of one's own humanity.

The proponent of the aesthetic defence is thus drawn into the vertiginous feat of arguing that art, as the prime arena of communally aesthetic value, is an absolute good in itself. Kant's thinking here is suggestive but difficult: making judgements of beauty supposedly exemplifies a supersensible harmony between our fundamental cognitive abilities and nature, and, by manifesting our freedom in the phenomenal realm enables us to reconcile our own place in nature with our status as rational

[22] The point and the terminology are taken from Diffey, 165 ff.

moral agents.[23] This has first to be shown to apply to art in particular, and then to be rendered intelligible. The same applies to Hegel's view that the value of art is explained by a fundamental human need for self-realization ('man's rational impulse to exalt the inner and outer world into a spiritual consciousness for himself, as an object in which he recognizes his own self'[24]). Is this difficult notion a true reflection of reality, and to what extent is the general need for self-realization one whose fulfilment requires art as such? We may look to the idea that art presents in sensuous terms the reconciled opposition of particular and universal,[25] or to Schiller's notion of the aesthetic as the site of freedom or play which unifies the sensuous and the intellectual and realizes the human potential to the fullest.[26] On the way to making such thoughts perspicuous, we shall have discovered that the task before us is not that of clearing up some quirky blind spot of Plato's, local to what we call aesthetics. Only by confronting Plato's notion of human excellence on the grandest scale can the aesthetic defence hope to succeed.

The aesthetic defence, again calling on Kant and Schiller,[27] also has on its side the argument that a culture depends on the aesthetic, and that our being fully human depends on our belonging to a culture: only if we can aim to converge in judgements that are made in a realm of freedom are we fully human. If this is true, then even though particular individuals may turn their backs on the aesthetic to a greater or lesser extent, their other ethical, social or cognitive ends depend on their living in a culture in which artworks are produced and evaluated aesthetically. It will, again, be quite difficult to determine whether this elevated claim is one we should believe. If it is, the aspirations embodied in Plato's own thinking may be owed to his belonging to the culture of tragedians, rhapsodes, and the lovers of sights and sounds—and that would be an impressive point to be able to make in the debate we are imagining.

Suppose that we have a convincing story about the fundamental importance of the aesthetic value of art, what would it have achieved against Plato? He might (let us imagine) concede that aesthetic evaluation is autonomous, and agree that engaging in some activities of aesthetic value is a species of absolute good for any human being, and that only in an aesthetically enriched culture can other human endeavours be

---

[23] Cf. Savile, 103.   [24] Hegel, 36.
[25] Ibid. 59–61.   [26] Schiller, esp. 94–109.
[27] Here I am assisted especially by Hampshire (1960) and (1989).

realized. He would not need to change his views radically: recall the love of beauty, order, and harmony which he would inculcate into his citizens in *Republic* 3 and *Laws*.[28] But his critique is not necessarily silenced. His line will still be that the aesthetic cannot be allowed to dominate in a healthy life, whether individual or communal. The aesthetic, he will say, cannot be that around which our lives are structured, and it cannot alone set the standard for art. Truth and the good, once our culture can grasp them as distinct ends, are more important. So although we will now have reason to recognize the aesthetic as a self-contained value, and reason not to expunge it from our ideal community (as Plato never really wished to do anyway), we will still have reason to regulate its particular instances in the light of our other values. And particular instances were always the point: if tragic poetry or some other form of *mimēsis*—irrespective of its being a fine instance of aesthetic value—is, by its nature and by its characteristic psychological effects, detrimental to the search for truth and the good, then we should still be concerned not to let it rule in our souls, but ward off its powerful spell with argumentative remedies. Plato's arguments for this appraisal of tragedy still stand awaiting a reply.

The total non-aesthete might be ethically and cognitively impoverished. Lacking all propensity to respond disinterestedly to pattern or order, he or she would arguably have a diminished capacity to understand his or her fellow humans, or indeed the world: he or she might be less able to reason, to do science, history, mathematics, or philosophy. Plato could concur: he never advocated or even conceived of a total non-aesthete. But how clear is it that these other endeavours would be hampered by one's failing to confront beautiful *works of art*? The claim that someone involved with aesthetically valuable art would be *morally* better than someone not so involved is questionable. It could turn out to be an empirical truth that those with their aesthetic sensibilities directed specifically towards the arts tend to have a better all-round responsiveness in human or ethical terms. (It could turn out not to be the case.) But if so, we should not know how to explain the correlation, since it is possible that having some generalized human responsiveness disposes one well towards the arts, and not the other way round.[29] Concern with the aesthetic in art might be a symptom of being morally sensitive; Kant thought something parallel when he wrote that an interest

[28] Halliwell (1991, 330) suggests that in *Rep.* 3 (400c–402a, 403c) Plato has in effect accepted something congenial to Schiller's notion of an aesthetic culture.

[29] Also a point made by Diffey, 114.

in contemplating natural beauty 'is at least indicative of a temper of mind favourable to the moral feeling' and requires that someone 'has *previously* set his interest deep in the foundations of the morally good'.[30] (Note, incidentally, that here interest in *art* is excluded from such a connection with moral goodness.) We might suggest that the art-free life must lack something in understanding of human psychology, and that art is of value in helping us to know the nature of courage and justice, or in understanding the intricacies of the ways people think and feel. But would art make this contribution in virtue of having *aesthetic* value? We have explained the aesthetic in a more or less Kantian way, in terms of non-moral, non-cognitive judgements that are founded on disinterested responses to objects perceived. Aesthetic value is something like beauty, on this account. But, although the two may often be found together, it is not clear that a concern for beauty in art improves one's understanding of human behaviour.

Thus we are led to the second line of defence, which I have called the cognitive/ethical defence. It will not be concerned to dispute whether the value of tragedy and its kindred arts is aesthetic. It need make no use of that concept at all, as (on a plausible reading[31]) Aristotle does not in his reply to Plato. Instead, it undertakes to show by a direct route that tragedy and other fictional representations of human behaviour make a fundamental contribution to our ethical life and to our knowledge. What kind of knowledge, though? It seems unlikely that there is class of true propositions which only artworks can put us in touch with—artworks could be at best the most effective means of coming to know them. But there is a further difficulty here: if we ask *which* propositional truths a particular drama or novel teaches us, answers tend to be either banal or implausible.[32] Even supposing that we manage to cull some useful piece of wisdom (such as, perhaps: 'When retiring as head of a family or government, it is unwise to yield your authority too early to whoever puts up the best show of affection')—we ought to wonder whether the dramatist could not have conveyed that proposition in less labour-intensive fashion. The conclusion should be, not that there is nothing

[30] Kant, §42, 157, 160 (my emphasis).

[31] Well presented by Halliwell (1991), 339–42.

[32] As Stolnitz illustrates, by considering *Pride and Prejudice* (with its 'psychological truth': 'Stubborn pride and ignorant prejudice keep attractive people apart') and *Crime and Punishment* ('Punishment for a crime frightens a criminal less than we think because the criminal himself demands it'). These are probably truths, in that what they describe happens, but the value of the respective works does not lie in their putting us in mind of these propositions.

to learn from drama, but that not all learning is the mastery of true propositions.

The 'knowledge' that we may more plausibly claim for tragedy is an understanding of human behaviour through imagining possible human behaviour and being impressed by its emotional significance. This is a kind of understanding whose attainment is an ethical gain, and part of what being a good person is. So the point is not that tragedy has two values, one cognitive and one ethical: rather that it enables us to attain a kind of knowledge in a way which is ethically valuable.[33] We are required to disagree with Plato over the nature of ethical understanding, affirming that we learn best when allowed to explore ideas of jealousy, lust, stupidity, confusion, and despair as they affect passages of people's lives, not when kept on a restricted diet of artificially rational paradigms. Secondly, we must disagree with Plato over the nature of *mimēsis*. In a nutshell, the claim will be that fictional representation involves the creative use of the imagination, that the imagination, by showing us how it *would feel* to be a person in multifarious circumstances which we will never in fact occupy, helps us eventually learn how *to feel*,[34] and that learning to feel in just this way is an irreplaceably valuable part of ethical development.

For all his imaginative writing, Plato does not do justice to imagination's role in the human make-up.[35] Yet how basic it is to entertain a thought about how the world is not but could be—to compose an intelligible picture or story about intelligible people who do not exist. *Not* to imagine would be exceedingly strange for a member of the human species. Aristotle corrects Plato in devastating manner with the simple utterance that 'man differs from the other animals in being most mimetic'; imaginative production is something *kata phusin*—in accordance with our nature.[36] That we are all natural and skilful imaginers is, however, something Plato appears, or affects, to overlook. Again and again we have seen him not grasping the point of representation in the arts: a painter makes a bed which strangely happens not to be a real one,

---

[33] I have found Nussbaum (1990) suggestive here (see esp. 23–9).

[34] I am influenced here by Scruton (unpublished): 'We learn by example what to feel, and what not to feel. Involved in this process incidentally, is another kind of knowledge: knowing what it's like. Shakespeare's *King Lear* teaches us what it's like to undergo the extremes of ingratitude, by enabling us to *imagine* what it's like. What we acquire is not propositional knowledge of some "subjective" fact, but familiarity with a state of mind.'

[35] His critique of drama seems indeed to be 'rooted ultimately in a fear of imagination'—Halliwell (1992), 69.

[36] *Poetics* 1448b4–20.

Homer mysteriously tries to 'persuade us' that he is someone else, audiences and actors weep and shudder at distressing events which they perversely enjoy. Why not say that they are using their imaginations and making or enjoying a representation? As Aristotle's other well-known dictum has it, 'objects which in themselves we view with pain, we delight to contemplate when reproduced in a likeness with minute fidelity'.[37] Plato recognizes that people tend to think pleasure in *mimēsis* is a good thing for its own sake. But he denies the possibility that we both benefit from experiencing the contents of our imaginings and at the same time happily recognize them as only imaginings.

Plato thinks that taking pleasure in representations of actions is never clearly distinguished from approving actions of the same kind in real life. So poets who aim to benefit their audience ought not to write about baseness, excessive grief, or unpunished injustice, because these will simply escape beyond the confines of the image. What we enact and see enacted we will become ourselves; whether the enactment is in or out of a story makes, for him, no difference. It is as if drama has no containing skin around it, so that despicable things leak out and are soaked up by the defenceless psyche.[38] The truth, however, is that imaginings interact in a much more subtle way with other thoughts and emotions. We exercise our full understanding on Thebes, Oedipus, and Jocasta. Although they are only an image, our thinking about them is no less systematic or fruitful than our thought about the real world. In this way imagination is not a wholly separate capacity from those of ordinary belief-formation and reasoning, which is why there is no barrier to our learning about real actions, motivations, and conflicts through watching a drama. But on the other hand, we are not always at the mercy of whatever appears before us. We can—effortlessly, *kata phusin*—approve the representation without simply approving or copying what is represented. That is the first massive achievement of Aristotle's theory as a reply to Plato.

The second is the hint that tragedy's engagement with our *emotions* is both an essential and a beneficial feature of it. It is difficult to know exactly what to say here. Somehow our feelings for the situation of

[37] Ibid. 1448b10–11.

[38] Danto (1987, 4) uses the same metaphor for the opposite view from Plato's: 'The concept of art interposes between life and literature a very tough membrane, which insures the incapacity of the artist to inflict moral harm so long as it is recognized that what he is doing is art.' I owe this quote to Nehamas (1991), 350. See also Nehamas (1988) on the 'transparency' of representation in Plato.

Oedipus are not cordoned off from the rest of our feelings; they are not mere pretence, for 'fearing' and 'pitying' here really can—as Plato over-insists—affect our attitudes in ordinary life. And yet these are not straightforwardly real emotions, since they cannot initiate action towards Oedipus, and are not unbearably painful to experience. We are on the edge between safety and vulnerability here: safe because we handle *mimēsis* with ease, vulnerable because an understanding of the scene's bearing on our own emotional life is forced upon us. Plato would see this doubleness as bearing out his worst fears about tragedy, but the cognitive/ethical defence seeks to transform this very feature into a positive one.

On this account artistic *mimēsis* is continuous both with the life in which we act and suffer, and with the educative aims of other forms of discourse—the sermon, the philosophical treatise. It presents us with an opportunity to learn how to live, what to seek, what comforts not to expect. It differs, however, both from ordinary life and from these other forms of discourse. As against life, it offers both objectivity, and intimacy without predicament. Flint Schier is helpful here:

In real life close knowledge entails intimacy, but intimacy entails predicament; to be inward with someone's feelings usually entails that we begin to care about those feelings . . . but then when we care about them, we naturally want to do something. . . . In the theatre, we can achieve an intimate knowledge of characters without really finding ourselves sharing their predicament. . . . But there is a second advantage for art over reality which I think is even more important than the disinterest of the spectator: that is the disinterest or objectivity of the artist. Obviously, if someone is in the throes of agony they will not so conduct themselves that we will be provided with a maximally acute sense of their distress. Real distress is often much less powerfully expressed than theatrical distress—partly because people rarely want to stare their own situation in the face. . . . The great artist can escape this restriction; and therefore his characters will speak and act in a much more revealing way than would an actual victim of disaster.[39]

We may add that actual victims tend either to perish or to carry away with them some kind of impairment. To survive as an enriched spectator in a real version of Lear's Britain would be inhuman.

As against life, then, tragic *mimēsis* offers us clear vision and freedom to think. As against the sermon or philosophical treatise, it offers us not generalities but the image of humanity in the particularity of

[39] Schier (1989), 24.

action. And Plato was right: part of us must submit to the image with a trusting, uncritical sensitivity to the feelings it portrays—this submission helps us begin to learn what it feels like to suffer at the very limits of endurance, to inflict suffering, or to allow it to happen. In that worn-out metaphor, drama 'brings home' the truth. It feeds into our understanding of our own lives at a level which mere argument and exhortation cannot penetrate. This, in outline, is the cognitive/ethical defence. Its strength is that it combines an end—learning how to live a better life—that Plato could not fault, with an account of why *mimēsis* is a uniquely valuable means to it. Neither philosophy nor the events of life itself could replace the satisfying and natural combination of emotional involvement and dispassionate contemplation that *mimēsis* of human action has to offer.

We have now prepared two different replies for our defenders of the arts. Art has aesthetic value, which is an important human achievement irreducible to other values. Art presents to us images from which we learn in a unique way about ethical matters. Both seem true. Aesthetic value and cognitive/ethical value are compatible—many artworks obviously score on both counts. Nor can these two kinds of value always be isolated from one another: we know that relations between form and content, for example, are various and complicated. But can either defence be collapsed wholly within the other? I would argue not. One reason for pressing the two accounts together would be the thought that the pleasure in representations and the pleasure in beauty are of a kind, or, as Roger Scruton puts it, 'interest in representation is a special case of aesthetic interest'.[40] The ease with which Aristotle has so often been co-opted into the aesthetic defence suggests that such a view is widespread. But although the cognitive/ethical defence claims that fictional representation has the advantage of 'distancing' us from real-life predicament (Schier talks of the 'disinterestedness' of artist and spectator as a cognitive/ethical benefit), it makes no mention of aesthetic judgement or beauty. We attend for the sake of learning and expanding our ethical awareness, and 'to learn gives the greatest pleasure'.[41] Attending for the sake of learning may marry happily with taking an aesthetic interest in the drama, even to the extent that in experience we cannot clearly discriminate the two as separate attitudes. Nevertheless they are separate, and in practice we retain the right to shift from one to the other. Opera is full of examples. Someone may find the mental lives of

[40] Scruton (1974), 167.   [41] *Poetics* 1448b13.

Tristan and Isolde incoherent and unedifying or the moral sentiments of *The Magic Flute* reprehensibly paternalistic, and yet see this as detracting hardly at all from the greatness of the respective works. In the face of supreme aesthetic excellence, it is boring and over-earnest to press the cognitive/ethical line too hard. Yet if we decide that the point of some artwork has been to justify racial hatred, say, we may suddenly change tack and regard with great suspicion the person who claims to embrace it wholeheartedly on its 'purely aesthetic' merits.

This chapter has been a series of sketches, and no doubt there are other strategies for arguing against Plato in the philosophy of art. But we already have enough to be able to conclude. We may claim to have shown that countering Plato's critique of the arts is an ambitious philosophical undertaking. We must pay attention to questions about the nature of philosophical enquiry itself and its relations to artistic practices from which it claims to distinguish itself. We must question Plato's notion of human excellence and his conception of knowledge, build up our own conception of the aesthetic, decide how it relates to other values he recognizes, and fashion some alternative to his account of the healthy working of the psyche, showing the importance of imagination and the capacity for aesthetic response, and facing up to the idea that what is not rationally explicable to us can have a proper place in our psychological well-being. This is vindication enough of the idea that Plato's philosophy of art is a monumental contribution to the subject. For if he is wrong, it is scarcely about anything small or easy.

The most satisfying reply will have a number of components. We must explain that no single defence can be demanded of the arts, and insist that our natural involvement with them from within be allowed to inform our account. Let us then assert that there is aesthetic value, that artistic products often provide it, and that the best of them, in so doing, address something of irreducible importance to us. Let us agree that the imaginative portrayal of human action, thought, and feeling is a unique contribution to our natural moral growth and self-understanding. Let us also admit that the arts have a separate origin from philosophy, and that they do not have to harmonize with any given set of philosophical preconditions on pain of being valueless. But finally, let us wonder whether the whole point of the arts is not deeply anti-Platonic in another way. We have asserted that a plurality of values may be found in the arts. It is not just that some works have one kind of value, others another—though that is true. Rather, even the single works that seem most to merit the title of art have a fullness and richness which resists our puny attempts to compartmentalize them. When we embark on artistic ventures, we take the risk of being seduced by pleasing images, and the opposite risk of confronting a horribly truthful likeness. It would be a security to know that what happened in art did not matter to anything outside it, and equally a security to know that it mattered a great deal. But, it seems, we must always engage with art in insecurity over these questions. Plato's face would be a mask of incomprehension, but let us put it to him that the final secret of art's value lies in our being able to embrace it whole without knowing exactly what its value is, its contribution to the good life residing in a unique openness to possibilities and a freedom from having to be merely one definite thing.

Bibliography

Items marked * contain those translations of Plato which I have used unless otherwise stated.

ADAM, J., *The Republic of Plato* (2 vols.; Cambridge, 1902).

ANNAS, J., *An Introduction to Plato's Republic* (Oxford, 1981).

—— 'Plato on the Triviality of Literature', in Moravcsik and Temko (eds.), *Plato on Beauty, Wisdom, and the Arts* (1982), 1–28.

AQUINAS, ST THOMAS, *Summa Theologiae* (Blackfriars edn.; London, 1967), vol. xix, 1a. 2ae, 22–30.

ARISTOTLE, *Poetics*, in S. H. Butcher, *Aristotle's Theory of Poetry and Fine Art* (1911; repr. New York, 1951).

BARNES, J., *The Presocratic Philosophers* (London, 1982).

BEARDSLEY, M. C., *Aesthetics from Classical Greece to the Present: A Short History* (University of Alabama, 1966).

BELFIORE, E., 'Plato's Greatest Accusation against Poetry', in *New Essays on Plato, Canadian Journal of Philosophy*, Supplementary Vol. IX (1983), 39–62.

—— 'A Theory of Imitation in Plato's *Republic*', *Transactions of the American Philological Association*, 114 (1984), 121–46.

—— '"Lies Unlike the Truth": Plato on Hesiod, *Theogony* 27', *Transactions of the American Philological Association*, 115 (1985), 47–57.

BELL, C., 'Significant Form', in J. Hospers (ed.), *Introductory Readings in Aesthetics* (New York, 1969), 87–99.

BOSANQUET, B., *A History of Aesthetic* (London, 1892).

BUDD, M., 'Belief and Sincerity in Poetry', in E. Schaper (ed.), *Pleasure, Preference and Value* (Cambridge, 1983), 137–57.

—— *Music and the Emotions: The Philosophical Theories* (London, 1985).

—— 'How Pictures Look' (Inaugural Lecture at University College London, 1991).

BURNYEAT, M., 'Plato on the Grammar of Perceiving', *Classical Quarterly*, 26 (1976), 29–51.

—— *The Theaetetus of Plato* (Indianapolis, 1990).

—— 'The Passion of Reason in Plato's Phaedrus' (unpublished).

CALLOW, S., *Being an Actor* (Harmondsworth, 1985).

CHERNISS, H., 'On Plato's *Republic* X 597B', *American Journal of Philology*, 53 (1932), 233–42.

CLAY, D., 'The Tragic and Comic Poet of the *Symposium*', in J. P. Anton and A. Preus (eds.), *Essays in Ancient Greek Philosophy*, vol. 2 (Albany, NY, 1983), 186–202.

COLLINGWOOD, R. G., 'Plato's Philosophy of Art', *Mind*, 34 (1925), 154–72.

—— *The Principles of Art* (Oxford, 1938).

CORNFORD, F. M., *Plato's Theory of Knowledge: The Theaetetus and the Sophist of Plato translated with a running commentary* (London, 1935).

—— Sophist, in Hamilton and Cairns (eds.), *Plato: Collected Dialogues*, 957–1017.

—— *The Republic of Plato* (Oxford, 1941).

CROMBIE, I. M., *An Examination of Plato's Doctrines* (2 vols.; London, 1962–3).

CROSS, R. C., and WOOZLEY, A. D., *Plato's Republic: A Philosophical Commentary* (London, 1964).

DAICHES, D., *Critical Approaches to Literature* (London, 1956).

DANTO, A. C., *The Transfiguration of the Commonplace* (Cambridge, Mass., 1981).

—— *The Philosophical Disenfranchisement of Art* (New York, 1986).

—— *The State of the Art* (New York, 1987).

DEMAND, N., 'Plato and the Painters', *Phoenix*, 29 (1975), 1–20.

DERRIDA, J., 'Plato's Pharmacy', in *Dissemination*, trans. B. Johnson (London, 1981), 61–171.

DICKIE, G., *Art and the Aesthetic: An Institutional Analysis* (Ithaca, NY, and London, 1974).

DIELS, H., and KRANZ, W., *Die Fragmente der Vorsokratiker*, 3 vols. (Berlin, 1951–4).

DIFFEY, T. J., *The Republic of Art and Other Essays* (New York, 1991).

DODDS, E. R., *The Greeks and the Irrational* (Berkeley, Calif., 1951).

—— *Plato: Gorgias* (Oxford, 1959).

—— *The Ancient Concept of Progress and Other Essays on Greek Literature and Belief* (Oxford, 1973).

DORTER, K., 'The Ion: Plato's Characterization of Art', *Journal of Aesthetics and Art Criticism*, 32 (1973–5), 65–78.

DOVER, K. J., *Greek Popular Morality in the time of Plato and Aristotle* (Oxford, 1974).

—— *Plato: Symposium* (Cambridge, 1980).

ELIAS, J. A., *Plato's Defence of Poetry* (London, 1984).

ELSE, G. F., ' "Imitation" in the Fifth Century', *Classical Philology*, 53 (1958), 73–90.

—— *Plato and Aristotle on Poetry* (Chapel Hill, NC, 1986).

EVERSON, S. (ed.), *Epistemology* (Companions to Ancient Thought, 1; Cambridge, 1990).

FERRARI, G. R. F., *Listening to the Cicadas: A Study of Plato's Phaedrus* (Cambridge, 1987).

—— 'Plato and Poetry', in G. A. Kennedy (ed.), *The Cambridge History of Literary Criticism*, i. *Classical Criticism* (Cambridge, 1989), 92–148.

FINE, G., 'Knowledge and Belief in *Republic* v', *Archiv für Geschichte der Philosophie*, 60 (1978), 121–39.

206   *Bibliography*

FINE, G., 'Knowledge and Belief in *Republic* v–vii', in S. Everson (ed.), *Epistemology* (1990), 85–115.

FLASHAR, H., *Der Dialog Ion als Zeugnis platonischer Philosophie* (Berlin, 1958).

FORSTER, E. M., 'The Duty of Society to the Artist', in *Two Cheers for Democracy* (London, 1972), 94–8.

GADAMER, H.-G., 'Plato and the Poets', in *Dialogue and Dialectic: Eight Hermeneutical Studies on Plato*, trans. P. C. Smith (New Haven, Conn., 1980), 39–72.

GALLOP, D., *Plato: Phaedo* (Oxford, 1975).

GAUDREAULT, A., 'Mimésis et Diègèsis chez Platon', *Revue de Metaphysique et de Morale*, 94 (1989), 79–92.

GOLDEN, L., 'Plato's Concept of *Mimesis*', *British Journal of Aesthetics*, 15 (1975), 118–31.

GOMBRICH, E. H., *Art and Illusion* (London, 1960).

—— 'Illusion and Art', in R. L. Gregory and E. H. Gombrich (eds.), *Illusion in Nature and Art* (London, 1973).

GOODMAN, N., *Languages of Art* (New York, 1968).

GOSLING, J. C. B., '*Republic* v; *Ta Polla Kala* etc.', *Phronesis*, 5 (1960), 116–28.

*—— *Plato: Philebus* (Oxford, 1975).

GOULD, T., *The Ancient Quarrel between Poetry and Philosophy* (Princeton, NJ, 1990).

GREENE, W. C., 'Plato's View of Poetry', *Harvard Studies in Classical Philology*, 29 (1918), 1–75.

GREY, D. R., 'Art in the *Republic*', *Philosophy*, 27 (1952), 291–310.

GRISWOLD, C. L., 'The Ideas and the Criticism of Poetry in Plato's *Republic*, Book 10', *Journal of the History of Philosophy*, 19 (1981), 135–50.

—— 'Plato's Metaphilosophy: Why Plato Wrote Dialogues', in C. L. Griswold (ed.), *Platonic Writings, Platonic Readings* (New York and London, 1988), 143–67.

GRUBE, G. M. A., 'Plato's Theory of Beauty', *The Monist*, 37 (1927), 269–88.

—— *Plato's Thought* (1935; repr. London, 1980).

*—— *Plato: The Republic* (London, 1981).

*GUTHRIE, W. K. C., *Plato: Protagoras and Meno* (Harmondsworth, 1956).

—— *The Sophists* (Cambridge, 1971).

—— *A History of Greek Philosophy*, iv. *Plato the Man and His Dialogues: Earlier Period* (Cambridge, 1975).

HACKFORTH, R., *Plato's Phaedrus* (1952; repr. Cambridge, 1972).

—— *Plato's Philebus* (1958; repr. Cambridge, 1972).

HALLIWELL, S., 'Plato and Aristotle on the Denial of Tragedy', *Proceedings of the Cambridge Philological Society*, 30 (1984), 49–71.

—— *Aristotle's Poetics* (London, 1986).

—— *Plato: Republic 10* (Warminster, 1988).

—— 'The Importance of Plato and Aristotle for Aesthetics', *Proceedings of the Boston Area Colloquium in Ancient Philosophy*, 5 (1991), 321–57.

—— 'Plato and the Psychology of Drama', in B. Zimmermann (ed.), *Antike Dramentheorien und ihre Rezeption* (Stuttgart, 1992), 55–73.

HAMILTON, E., and CAIRNS, H. (eds.), *Plato: Collected Dialogues* (Princeton, NJ, 1963).

*HAMILTON, W., *Plato: Symposium* (Harmondsworth, 1951).

HAMPSHIRE, S., 'The Conflict between Art and Politics', *The Listener*, Oct. 13, 1960, 629–36.

—— 'The Social Spirit of Mankind', in E. Förster (ed.), *Kant's Transcendental Deductions* (Stanford, Calif., 1989), 145–56.

HAVELOCK, E. A., *Preface to Plato* (Cambridge, Mass., 1963).

HEGEL, G. W. F., *Introductory Lectures on Aesthetics*, trans. B. Bosanquet, ed. M. Inwood (Harmondsworth, 1993).

HESIOD, *Theogony*, in *Hesiod's Theogony*, trans. with introduction, etc.; by R. S. Caldwell (Cambridge, Mass., 1987).

—— *Works and Days*, trans. A. N. Athanassakis, in *Hesiod: Theogony, Works and Days, Shield* (Baltimore and London, 1983).

HOFSTADTER, A. and KUHNS, R., *Philosophies of Art and Beauty* (Chicago, 1964).

IRWIN, T. H., *Plato's Moral Theory* (Oxford, 1977a).

—— 'Plato's Heracleiteanism', *Philosophical Quarterly*, 27 (1977b), 1–13.

*—— *Plato: Gorgias* (Oxford, 1979).

—— Review of M. Nussbaum, *The Fragility of Goodness*, *Journal of Philosophy*, 85 (1988), 376–83.

JAEGER, W., *Paideia: The Ideals of Greek Culture*, vol. ii, trans. G. Highet (Oxford, 1944).

JANAWAY, C., 'Recent Work in Aesthetics', *Philosophical Books*, 30 (1989), 193–201.

—— 'Plato's Analogy between Painter and Poet', *British Journal of Aesthetics*, 31 (1991), 1–12.

—— 'Arts and Crafts in Plato and Collingwood', *Journal of Aesthetics and Art Criticism*, 50 (1992a), 45–54.

—— 'Craft and Fineness in Plato's *Ion*', *Oxford Studies in Ancient Philosophy*, 10 (1992b), 1–23.

—— 'Beauty in Nature, Beauty in Art', *British Journal of Aesthetics*, 33 (1993), 321–32.

JOWETT, B., *Republic*, in *The Dialogues of Plato: translated into English with analyses and introductions*, vol. ii (Oxford, 1953), 1–499.

KAHN, C., 'The Beautiful and the Genuine: A Discussion of Paul Woodruff, *Plato, Hippias Major*', *Oxford Studies in Ancient Philosophy*, 3 (1985), 261–87.

KANT, I., *Critique of Judgement*, trans. J. C. Meredith (Oxford, 1928).

KERFERD, G. B., *The Sophistic Movement* (Cambridge, 1981).

KEULS, E. C., *Plato and Greek Painting* (Leiden, 1978).

KOLLER, H., *Die Mimesis in der Antike* (Berne, 1954).

KOSMAN, L. A., 'Silence and Imitation in the Platonic Dialogues', in J. C. Klagge and N. D. Smith (eds.), *Oxford Studies in Ancient Philosophy*, suppl. vol. 1992: *Methods of Interpreting Plato and his Dialogues* (Oxford, 1992), 73–92.

KRISTELLER, P. O., 'The Modern System of the Arts: A Study in the History of Aesthetics (I)', *Journal of the History of Ideas*, 12 (1951), 496–527.

—— 'The Modern System of the Arts: A Study in the History of Aesthetics (II)', *Journal of the History of Ideas*, 13 (1952), 17–46.

LADRIÈRE, C., 'The Problem of Plato's *Ion*', *Journal of Aesthetics and Art Criticism*, 10 (1951), 26–34.

LEE, H. D. P., *Plato: The Republic* (Harmondsworth, 1955).

*—— *Plato: Timaeus* (Harmondsworth, 1965).

*LEVETT, M. J. (rev. M. Burnyeat), 'Plato's *Theaetetus*', in M. Burnyeat, *The Theaetetus of Plato*.

LEVI, P., 'Greek Drama' in J. Boardman, J. Griffin, and O. Murray (eds.), *The Oxford History of the Classical World* (Oxford, 1986), 156–85.

LEVINSON, G., 'Defining Art Historically', *British Journal of Aesthetics*, 19 (1979), 232–50.

LIDDELL, H. G., and SCOTT, R., *A Greek-English Lexicon*, rev. H. S. Jones (Oxford, 1968).

LODGE, R. C., *Plato's Philosophy of Art* (1953; repr. New York, 1975).

LOVIBOND, S., 'Plato's Theory of Mind', in S. Everson (ed.), *Psychology* (Companions to Ancient Thought, 2; Cambridge, 1991), 35–55.

LUCAS, D. W., *Aristotle: Poetics* (Oxford, 1968).

LYONS, J., *Structural Semantics: An Analysis of Part of the Vocabulary of Plato*, Publications of the Philological Society, 20 (Oxford, 1963).

MCKEON, R., 'Literary Criticism and the Concept of Imitation in Antiquity', in R. S. Crane (ed.), *Critics and Criticism* (Chicago, 1957), 117–45.

MOLINE, J., 'Plato on the Complexity of the Psyche', *Archiv für Geschichte der Philosophie*, 60 (1978), 1–26.

MORAVCSIK, J. M. E., 'Reason and Eros in the "Ascent"-passage of the *Symposium*', in J. P. Anton and G. L. Kustas (eds.), *Essays in Ancient Greek Philosophy* (Albany, NY, 1971), 285–302.

—— 'Noetic Aspiration and Artistic Inspiration', in Moravcsik and Temko (eds.), *Plato on Beauty, Wisdom, and the Arts* (1982), 29–46.

—— 'On Correcting the Poets', *Oxford Studies in Ancient Philosophy*, 4 (1986), 35–47.

—— and TEMKO, P. (eds.), *Plato on Beauty, Wisdom, and the Arts* (Totowa, NJ, 1982).

MOTHERSILL, M., *Beauty Restored* (Oxford, 1984).

MURDOCH, I., *The Fire and the Sun* (Oxford, 1977).

MURPHY, N. R., *The Interpretation of Plato's Republic* (Oxford, 1951).

MURRAY, P., 'Poetic Inspiration in Early Greece', *Journal of Hellenic Studies*, 101 (1981), 87–100.

NEHAMAS, A., 'Plato on Imitation and Poetry in *Republic* 10', in Moravcsik and Temko (eds.), *Plato on Beauty, Wisdom, and the Arts* (1982), 47–78.

—— 'Plato and the Mass Media', *The Monist*, 71 (1988), 214–34.

—— 'Commentary on Halliwell', *Proceedings of the Boston Area Colloquium in Ancient Philosophy*, 5 (1991), 349–57.

NIETZSCHE, F., *On the Genealogy of Morals*, trans. W. Kaufmann, in *Basic Writings of Nietzsche* (New York, 1968), 449–599.

—— *The Birth of Tragedy*, ibid. 15–144.

—— *The Will to Power*, ed. W. Kaufmann, trans. W. Kaufmann and R. J. Hollingdale (New York, 1968).

NUSSBAUM, M. C., ' "This Story Isn't True": Poetry, Goodness, and Understanding in Plato's *Phaedrus*', in Moravcsik and Temko (eds.), *Plato on Beauty, Wisdom, and the Arts* (1982), 79–124.

—— *The Fragility of Goodness* (Cambridge, 1986).

—— *Love's Knowledge: Essays on Philosophy and Literature* (New York and Oxford, 1990).

OATES, W. J., *Plato's View of Art* (New York, 1972).

OSBORNE, C., 'The Repudiation of Representation in Plato's *Republic* and its Repercussions', *Proceedings of the Cambridge Philological Society*, 33 (1987), 53–73.

PARTEE, M. H., 'Inspiration in the Aesthetics of Plato', *Journal of Aesthetics and Art Criticism*, 30 (1971), 87–95.

PENNER, T., 'Thought and Desire in Plato', in G. Vlastos (ed.), *Plato: A Collection of Critical Essays* (New York, 1971), ii. 96–118.

—— *The Ascent from Nominalism* (Dordrecht, 1987).

PICKARD-CAMBRIDGE, A. W., *Dithyramb Tragedy and Comedy* (Oxford, 1927).

PLOTINUS, *The Enneads*, trans. S. MacKenna (London, 1962).

POHLENZ, M., 'Die Anfänge der griechischen Poetik' (1920; repr. in *Kleine Schriften*, ii (Hildesheim, 1965), 436–72.

POUND, E., 'The Serious Artist', in *Literary Essays of Ezra Pound* (London, 1954), 41–57.

PRICE, A. W., *Love and Friendship in Plato and Aristotle* (Oxford, 1989).

READ, H., *The Meaning of Art* (1931; repr. Harmondsworth, 1949).

REEVE, C. D. C., *Plato: Republic*, trans. G. M. A. Grube, rev. C. D. C. Reeve (Indianapolis, 1992).

ROOCHNIK, D. L., 'Socrates's Use of the Techne-Analogy', *Journal of the History of Philosophy*, 24 (1986), 295–310.

*ROWE, C. J., *Plato: Phaedrus* (Warminster, 1986).

RUSKIN, J., 'Sesame and Lilies', in *Sesame and Lilies, The Two Paths and The King of the Golden River* (London, 1907), 1–79.

SAINTSBURY, G., *A History of Criticism and Literary Taste in Europe*, i. *Classical and Mediaeval Criticism* (Edinburgh and London, 1908).

SAUNDERS, T. J. (ed.), *Plato: Early Socratic Dialogues* (Harmondsworth, 1987).

*—— *Plato: Ion*, in Saunders (ed.), *Plato: Early Socratic Dialogues* (1987), 39–65.

*—— *Plato: The Laws* (Harmondsworth, 1975).

SAVILE, A., *The Test of Time: An Essay in Philosophical Aesthetics* (Oxford, 1982).

SCHAPER, E., *Prelude to Aesthetics* (London, 1968).

SCHIER, F., *Deeper into Pictures* (Cambridge, 1986).

—— 'The Claims of Tragedy: An Essay in Moral Psychology and Aesthetic Theory', *Philosophical Papers*, 18 (1989), 7–26.

SCHILLER, F, *On the Aesthetic Education of Mankind: In a Series of Letters*, ed. and trans. E. M. Wilkinson and L. A. Willoughby (Oxford, 1967).

SCHOPENHAUER, A., *The World as Will and Representation*, trans. E. F. J. Payne (2 vols.; New York, 1969).

SCHUHL, P.-M., *Platon et l'art de son Temps* (Paris, 1933).

SCRUTON, R., *Art and Imagination* (London, 1974).

—— 'On "knowing what"' (unpublished).

SHELLEY, P. B., *The Complete Works of Percy Bysshe Shelley*, vii (London, 1965).

SHOREY, P., *Republic*, in Hamilton and Cairns (eds.), *Plato: Collected Dialogues*, 575–844.

SIDNEY, SIR PHILIP, 'A Defence of Poetry', in K. Duncan-Jones and J. van Dorsten (eds.), *Miscellaneous Prose of Sir Philip Sidney* (Oxford, 1973), 73–121.

*SKEMP, J. B., *Statesman*, in Hamilton and Cairns (eds.), *Plato: Collected Dialogues*, 1018–85.

SÖRBOM, G., *Mimesis and Art* (Uppsala, 1966).

SPRAGUE, R. K. (ed.), *The Older Sophists* (Columbia, SC, 1972).

—— *Plato's Philosopher-King* (Columbia, SC, 1976).

STEVEN, R. G., 'Plato and the Art of His Time', *Classical Quarterly*, 27 (1933), 149–55.

STEWART, J. A., *The Myths of Plato* (1905; repr. Fontwell, Sussex, 1960).

STOLNITZ, J., 'On the Cognitive Triviality of Art', *British Journal of Aesthetics*, 32 (1992), 191–200.

TATE, J., '"Imitation" in Plato's *Republic*', *Classical Quarterly*, 22 (1928), 16–23.

—— 'Plato and "Imitation"', *Classical Quarterly*, 26 (1932), 161–9.

TAYLOR, A. E., *Plato: The Man and his Work* (London, 1926).

TIGERSTEDT, E. N., *Plato's Idea of Poetical Inspiration* (Helsinki, 1969).

—— '*Furor poeticus*: Poetic Inspiration in Greek Literature before Democritus and Plato', *Journal of the History of Ideas*, 31 (1970), 163–78.

TOLSTOY, L., *What is Art?*, trans. A. Maude (Indianapolis, 1960).

*TREDENNICK, H., *Apology*, in *The Last Days of Socrates* (Harmondsworth, 1969).

URMSON, J. O., 'Plato and the Poets', in Moravcsik and Temko (eds.), *Plato on Beauty, Wisdom, and the Arts* (1982), 125–36.

—— 'Pleasure and Distress: A Discussion of J. C. B. Gosling and C. C. W. Taylor, *The Greeks on Pleasure*', in *Oxford Studies in Ancient Philosophy*, 2 (1984), 209–21.

VERDENIUS, W. J., *Mimesis: Plato's Doctrine of Artistic Imitation and its Meaning to us* (Leiden, 1949).

—— 'Der Begriff der Mania in Platons *Phaidros*', *Archiv für Geschichte der Philosophie*, 44 (1962), 132–50.

—— 'The Principles of Greek Literary Criticism', *Mnemosyne*, 36 (1983), 14–59.

VLASTOS, G., 'The Disorderly Motion in the "Timaeus"' (1939), repr. in R. E. Allen (ed.), *Studies in Plato's Metaphysics* (London, 1965), 379–99.

—— 'Degrees of Reality in Plato' (1965), repr. in Vlastos, *Platonic Studies*, 58–75.

—— 'Reasons and Causes in the *Phaedo*' (1969), repr. in Vlastos, *Platonic Studies*, 76–110.

—— *Platonic Studies* (Princeton, NJ, 1981).

WALTON, K., 'Fearing Fictions', *Journal of Philosophy*, 75 (1978), 5–27.

WARRY, J. G., *Greek Aesthetic Theory* (London, 1962).

WATT, D., *Charmides*, in Saunders (ed.), *Plato: Early Socratic Dialogues*, 163–209.

WHITE, N. P., *A Companion to Plato's Republic* (Oxford, 1979).

WILDE, O., 'The Critic as Artist', in R. Ellman (ed.), *The Artist as Critic: Critical Writings of Oscar Wilde* (New York, 1968), 371–408.

WOLLHEIM, R., *Art and its Objects* (2nd edn.; Cambridge, 1980).

*WOODRUFF, P., *Plato: Hippias Major* (Oxford, 1982*a*).

—— 'What Could Go Wrong with Inspiration? Why Plato's Poets Fail', in Moravcsik and Temko (eds.), *Plato on Beauty, Wisdom, and the Arts* (1982*b*), 137–50.

—— 'Plato's Early Epistemology', in S. Everson (ed.), *Epistemology* (1990), 60–84.

XENOPHON, *Memorabilia* (*Memoirs of Socrates*), trans. H. Tredennick and R. Waterfield, in *Conversations of Socrates* (Harmondsworth, 1990).

Glossary of Greek Terms

The main text of the book does not assume that the reader knows Greek: when Greek words are introduced they are always explained. However, some Greek terms are used without a translation on every occurrence. The following is a list of such terms, with preferred English equivalents.

agathos	good
alogon	without a rational account (*logos*)
alogon pragma	a thing without a rational account
aporia	perplexity
aretē	excellence, virtue
aulos	'flute'—in fact a reed instrument
dēmiourgos, (pl. *dēmiourgoi*)	craftsman, maker
diēgēsis	narration
eidōlon (pl. *eidōla*)	image
eikōn (pl. *eikones*)	likeness
epainetēs (pl. *epaineteis*)	eulogist
epistēmē (pl. *epistēmai*)	knowledge, branch of knowledge
erōs	love
euschēmosunē	grace, well-formedness
harmonia (pl. *harmoniai*)	musical mode, tuning, harmony
kalos	fine, beautiful (masculine)
kalon (pl. *kala*)	fine, beautiful (neuter)
to kalon; auto to kalon	fineness, beauty; fineness itself, beauty itself
kallistos	finest, most beautiful (masculine)
kalliston	finest, most beautiful (neuter)
kalōs	finely
kalos kagathos	'fine and good', noble
lexis	mode of discourse
logismos	reasoning, calculation
logistikon	the rational part (of the soul)
logos (pl. *logoi*)	word, account, argument
mania	madness
mimēsis (pl. *mimēseis*)	representation, artistic image-making, dramatic enactment, imitation
mimeisthai	to represent, imitate
mimētikē, to mimētikon	the mimetic arts
mimēma (pl. *mimēmata*)	representation, copy, imitation
mimētēs (pl. *mimētai*)	mimetic artist, practitioner of *mimēsis*
mousikē	music, the arts, culture
mousikos	cultured, educated

muthos (pl. *muthoi*)	story, myth
paidia	amusement, play
phantasma (pl. *phantasmata*)	semblance
pharmakon	drug, spell, remedy
poiētēs	poet, maker
poiētikos	poetic
poiētikōtatos	most poetic
poiētikē technē	poetic craft or expertise
polis	city, state
pseudeis logoi	false stories, accounts
pseudos	falsehood
rhētōr	public speaker, rhetorician
skiagraphia	'shadow-painting', illusionistic painting technique
technē (pl. *technai*)	craft, expertise, expert knowledge
technikos	possessing craft, expertise
theios	divine
theia moira	divine dispensation

General Index

Index of Passages in Plato